Without Education or Encouragement

Without Education or Encouragement

The Literary Legacy of Flora Thompson

Ruth Collette Hoffman

Madison • Teaneck
Fairleigh Dickinson University Press

Associated University Presses
2010 Eastpark Boulevard
Cranbury, NJ 08512

The paper used in this publication meets the requirements of the American National Standard for Permanence of Paper for Printed Library Materials Z39.48-1984.

Library of Congress Cataloging-in-Publication Data

Hoffman, Ruth Collette, 1951–
Without Education or Encouragement: the literary legacy of Flora Thompson / Ruth Collette Hoffman
p. cm.
Includes bibliographical references and index.
ISBN 978-0-8386-4206-1 (alk. paper)
1. Thompson, Flora—Criticism and interpretation. 2. Thompson, Flora—Knowledge and learning. 3. Pastoral literature, English—History and criticism. 4. Country life in literature I. Title.
PR6039.H653Z68 2009
828'.91209—dc22

2008048352

PRINTED IN THE UNITED STATES OF AMERICA

For George

and for our children

Christopher, Ian, Dylan, Julia, Claire, Anissa, Dakhita, and Imani

Contents

Acknowledgments

THIRTY FIVE YEARS AGO, I FIRST ENCOUNTERED FLORA THOMPSON'S *Lark Rise to Candleford* in a Chicago bookstore. At the time, I was an undergraduate student in English at Loyola University and an aficionado of the English rural novel. I remember being fascinated by *Lark Rise to Candleford*, particularly its detailed descriptions of English country life. I did not reread *Lark Rise to Candleford* until 2002 when I was a graduate student at Northern Illinois University. Once again, I was charmed by Thompson's trilogy and eager to discover more about the author and her published work. With the encouragement of my dissertation director, Professor William Baker, I soon decided to make Flora Thompson the subject of my doctoral dissertation. Thanks to the support of colleagues, friends, and family, that doctoral dissertation has now become a book.

I must first acknowledge my gratitude to Flora Thompson's biographer, Gillian Lindsay. Gillian's excellent book, *Flora Thompson: The Story of the Lark Rise Writer*, provided crucial background information on Thompson, as well as tantalizing glimpses of her early work for the *Lady's Companion* and the *Catholic Fireside*. When I first began my research, Gillian responded generously to my frequent emails and shared her personal copies of Thompson's essays and short stories with me. Her husband, David, devoted one rainy weekend in May of 2005 to photocopying over fifty of Thompson's nature essays for me in his surgery. Gillian read my manuscript when it was still a dissertation and has continued to be a source of information, encouragement, and support.

Like Gillian Lindsay, John Owen Smith has become a treasured colleague and friend. John's book, *On the Trail of Flora Thompson*, and his knowledge of the author's life in Hampshire have been invaluable. His website devoted to Flora Thompson continues to be an excellent source of information and resources for those interested in learning more about this author. John kindly read a late draft of my manuscript and helped me to eliminate a few lingering errors. When my husband and I traveled to England in May of 2007 and in July of 2008, John and his wife Dil, as well as Gillian and David Lindsay, acted as our guides as we visited the places from which Thompson drew her inspiration.

Thanks is also due to Tony Webster, marketing trustee and Web master at the Old Gaol Museum in Buckingham, for sharing material related to Flora Thompson from the museum collection. In May 2007, I was privileged to attend the grand opening ceremony of the Flora Thompson Exhibition at the Old Gaol Museum. Tony welcomed my husband and I to this special event, and museum trustee Pat Brook took us on a guided tour of Buckingham, pointing out locations associated with Thompson's extended family.

I would also like to thank Flora Thompson's granddaughter, Mrs. Elizabeth Swaffield, for allowing me to include poems from *Bog Myrtle and Peat* in this volume. A special thanks is also due to Henry Westbury, who gave me permission to use the cover photograph of Flora Thompson and to quote from a letter Thompson wrote to his uncle, Leslie Castle. The Oxford University Press has granted permission for the quotations from *Lark Rise to Candleford* and *A Country Calendar* that appear in this volume.

This book began as a doctoral dissertation prepared under the direction of Presidential Research Scholar, William Baker. Professor Baker read many drafts of this manuscript and was a continuing source of advice and support. I would also like to thank Professor John Knapp and Professor David Gorman, who served on my dissertation committee, for their many helpful suggestions. I was also assisted in the preparation of this manuscript by two excellent proofreaders: my father, Harold H. Holtmeyer, and my daughter, Claire M. Hoffman. Thanks are also due to Melissa Birks for her valuable editorial advice.

My greatest thanks go to my husband and my children. My husband, George, accompanied me to the Colindale in May 2007 and spent one day helping me to sift through back issues of the *Catholic Fireside*. Happily, on that day we discovered two previously unidentified short stories by Thompson, "The Mervyn Mystery" and "The Hidden Power." I am also grateful to my husband and children for suffering my frequent absences from family activities with amazing patience.

1
Flora Thompson: An Introduction

For over sixty years, Flora Thompson has been celebrated as the author of *Lark Rise to Candleford*, a trilogy based on the author's memories of growing up in rural Oxfordshire during the late nineteenth century. *Lark Rise*, the first book of the trilogy, was published by the Oxford University Press in 1939. Urged on by readers who were eager to know "what happened next" to Laura, the book's protagonist, Thompson quickly published two sequels to *Lark Rise*: *Over to Candleford* (1941) and *Candleford Green* (1943). To this day, Thompson's trilogy is considered a minor classic among writings about the English countryside. And, since it continues to attract readers who enjoy accounts of English country life, *Lark Rise to Candleford* is still periodically republished.

Since the publication of *Lark Rise to Candleford* as a one-volume trilogy in 1945, Flora Thompson's life and works have inspired plays, audio recordings, and a television series produced for BBC One. Keith Dewhurst authored the first two plays based on Thompson's trilogy. His two-act *Lark Rise* was first performed by the National Theatre as a promenade production in 1978. The first performance of *Candleford* followed in 1979.[1] During the 1990s, Hampshire historian John Owen Smith authored two plays based upon Thompson's life in Hampshire and her early work as a freelance journalist. Smith's two-act play, *Flora's Peverel*, was first performed as a community play project in 1997, followed by the first production of *Flora's Heatherley* in 1998. Two audio recordings of the trilogy were also released during the 1990s. Isis Audio Dimensions released an unabridged recording of *Lark Rise to Candleford* in 1994. The following year, Penguin Audiobooks released an abridged recording of the trilogy, performed by Dame Judy Dench. Thompson's trilogy is sure to find a host of new readers in the twenty-first century, following BBC One's production of *Lark Rise to Candleford*, a ten-part television series that debuted on January 13, 2008.

To this day, references to Thompson and excerpts from *Lark Rise to Candleford* can be found in a wide variety of anthologies and popular books. Memorial plaques have also been placed outside homes associated with the author in Oxfordshire, Hampshire, and Devon. A plaque can be found outside Thompson's childhood home in Juniper Hill, Oxfordshire, and inside the Church of St. Mary in Cottisford where her family worshipped. In Liphook, Hampshire, a plaque has been mounted outside the home where Thompson lived with her postmaster husband from 1916 to 1927. Liphook paid further tribute to the author in May 1981 when a bust of Thompson, sculpted by Philip Jackson, was unveiled outside the Liphook Post Office.[2] In 2000 the Dartmouth and Kingswear Society installed a blue memorial plaque outside Thompson's former home in Dartmouth, Devon, where she lived from 1928 to 1940. In April 2008, following the successful debut of the BBC's *Lark Rise to Candleford,* a blue memorial plaque was installed outside a home in Winton, Bournemouth, where Thompson lived from 1909 to 1915. The first permanent exhibition dedicated to Thompson's life and works was opened at the Old Gaol Museum in Buckingham in April 2005. In May 2007, the sixtieth anniversary of Thompson's death was marked by a series of cultural events in Oxfordshire and Hampshire. These events included the grand opening of an audiovisual exhibition at the Old Gaol Museum, a performance of Keith Dewhurst's *Lark Rise* under a marquee in Juniper Hill, and a *Lark Rise* folk night, featuring a performance by Ashley Hutchings and the Lark Rise Band. The week of special events concluded with the unveiling of a memorial plaque outside The Ferns in Grayshott, Hampshire, where Thompson lived from 1899 to 1900, when she worked as an assistant to the Grayshott postmaster.

Flora Jane (Timms) Thompson was born on December 5, 1876, the daughter of Albert Timms, a stonemason, and Emma (Dibber) Timms, a former nursemaid. Albert and Emma Timms lived the whole of their married life in Juniper Hill, a poor agricultural hamlet in northeast Oxfordshire. Flora Jane was the first of six surviving children born to the couple. Beginning in 1882, she attended a tiny village school in the neighboring village of Cottisford, leaving at the age of fourteen (in 1891) to take her first job at a post office in nearby Fringford. Flora worked at the Fringford post office until 1897, when she left to take a series of temporary post office positions. She married John Thompson, a fellow post office employee, on January 7, 1903. Three children were born to Flora and John Thompson: Winifred in 1903, Basil in 1909, and Peter in 1918. Because married women were not allowed to work for the post office at this time, Thompson devoted herself to keeping house and raising children during the early years of her marriage. In 1916, her husband became the subpostmaster in Liphook, Hampshire, and Thompson added (unofficial) postal work to her duties as a wife and mother. In 1927, when John was appointed postmaster, the Thompsons made what they expected to be a final move to Dartmouth in Devon. However, with the beginning of World War II, they moved once again for safety reasons to a more secluded home in Brixham. In 1941 Flora and John lost their youngest son, Peter, (who had joined the Merchant Navy) when his ship, the *Jedmoor,* was torpedoed. With the combined pressures of wartime and grief, Thompson began to experience bouts of ill health until her death of a heart attack on May 21, 1947, at age seventy.

When they were first published by the Oxford University Press, the books of *Lark Rise to Candleford* were classified as autobiography. Consequently, scholars have studied the trilogy as a work of nonfiction. Agricultural historians, social historians, and folklorists have all found *Lark Rise to Candleford* to be a valuable source of information about rural life at the end of the nineteenth century. However, the continuing assumption that *Lark Rise to Candleford* is essentially autobiographical has limited the critical response to Thompson's trilogy and the understanding of her reputation as a writer. The autobiographical approach to Thompson and her work was initially based on the assumption that she was a simple countrywoman and first-time writer who, in the last eight years of her life, decided to record her memories of growing up in Oxfordshire during the 1880s and 1890s. Thompson was a woman from the rural working classes who (it was assumed) had been crippled by a poor education, unrelenting toil, and an oppressive marriage, all of which had made it impossible for her to follow her creative impulses until the last few years of her life when she was old and infirm. Thompson's first biographer, Margaret Lane, characterized Thompson as a writer whose life was "obscure" and whose literary gifts only "blossomed into fulfillment in old age."[3] Thompson's decision to adopt a flimsy disguise, calling herself "Laura" rather than "Flora" in the books of her trilogy, seemed a charmingly naïve touch in what one reviewer called her "delicately disguised autobiography."[4] In his 1979 review of *A Country Calendar*, a posthumous collection of Thompson's work, English writer and editor Ronald Blythe further characterized Flora Thompson's writing as a "spiritual escape"—a strategy "to protect her inner life" from a husband who "was crushing in his attitude towards her."[5] The short stories that Thompson had published in women's magazines (known only by a few critics) were rather an embarrassment. In the words of Marxist critic Rebecca O'Rourke, this work was "simply writing that would sell" rather than the "writing she wanted to do."[6] Sadly, Thompson's short fiction seemed to confirm that the author's genius emerged only at the end of her life when she was writing (less creatively) about her childhood.

Although there is an element of truth in some of these unchallenged assumptions about Thompson, their effect has been to misrepresent the author's life and literary legacy. Beginning in the 1990s, a new generation of Thompson biographers provided a more accurate and detailed record of the author's life and writing career. Reading Gillian Lindsay's *Flora Thompson: The Story of the Lark Rise Writer* (1990), John Owen Smith's *On the Trail of Flora Thompson: Beyond Candleford Green* (1998), or Christine Bloxham's *The World of Flora Thompson* (1998), one discovers, for example, that the Oxford University Press's decision to publish *Lark Rise* as an autobiography was merely a strategy designed to circumvent the press's official policy (in 1939) of not publishing fiction. One also learns from Thompson's biographers that, although she attended only a tiny village school until the age of fourteen, Thompson was an avid reader and lifelong autodidact. In her early childhood, she shared her deep love of literature and her rich imaginative life with her brother Edwin. Both children devoured every printed text that they encountered in the poor agricultural hamlet where they lived. After she left home to take her first job in a village post office, and even after her marriage, Thompson continued to educate herself by borrowing books from other book lovers and from mechanics' institutes and local libraries, all of which she read in moments between postal work, housekeeping, and childrearing. And, although Thompson was born into the rural working classes, after her marriage she rose up the social ladder through her husband's professional promotions at the post office, eventually becoming a member of the lower middle class.

A Working Writer

Thompson's career as a working writer did not begin in 1939, when her first novel was published, but in February of 1911 when the author (then thirty-four) entered a writing competition sponsored by the *Lady's Companion.*[7] She immediately won first prize for a three-hundred-word literary essay. Thompson published her first short story in the *Lady's Companion* in 1912. For the next few years, Thompson continued to publish essays and short stories in the *Lady's Companion,* the *Literary Monthly,* and other (unfortunately unidentified) magazines. In 1919 Thompson enrolled in a writing course offered by the Practical Correspondence College of London. That same year, she also submitted a short story to the *Catholic Fireside.* During 1920 the *Catholic Fireside* published six short stories by the author. In 1921 Thompson published a small book of verse, *Bog Myrtle and Peat,* and began to write monthly nature essays for a series in the *Catholic Fireside* that she eventually named *The Peverel Papers.* From 1921 to 1927, she wrote a total of eighty-four essays for this series. In 1923 Thompson began writing monthly literary essays for the *Catholic Fireside*, for a new series that she named *The Fireside Reading Circle.* From January 1923 until November 1925, she published one essay in *The Fireside Reading Circle* and one essay in *The Peverel Papers* each month.

In 1925 Thompson ended *The Fireside Reading Circle* and founded the Peverel Society, a postal writing society through which she offered advice to inexperienced writers and conducted correspondence classes on general culture, literary genres, and literary techniques. In 1926 the Peverel Society published *The Peverel Society Book of Verse*, a collection of poetry written by society members and selected by Thompson. Thompson ended her professional association with the *Catholic Fireside* in 1927, when she and her family moved to Dartmouth in Devon.

In the 1930s, Thompson published three articles based on her memories of growing up in Juniper Hill: "Old Queenie" (published in the *Lady* in 1937), "An Oxfordshire Hamlet in the 'Eighties" (published in the *National Review* in 1937), and "May Day in the 'Eighties" (published in the *National Review* in 1938). These three articles became the foundation of three chapters in Thompson's first novel, *Lark Rise.* After *Lark Rise* and its sequels were published together as *Lark Rise to Candleford* in 1945, the Oxford University Press published a new novel by Thompson entitled *Still Glides the Stream*. This book was published in 1948, the year following the author's death. Thompson had completed another novel, entitled *Heatherley*, in 1944, but she never submitted it for publication. In 1979 *Heatherley* was finally published by the Oxford University Press in *A Country Calendar,* a book that also featured a selection of Thompson's nature essays and poetry. In 1986 a wider selection of Thompson's nature essays was published by the Century Hutchinson Press as *The Peverel Papers.* John Owen Smith published the first full-text edition of *The Peverel Papers* in 2008.

Thompson's desire to become a writer emerged in early childhood. In 1947 she wrote of her first literary efforts in "A Country Child Taking Notes," an article published in the *Readers News*: "I never could remember in after-life when I began to write, but, at seven years old I was penning letters in rhyme to Santa Claus, to be attached to my own and my brother's Christmas stockings, and a little later, I was running a family magazine, which continued until my mother's grocer changed the colour of his sugar wrapping-paper from greyish white to a very dark blue, upon which no ink would show, and so caused me to experience my first paper shortage."[8]

When *Bog Myrtle and Peat* was published in 1921, Thompson also spoke candidly of her early years as a wife and mother in an interview with the *Civilian*, a publication for government employees. In the resulting full-page article, Thompson, then forty-four, stated that even when "the cares and anxieties of bringing up a young family, and trying to run a home decently" upon a "pitiful salary" had "strained nerves and energy to breaking point," she found time for "a little reading."[9] During these difficult years, Thompson says, "I never quite gave up my hope of writing either." Pointing to the immediate success of "the first short story, the first newspaper article," and "even the first poem" that she submitted to various periodicals during the 1910s, Flora Thompson portrayed herself as a writer without literary struggles "in the ordinary sense." All of these first writing attempts, Thompson noted, were "accepted and paid for."

In her interview with the *Civilian*, Thompson also revealed her fierce determination to improve her education, a determination that gained in intensity when she moved with her husband to Bournemouth in 1903. The Bournemouth public library, Thompson says, quickly became her "Alma Mater." With nothing to guide her but her own desire for learning, Thompson says, "I went right back to the beginning, read the Greeks and Romans in translations; read the English poets; the English Novelists; the English Critics; nibbled at translations of the French writers; even tried my teeth upon philosophy and mysticism! Read Ibsen, Shaw, Yeats, and all the Celts. Became enamoured of the new poetry, at least of the work of those poets who passed as new in pre-war time."[10] Thompson also revealed her frequent feelings of isolation, both as a poet and as a lover of literature, in an interview with the *Daily Chronicle* where she stated, "I started writing little things long ago . . . No one helped me, and I have carried on my passion for literature quite alone."[11] Thompson projected this sense of loneliness and isolation in much of her published work, especially in *The Peverel Papers* and in the novels of *Lark Rise to Candleford* and *Heatherley*.

It is obvious from the record of her published work and from her statements to the *Civilian* that Thompson was not a simple countrywoman or inexperienced writer when she wrote the trilogy that made her famous. Moreover, the work that she published in various women's magazines during the 1910s and 1920s was not limited to conventional love stories. Thompson also published an impressive number of nature essays and literary essays in the 1920s, and in the 1930s, she published three short articles that were, in essence, early drafts of three chapters of her most famous novel, *Lark Rise*.

The Early Critical Response

Thompson enjoyed immediate critical and popular success when she published the three novels that became *Lark Rise to Candleford*.[12] Upon publication, *Lark Rise*, *Over to Candleford*, and *Candleford Green* were hailed in book reviews published in Britain and in the United States.[13] In May 1939, the Oxford University Press announced the publication of *Lark Rise* in *Literature and Life*, claiming it would "rank beside" Mary Russell Mitford's *Our Village* "for its joy in the details of village lives, its humour and observation, and the quiet potent memories of ways of life which are gone."[14] E. A. Wolfe's review in *Time and Tide* described *Lark Rise* as "a very remarkable picture of village life" and noted Thompson's description of "country civilization": the "children's rhymes and games, full of echoes of the past," the "old songs sung at the 'Wagon and Horses,'" and the "country festivals of May Day and Harvest Home."[15] *Lark Rise* was also reviewed in more prestigious literary publications. The review in the *Times Literary Supplement* characterized *Lark Rise* as the author's "reminiscences" of "the end of an era in the English countryside," told in "a quiet, easy and unpretentious style," and declared *Lark Rise* to be "a welcome contribution to the social history of the English countryside."[16] The review in the *New York Times* described *Lark Rise* as "an original and significant book . . . in being a bit of history: social history of yesterday in rural England."[17] The review praised Thompson for the originality of her point of view and for her prose, described as "touched by beauty and grounded in good common sense." George Dangerfield, in his review for the *Saturday Review,* noted that *Lark Rise*'s portrayal of village life was unique because it offered the minute details of daily life as seen by the villagers themselves, not "through the windows of the Rectory."[18]

Over to Candleford, like its predecessor, *Lark Rise*, proved to be another critical and popular success. The success of the novel was partially due to its power to remind a nation at war of a simpler and more serene time in English history.[19] At the same time, reviewers and readers appreciated Thompson's refusal to romanticize the past. The review in the *Spectator* noted that Thompson had written of the hamlet in which she had spent her childhood "with that objectivity possible after long love" and of her childhood with "a proud care not to romanticise."[20] The *Times Literary Supplement* also praised Thompson's ability to look back with "serenity and exquisite detachment" on her childhood and to "distil this very essence of English life."[21] The reviewer further observed, "It is rare for a sequel to follow a pattern so unwaveringly, to maintain a high standard so constantly, as does this present volume." The review in the *Times Literary Supplement* also quoted Thompson's introductory note to *Over to Candleford*, in which she described her work as less autobiography than a record of "impressions." She wrote in the third person, Thompson said, "because the writer can best see objectively, across the gulf of time and war and change, the child who was herself moving in that now vanished world."

Like its predecessors, *Candleford Green* was received enthusiastically by readers and reviewers alike when it was published in 1943. The reviews that appeared in Great Britain in the *Times Literary Supplement* and in the *Spectator* were typical of the admiring reviews this new work earned on both sides of the Atlantic. The review in the *Times Literary Supplement* identified Thompson's reading public as a "faithful band of followers" and noted, once again, that Thompson had stated that her novels were "intended less as autobiography than as a record of the impressions of a child brought up in a remote country hamlet in the eighteen-eighties." *Candleford Green* was praised for "the exactness and detail of the outward scene" as well as for "the rare objectivity" with which the protagonist, Laura, observed the village personalities around her.[22] The *Spectator* pronounced *Candleford Green* "a delightful book" and "a further fascinating installment in the life of her [Thompson's] young heroine."[23] Writing in the *New York Times Book Review,* Jane Spence Southron described *Candleford Green* as a "fascinating and informative study of English village life," praising Thompson for her ability to "delineate character" and for "seizing, selectively, the salient features of a scene, an epoch and a trend."[24] Southron proclaimed Thompson's novels "as readable as choice fiction" and praised the novel's dramatic presentation of village life as seen "clear-eyed, by a realist of poetic temperament." Southron also predicted that Thompson's work would become "a source book from which future historians may draw with utter confidence," a prediction that was to be borne out in years to come. The review in the *New York Herald Tribune* referred to *Candleford Green* and its predecessors (*Lark Rise* and *Over to Candleford*) as the "Candleford idylls" and predicted that Thompson's "delicately disguised autobiography" would become a valuable historical source that would "outlast current fiction in historical collections."[25]

When *Lark Rise*, *Over to Candleford*, and *Candleford Green* were first published together as *Lark Rise to Candleford,* the first edition of five thousand copies was sold out in advance of the April 12, 1945, publication date.[26] Not surprisingly, since *Lark Rise to Candleford* was the republication of three popular novels in one volume, book reviews were brief but positive. In the *Spectator*, V. C. Clinton-Baddeley noted the "very welcome" publication of books that "have already established themselves as classics of the English countryside."[27] In the *Christian Science Monitor*, Harold Hobson, calling *Lark Rise to Candleford* "an achievement both as social history and as a work of literature," stated that the new trilogy "enshrines as no other book has ever done, the nature of a village life now passed away."[28] John T. Frederick began his review in the *Chicago Sun Book Week* with the question, "How good were the good old days?"[29] Noting that "treatment of the horse and buggy days has tended to be either idyllic or contemptuous, lacking the balance and the clearness of vision so notable in *Lark Rise to Candleford,*" Frederick praised Thompson for giving her readers a candid account of life in late nineteenth-century England. Struthers Burt's review in the *New York Times Book Review* struck a different note. He not only used the publication of the trilogy to express his admiration for America's British Allies during World War II, but he also identified *Lark Rise to Candleford* as a novel. "The English," Burt stated, "are a stalwart and trustworthy people. A good people. The material of allies."[30] In *Lark Rise to Candleford,* Burt states, he found "none of that stark hatred and horror of the land so often found in American novels." Instead the trilogy offered a "real evocation . . . the summoning up of people and places and events, which is the inner and final magic of the novel." Burt concluded his review by proclaiming Thompson "the Anthony Trollope of the English farm hand" and her trilogy a "'Barchester Towers' in reverse."

British reviewers were less complimentary when the new Thompson novel, *Still Glides the Stream*, was published posthumously in 1948. The review in the *Times Literary Supplement* noted that most of the characters in *Still Glides the Stream* were of a "familiar type" and that Charity Finch, the protagonist, was "as prim a little heroine as the Candleford Laura."[31] The reviewer found particular fault with Thompson's use of the metaphor of an "ever gliding stream" that is "ever changing yet ever the same." Thompson intended this metaphor, which is found in the last paragraph of the novel, to be a source of "comfort and reassurance."[32] Undoubtedly, such bland reassurance rang hollow in a devastated post–World War II England, perhaps accounting for the reviewer's reaction: "If there is, as Miss Thompson intends there should be, a poignancy behind this chronicle of minima, it takes shape on account of her own and her reader's awareness that nothing reassuring is taking its place."

Reviews of *Still Glides the Stream* in the United States were more flattering. Ernestine Evans of the *New York Herald Tribune* characterized this novel as a "gentle refreshment at an ancient spring, the village life of England" akin to Thompson's "other memoir, 'Lark Rise to Candleford.'"[33] Eric Forbes-Boyd of the *Christian Science Monitor* declared that *Still Glides the Stream* was no "flimsy pastoral nor halcyon vision of a Merrie England that never was, but a completely honest picture of . . . yeoman and peasant society."[34] Forbes-Boyd also noted the "literary quality" of the novel, particularly the "artistry" in Thompson's choice of "significant detail" and her "economy in the handling of it" that he deemed "very nearly perfect." *Still Glides the Stream,* he asserted, was both a literary triumph and a "social document that may well have enduring value." Pamela Taylor of the *Saturday Review* praised Thompson's "artful and engagingly casual interweaving of human drama, of charming bits of folklore . . . and descriptive details," comparing the novel to a "cottage-worked sampler or bit of needlework" that "fixes for us a golden time which will not come again."[35] Unlike the reviewer in the *Times Literary Supplement*, Taylor found Thompson's characters to be sensitive "human portraits."

Thompson and Her Interpreters

To mark the publication of *Lark Rise to Candleford*, the Oxford University Press asked H. J. Massingham to write an introduction to the volume.[36]

Massingham was to be the first of Thompson's British admirers (such as Margaret Lane, Sir Hugh Casson, and Julian Shuckburgh) to interpret her life and work. Harold John Massingham (1888–1952), a prolific writer known for his books on nature and English country life, shared Thompson's view that technological progress had irrevocably altered the English countryside and English country life.[37] Consequently, when Massingham accepted the invitation to write an introduction to the trilogy, Thompson was delighted. In a letter to Massingham, Thompson wrote, although "reviewers have been kind and I have had a few letters of appreciation from readers, no one but you has recognized my aims and intentions in writing of that more excellent way of life of our forefathers."[38]

In his introduction to *Lark Rise to Candleford*, Massingham praised the novels of the trilogy for their evocation of life in the English hamlet, village, and market town at a time when a "local self-acting society" lived by a "fixed pattern of behaviour and with its roots warmly bedded in the soil."[39] Massingham placed the trilogy in the historical and social context of the modern world and used his review as a personal platform from which to blame the Industrial Revolution and the Enclosures for destroying English country life and for bringing about "the day of an emptied countryside harvested by machines and chemicals"[40] *Lark Rise to Candleford*, he declared, was the story of "the irreparable calamity of the English fields" and of "the utter ruin of a closely knit organic society with a richly interwoven and traditional culture."[41] It provided "an index to social change, of great complexity and heavy with revolutionary meaning." Ultimately, Thompson's story was "tragic" since "nothing has taken and nothing can take the place of what has gone." The "supreme value" of *Lark Rise to Candleford*, Massingham declared, was that Thompson "makes us see the passing of this England, not as a milestone along the road of inevitable progress, but as the attempted murder of something timeless in and quintessential to the spirit of man."[42]

English journalist and biographer Margaret Lane was the first writer to attempt a biographical sketch of Thompson. Margaret Winifred Lane (1907–94), the daughter of newspaper editor Harry George Lane, was educated at St. Stephens College, Folkstone, and at St. Hugh's College, Oxford. After receiving her B.A., she became a journalist, working in London and in New York from 1928 to 1938. Today, she is known primarily for her biographies of English writers.[43] Her brief biography of Thompson was originally published in the *Cornhill* magazine in January 1957 as a memorial article, written to mark the ten-year anniversary of Thompson's death.[44] Two years later, this article was republished in *Purely for Pleasure* (1959), a collection of Lane's biographical essays.

In 1979 Lane selected and edited a collection of Thompson's work for a book she entitled *A Country Calendar*. This volume contains a selection of Thompson's poems and nature essays, as well as the text of her previously unpublished novel, *Heatherley*. The poetry published in *A Country Calendar* had previously appeared in Thompson's *Bog Myrtle and Peat* (1921), and the nature essays had originally appeared in Thompson's monthly nature series, *The Peverel Papers*. Lane located the manuscript of *Heatherley* in the Flora Thompson archive at the Harry Ransom Humanities Research Center in Austin, Texas. An extended version of Lane's memorial article became the book's introduction.

In her introduction to *A Country Calendar*, Lane primarily addresses the relationship between Thompson's life and the events described in *Lark Rise to Candleford*. She describes Thompson's humble beginnings as "a cottage child, born in poverty, who wrote with a touch of genius."[45] Lane says little about the nature essays or the poetry in her introduction. However, in the book's foreword, she refers to Thompson's nature essays as a "somewhat secretive record" of the years she lived in Liphook with her postmaster husband and describes *Heatherley* as a "lightly disguised" and "somewhat fictionalized" account of the three years she worked at the post office in Grayshott, Hampshire, before her marriage.[46] According to Lane, Thompson did not submit *Heatherley* to her publisher because she felt "the magic of childhood and the old country life were missing."[47] Thompson's biographer, Gillian Lindsay, later confirmed Lane's assertion in *Flora Thompson: The Story of the Lark Rise Writer*, adding that Thompson wrote *Heatherley* only because fans of the trilogy wanted to know "what happened next" to her protagonist, Laura.[48]

Lane based her biography of Thompson on the events described in *Lark Rise to Candleford*, the information she gleaned from Thompson's correspondence, and the interviews she conducted with individuals who had known the author, including her daughter, Winifred. Lane quotes from a letter written by Thompson at the end of her life, in which she said of Lark Rise, "every one of the characters lived at Juniper and were just as described, with only the names altered."[49] Although Lane asserts that Thompson's childhood memories are "all faithfully set down, all true," she also states that Thompson did not intend to write the story of her life when she wrote the novels of the trilogy.[50] And, despite her reliance on the trilogy for biographical information, Lane sounds a note of caution: "Though much can be gathered from her work about her childhood and youth, the rest is obscure and has never been recorded."

In her introduction, Lane also addresses the tension between fact and fiction in *Lark Rise to Candleford* and attempts to arrive at a more accurate classification of the trilogy:

> Her three books . . . are not really novels, though fiction plays a part in them here and there. Nor are they autobiography pure and simple, for the

> personal element is evasive and oblique. They are better described, perhaps, as social history; though that, again, is a misleading name to give. They are more intimate, more personal, more alive than social history is usually allowed to be, for Flora Thompson dwells on the humble details which social historians either do not know, or else leave out. They are a simple yet infinitely detailed record of the life of the poor as it was lived in an obscure Oxfordshire hamlet.[51]

Lane's statement neatly summarizes ongoing debates over the reliability of *Lark Rise to Candleford* as a nonfiction account of rural life and source of biographical information about Flora Thompson.

A review of *A Country Calendar*, written by Ronald Blythe, appeared in the *Times Literary Supplement*. Declaring "hers was no ordinary talent," Blythe placed Thompson in the company of "[Gilbert] White and other village writers of rare quality."[52] Drawing on Lane's introduction, Blythe characterized Thompson as a woman who was "dragged into a prim suburban existence which she hated" by a husband who "was embarrassed by her writing."[53] In Thompson's nature essays, Blythe noted "the skillful weaving together of nature comment and Flora's own feelings of private involvement and intimacy." In *Heatherley*, Blythe approved Thompson's sympathy for farm laborers and her critical attitude toward "Georgian literary types" and "middle-class professional 'country writers' with their scholarly natural history and the absence of all that is instinctive in their observations." Blythe assessed Thompson's poetry in one terse comment: "A few representative poems . . . only prove that her poetry was in her prose." Throughout his review, Blythe focused primarily on the difficulties in Thompson's life that were the consequences of her gender, social class, limited education, and unsympathetic husband. He concluded, "Inherent in this last book is the plight of women of her background and the dull cult of the bottom drawer. She is all for the girl who raffled her bottom drawer and bought a bicycle."

In 1979 the Folio Society issued an edition of *Lark Rise*, introduced by Sir Hugh Casson and illustrated with twenty-four photographs.[54] In his seven-page introduction to this edition, Casson also provided a brief sketch of Thompson's life. He refers to her husband, John, as a man "who seems to have been as dull as an unstamped envelope" and states that John thought his wife's "constant reading and attempts to write pretentious and time-wasting."[55] Of Thompson's early writing career, Casson says that she was "tempted by [the] easy sales" of her "'sugared love stories' and trivial verses" that she wrote for women's magazines. Casson passes quickly over all of Thompson's work preceding *Lark Rise* and does not mention her substantial body of work for the *Catholic Fireside*. He compares her to the young John Ruskin, who "could spend half a day observing a colony of ants."[56] Thompson, Casson says, was able to assemble "a thousand small details, each diamond sharp, to form a total picture" and to create a portrait of "a vanished way of life" and a "self portrait" that was "as modest, firmly rooted and determined as a young blade of grass . . . and no less miraculous."[57]

In 1986 Julian Shuckburgh published *The Peverel Papers*, a further selection of the nature essays Thompson wrote for the *Catholic Fireside*. In his introduction to this collection, Shuckburgh announced his intention "to represent the full width of Flora Thompson interests, to avoid repetition, and to satisfy interest in the links between this work and her better-known books."[58] In Thompson's nature essays, published "fifteen years before she began *Lark Rise*," Shuckburgh noted the emergence of the "semi fictional" literary style that was to characterize Thompson's later novels. [59] Already evident in the nature essays, Shuckburgh adds, was Thompson's habit of "concealing names and places and events and to some extent her own personality." Shuckburgh credits Thompson for her "observant natural history, botany and country lore" and notes the influence of Gilbert White, Linnaeus, Huxley, and Darwin on her methods of observation and description.[60] Thompson's "detailed description of the landscape of south-eastern Hampshire" was so accurate, Shuckburgh reports, that local residents could still (in 1986) recognize the places she described in *The Peverel Papers*.

In his introduction to *The Peverel Papers,* Shuckburgh provides a brief sketch of Thompson's life and works. He acknowledges that what is known of the author's life is "almost entirely derived from her own writings" and further acknowledges that "since these writings all contain fictional elements their reliability is by no means clear."[61] However, despite these caveats, Shuckburgh continues in the tradition of Margaret Lane and Ronald Blythe, using Thompson's essays and novels to create a psychological portrait of Thompson and her marriage. Shuckburgh states that Thompson's life "can be seen, and may have been seen by her, as a succession of missed opportunities and unfulfilled yearnings."[62] He further states that Thompson "felt some fine destiny was awaiting but always somehow just eluding her" throughout her life. These statements seem to be based on Shuckburgh's sensitive appreciation for what he calls the "agony of yearning" and the "ache" of nostalgia in her work rather than on primary evidence.[63] Shuckburgh implies that Thompson's marriage was unhappy, based on two passages in *Heatherley*: one in which the fictional Laura has an "unfulfilled affair" with the sensitive and cultured Richard Brownlow and another passage in which Laura imagines writing a novel about "'a woman of fine, sensitive nature'" married to a man whose nature is "strong, coarse, and encroaching."[64] Based on his reading of the last chapter of *Candleford Green*, Shuckburgh also states that Thompson's taste for reading was considered "quite abnormal by her contemporaries, and positively disreputable by her husband and his family."[65] In reality, this chapter does not support Shuckburgh's statement, although the fictional Laura does critique "a class newly emerging" in which "much of [Laura's] life was to be spent," for its focus on "keeping up appearances," its lack of taste, and its "mass reading" of popular authors such as Maria Corelli and Nat Gould.[66] Finally, Shuckburgh interprets Thompson's invention of a fictional persona for *The Peverel Papers* (a doctor's daughter who reads Dante and who has retreated from the world to live in a cottage on the fictitious "Peverel Downs") as evidence that the author felt she had "to invent a fictitious Flora Thompson, worthy of being the author of these papers."[67] Rather than seeing the fictional persona as evidence of Thompson's creativity or her astute understanding of audience expectations, Shuckburgh concludes instead that it reveals "something deeply sad and attractive about [the] author"—that Thompson "had no confidence in her own personality."

The Scholarly Response

H. J. Massingham, Margaret Lane, Sir Hugh Casson, and Julian Shuckburgh interpreted Thompson's legacy by focusing on the autobiographical aspects of her *oeuvre* and on the accuracy of her descriptions of country life. Agricultural and social historians have also treated *Lark Rise to Candleford* as a work of nonfiction, using it as a primary source in their studies of late nineteenth-century rural life. In addition, the trilogy has been the focus of a handful of scholarly articles written by Marxist critics, feminists, and folklore scholars. Although critics and scholars have noted the artistic and literary quality of Thompson's prose, none has studied *Lark Rise to Candleford* as a literary work.

Although there has been no sustained interest in Thompson as a literary figure, a surprising number of literary reference works do include an entry for her among the entries for more famous writers. A brief entry for Thompson can be found in *The New Cambridge Bibliography of English Literature* (1972), *The Oxford Companion to English Literature* (1985), *The Feminist Companion to Literature in English (1990),* the *Oxford Guide to British Women Writers* (1999), and *The Cambridge Guide to Women's Writing in English* (1999). An appraisal of Thompson's poetry, written by John Ferns, is also found in the *Dictionary of Literary Biography.* In all of these reference works, Thompson is represented as a writer of rural memoirs or lightly fictionalized autobiography rather than as a literary figure. In *Women's Writing in English: 1900–1945* (1998), Anthea Trodd identifies Thompson as a rural working-class writer and praises *Lark*

Rise to Candleford for being "authentically a working-class record" rather than "a middle-class writer's attempt to mediate between the urban middle-class reader and the rural poor."[68] As a working-class, rural autobiographer, Thompson has also appeared in three unpublished doctoral dissertations, Susan Ann Hyman's *Green Fields: The Spirit of Place in Novels and Memoirs of the Victorian Countryside* (1994), Martin John Lovelace's *The Presentation of Folklife in the Biographies and Autobiographies of English Rural Workers* (1983), and Mary Margaret Magee's *A Dialectic of Submission and Revolt* (1987).[69]

Of Thompson's six published books, the *Lark Rise to Candleford* novels, especially *Lark Rise*, are the only works to have received critical attention. To this day, the trilogy occupies an uneasy ground between fact and fiction. *Lark Rise*, *Over to Candleford*, and *Candleford Green* are usually described as thinly veiled autobiography or social history. For this reason, Thompson is frequently compared to Fred Kitchen (1890–1969), a farm laborer who published his autobiography, *Brother to the Ox*, in 1940, and to George Sturt (1863–1927), a small country businessman who documented village life in Surrey in his famous *Change in the Village* (1912), published under his pseudonym, George Bourne. Thompson is sometimes mentioned in studies of rural fiction or regional writing, but only in passing. In *The Rural Tradition in the English Novel, 1900–1939*, Glen Cavaliero notes that few rural writers experienced country life as a means of livelihood like Thompson and her family. He refers to the "sober dignity" of her trilogy and praises it for being "probably the best account of late nineteenth century village life that we have, outside of the work of George Sturt."[70] This comparison, though flattering, is also telling, since George Sturt authored the decidedly nonfiction *Change in the Village*. W. J. Keith also mentions Thompson in *The Rural Tradition*, a study of nonfiction prose written about the English countryside. Keith praises Thompson's trilogy as a "minor classic" that is "refreshingly unsentimental."[71] Beyond the trilogy's historical value, Keith says, is the "artistic subtlety through which the carefully drawn figure of Laura acts as a filter between the personal reminiscence of Flora Thompson and the discriminating response of the reader." Stephen Wade, author of *In My Own Shire: Region and Belonging in British Writing, 1840–1970,* places *Lark Rise to Candleford,* along with Elizabeth Gaskell's *Cranford* and Mary Russell Mitford's *Our Village,* in the genre of "local communal writing," describing Thompson's trilogy as "the quintessential regional memoir in the category of the known community."[72] Although admiring the artistic and literary qualities of Thompson's work, Cavaliero, Keith, and Wade all treat *Lark Rise to Candleford* as a work of nonfiction.

To date, there have been no major studies of Thompson as a literary figure. Undoubtedly, scholarly interest in Thompson has been limited due to the perception of Thompson as an ordinary working-class woman (with a surprisingly poetic streak) who happened to write several popular books based on her childhood memories of rural Oxfordshire during the late nineteenth century. Although literary scholars have had little interest in Thompson, *Lark Rise to Candleford* is still being used as a primary source by scholars in a variety of fields such as agricultural history, folklore studies, and social history.

Lark Rise to Candleford is used as a primary source in *The Victorian Countryside* (1981), an exhaustive two-volume study of Victorian agriculture and country life published by G. E. Mingay, professor of agrarian history at the University of Kent at Canterbury. There are ten separate citations of Thompson's trilogy in this scholarly work, on topics ranging from childbirth practices to the behavior of farm laborers. In *Chilies to Chocolate*, the published proceedings of the American Academy of Sciences 1988 symposium on the introduction of New World crops into Europe, Alan Davidson uses an excerpt from *Lark Rise to Candleford* in his article "Europeans Wary Encounters with Tomatoes, Potatoes, and Other New World Foods" to illustrate how ordinary English men and women reacted to tomatoes when they were first introduced into the English market. Pamela Horn, the author of many studies of Victorian life, makes extensive use of Thompson's trilogy as a primary source in her work. In the index of *Victorian Countrywomen* (1991), there are twelve separate references to evidence found in Thompson's novels. In the index of Horn's *The Victorian Country Child* (1997), there are seventeen citations of Thompson documented, but there are also a number of unattributed "facts" from Thompson's trilogy in this work as well.[73]

Folklore scholars Deborah Kodish, Michael Pickering, and Roy Judge have also used Thompson's trilogy, particularly *Lark Rise,* as a primary source of evidence in their respective studies of English folkways. Deborah Kodish declares *Lark Rise to Candleford* to be "fine ethnography and splendid reading" in "Moving Towards the Everyday: Some Thoughts on Gossip and Visiting as Secular Procession."[74] In her study, Kodish describes the social calls that "occur every afternoon" when the women of Lark Rise "visit each other's kitchens" as a "secular" procession.[75] This secular procession, Kodish asserts, was "every bit as central to the lives of Lark Risers" as the processions associated with "festive" events such as May Day.[76] This was because visiting and gossiping allowed "individuals to manipulate or display their status," to form social networks, and to exercise social power.[77] In *Lark Rise to Candleford*, Kodish says, Thompson "reanimated" both "sacred and secular processions," thereby revealing the "continuities and complexities of hamlet life."[78]

Michael Pickering analyzes Thompson's description of village pub singing in "Popular Song at Juniper Hill." Pickering qualifies his use of

Thompson's account by classifying *Lark Rise* as both autobiography *and* autobiographical fiction–in both cases, a mediated source of evidence. Pickering holds Thompson's account (in chapter 4 of *Lark Rise)* to the evidentiary standards of his discipline, concluding that her depiction of men's singing in the taproom of the Wagon and Horses is a generalized account, rather than ethnography. Pickering notes that, as a young girl, Thompson could not have directly observed all that she writes about in this chapter. Pickering also states, "We may presume that she was attempting to give a more rounded and balanced portrait of such cultural life than would have been possible if she had confined herself to a description of one particular occasion."[79] Pickering emphasizes the creative and literary quality of Thompson's description of pub singing. He identifies her "portrayal of village labouring life" as "autobiographical fiction." [80] This "literary technique," Pickering states, "enabled her to extend her narrative scope beyond the range of her direct experience, to increase her sympathy and detachment, to give greater depth to other characters, and a symbolic feeling and value to significant events." Pickering does not dismiss Thompson's account for being fictional in part. Instead, he compares her favorably to Thomas Hardy, whose novels, he notes, are often cited by social and cultural historians.

In "Fact and Fancy in Tennyson's 'May Queen' and in Flora Thompson's 'May Day,'" Roy Judge studies Thompson's description of May Day celebrations in chapter 8 of *Lark Rise* and declares it a "classic description of rural garlanding."[81] Judge is concerned with the authenticity of Thompson's account, noting that since it supposedly came from Thompson's childhood memories, the description is "almost too good to be true." Judge concludes that, "since no memory could be that retentive," Thompson must have recreated some aspects of her account. Judge also notes an "idyllic quality" in Thompson's description of May Day activities, which he attributes to her "highly creative skill."[82] Although noting that Thompson's description of May Day activities is idiosyncratic, he still concludes that her account "conforms reasonably well with the local pattern of the area in the 1880s."[83]

Thompson's *Lark Rise to Candleford* makes a brief appearance in Raymond Williams's *The Country and the City* (1973). Williams links the trilogy to Ronald Blythe's distinctly documentary *Akenfield* (1969), describing both as "irreplaceable records."[84] Jonathan Rose, in *The Intellectual Life of the British Working Classes* (2001), associates Thompson's trilogy with William Lovett's *Life and Struggles* (1876) and describes them as "two classic proletarian memoirs" that have proven to be "reasonably (if not perfectly) accurate."[85] Rose, a professor of history at Drew University, uses Thompson's novels as evidence in his discussion of various aspects of working-class life, such as the inadequacies of country schools and the working man's view of Darwin's *On the Origin of Species.* Rose makes the most extensive use of *Lark Rise to Candleford* to document the "shared literary culture" that existed before public libraries appeared in rural areas—a time when books "were practically treated as public property."[86] Rose also uses passages from Thompson's trilogy to illustrate how popular literature could function as propaganda, conveying conservative values to working-class readers. Using a passage from *Candleford Green*, Rose also notes how the pious literature typically found in Sunday school libraries distorted the perception that "impoverished rural laborers" had about their own economic and social condition.[87] Even the poorest resident of Lark Rise would have concluded that the *real poor* lived in the slums after reading about the misery of urban slum life in such literature.

Barbara English questions scholars' use of *Lark Rise to Candleford* as a source of evidence in "*Lark Rise* and Juniper Hill: A Victorian Community in Literature and in History." English consulted various official records and documents (including parish and estate records, census returns, and Ordnance Survey maps) to challenge historians' uncritical acceptance of *Lark Rise to Candleford* as a primary source. As English points out, critics and scholars have always assumed that *Lark Rise* was not only an autobiography but also an accurate and factual record. In 1985, when she surveyed work published by historians in the forty years following the publication of *Lark Rise*, English reports that she found "one hundred and seventy-three references to the trilogy, in forty-five books or articles."[88] English states that "none of the books or articles using *Lark Rise* weighed up its value as a primary source."[89]

English contends that Flora Thompson was creating "a literary masterpiece" rather than a historical record when she wrote the novels of her trilogy.[90] English notes that when *Lark Rise* was first published, Thompson did not claim the book was a factual account of her childhood. Instead, Thompson referred to *Lark Rise* as a "story" in her introductory note to the first edition.[91] Because Thompson called *Lark Rise* "a story" and changed the names of people and places she had known as a child, English concludes that Thompson's intention was "to present a fictional account in a real setting." English further notes that when she examined three essays published in the 1930s that became the foundation for three chapters of *Lark Rise*, she discovered that the few alterations Thompson made to these texts were "for literary rather than historic reasons: that is to improve the construction and phrasing rather than to correct factual error."[92]

To further prove the fictional nature of Thompson's trilogy, English includes a statement from the introduction to *A Country Calendar* in which Thompson is quoted as saying, "In *Over to Candleford* and *Candleford Green* I wrote more freely than in *Lark Rise*, and do not think I described any house or place exactly as it existed."[93] Based on this statement, English concludes that historians should use these two books only "in confirmation of evidence found elsewhere; they cannot be regarded as primary sources, but only in the same light as fiction." Despite Thompson's claim that in *Lark Rise* her "aim throughout was to describe things exactly as they were, without sentimentalizing or dramatizing," English's close study of *Lark Rise* reveals that "some sections of *Lark Rise* can be shown to be true, some doubtful or suspect, others untrue."[94] English notes a number of discrepancies between Thompson's fictional Lark Rise and the hamlet of Juniper Hill, where Flora Thompson was born and spent her childhood. Noting that Thompson's novels are still used by her biographers as the chief source of information about the author's private life, English also points out several significant discrepancies between the fictional family Thompson created for *Lark Rise to Candleford* and Flora's family (the Timms family of record) living at Juniper Hill. English concludes that in *Lark Rise* Thompson "constructed a past which never really existed" and a village "with the violence left out, where no one went away, and children did not die."[95]

Thompson has been studied as a working-class writer by a variety of scholars. John Burnett, David Vincent, and David Mayall include Thompson in their seminal work on the British working-class autobiography, *The Autobiography of the Working Class*. Burnett, Vincent, and Mayall compiled and annotated the titles of published and unpublished working-class autobiographies written between 1790 and 1945 for this three-volume work. While calling Thompson's trilogy "a deservedly famous account," Burnett, Vincent, and Mayall conclude that *Lark Rise to Candleford* is "less a life history and more an evocative and vivid portrait of rural life and labour during a period of rapid transformation."[96] It is interesting to note that these authors include Thompson's *Still Glides the Stream* with the novels of *Lark Rise to Candleford*, calling all four "semi-autobiographical." Because *Still Glides the Stream* is set in a different Oxfordshire community and explores the lives of a totally different cast of characters, this description of *Still Glides the Stream* is somewhat misleading.

Rebecca O'Rourke and Sara Mills also identify Thompson as a working-class woman writer in their respective studies of the British working-class novel of the 1920s and 1930s. In "Were There No Women? British Working Class Women's Writing in the Inter-War Period," O'Rourke compares Thompson to Ethel Mannin, a socialist and prolific working-class writer of the same period. Unlike male working-class novelists, O'Rourke notes, women novelists such as Mannin and Thompson wrote of their early working-class experience, but "as women whose lives took them away from their class in later years."[97] O'Rourke says that Mannin and Thompson were both determined to become writers from an early age and "in very contrasted ways, achieved their ambition."[98] Unlike Ethel Mannin, who achieved "early success and prolificacy," Thompson, O'Rourke says, stands as an example of the thwarted writer who "comes late to writing and produces little."[99] O'Rourke characterizes Thompson as "the proper model of a working-class woman writer, simply because of her struggle to become one and the only partial realisation of her ambition."[100]

O'Rourke's evaluation clearly privileges Thompson the novelist over Thompson the essayist and short story writer. In fact, O'Rourke states that *Lark Rise to Candleford* is Thompson's "only substantive work."[101] She asserts that the work that Thompson published in the *Catholic Fireside* and the *Daily News* was "simply writing that would sell" rather than the "writing she wanted to do."[102] This is, perhaps, too broad a statement. Although Thompson was not happy with the "small sugared love tales" she wrote for various women's magazines, her writing for the *Catholic Fireside* was devoted to topics close to Thompson's heart: nature and literature.[103] O'Rourke concludes that *Lark Rise to Candleford* is "a self-conscious recollection of a community on the point of change" and a "social history of the life and times of the rural poor" rather than a novel.[104]

In her study of the working-class novel, Sara Mills asks why there were so few working-class women writing novels in the 1930s at a time when there was an outpouring of novels written by working-class men. In "Problems in the Analysis of British Working Class Women's Writing in the Thirties: Flora Thompson's *Lark Rise to Candleford*," Mills uses *Lark Rise to Candleford* and an essay Thompson published in the *Lady* to identify the constraints that prevented working-class women from writing as prolifically as working-class men.[105] Mills identifies four constraints that affected working-class women writers in general and Thompson in particular. Three of these constraints were finding time in which to write, establishing a political address, and creating an appropriate voice. The fourth constraint, imposed on working-class women writers by publishers and critics, was the assumption that their writing was essentially autobiographical.

Finding time in which to write was particularly difficult for working-class women, Mills states. Due to prevailing social conventions, "writing and solitude were not necessarily considered to be part of a 'woman's role.'"[106] Citing O'Rourke, Mills states that "women simply did not have the time to spend on writing."[107] To prove Thompson did not have time to write until the last decade of her life, Mills points to the fact that Thompson did not start writing *Lark Rise* until she was in her sixties. Certainly, domestic life, childrearing, working at the post office, and dealing with the hardships of World War I and World War II limited the time Thompson had to devote to her writing. However, she was publishing poetry, short stories, and essays for more than twenty years before *Lark Rise* was published, a fact that Mills does not acknowledge.

The second constraint Mills identifies is the inability of working-class women of the 1930s to identify with their own social class and with the class struggle. Although "few radicals" would consider Thompson a working-class writer, Mills says she has chosen to do so even though Thompson's work does not display a strong sense of class consciousness or "political address."[108] Mills is perplexed by Thompson's decision to write a "rural idyll" set in the 1880s at a time when "unemployment was a burning issue" and the theme of many working-class novels.[109] Instead, Mills says, Thompson wrote of a rural working-class community that was "unconcerned with political struggle."[110] Mills's identification of Thompson as a working-class writer is somewhat problematic. Thompson may have grown up in an impoverished rural hamlet as a child, but her father was a stonemason, not an agricultural worker, and her mother was a woman of some refinement. When a young girl living in Ardley, Thompson's mother had gone to the rector's house every day after school, where she received lessons in music and writing and absorbed the manners of the dignified and cultured rector and his sister.[111] Furthermore, Thompson married a fellow post office employee and, through her husband's professional promotions, eventually became a member of the lower middle class.

Mills says that the third constraint placed upon working-class women writers was the pressure to find an acceptable voice. In the 1930s, women were expected to write about certain topics (such as romance and domestic life) and only in certain genres. Mills says Thompson was discouraged from writing poetry and was "quite actively steered" into writing about traditionally feminine subjects in short stories and essays geared toward women's magazines like the *Lady*.[112] Thompson did this, Mills says, in order to "make a living." However, Thompson did not depend on the income from her short stories and essays for her livelihood. It is more accurate to say that Thompson chose to earn extra money in this way because, as both Margaret Lane and Gillian Lindsay have noted, she used her earnings to send her children to excellent schools. Furthermore, Thompson never restricted herself to one genre. As previously noted, she published poetry, short fiction, nature essays, and literary essays, and she even wrote a novel (*Gates of Eden*) well before her famous trilogy was published.

The fourth constraint placed on working-class women writers, Mills says, was the automatic classification of women's writing as autobiography. Mills expresses surprise at the persistent identification of *Lark Rise to Candleford* as an autobiography. The trilogy cannot be an autobiography, Mills says, because it is "a third person narrated text" and because it is "so little focused on the central protagonist [Laura]."[113] Mills further notes that the trilogy is written in two distinct, omniscient third-person voices: the "ethnographic" voice that reports on the life of the rural poor and the voice that focuses on Laura's life. Mills attributes the continued misclassification of *Lark Rise to Candleford* to prevailing "stereotypes of women's writing simply flowing forth in an unmediated way," as if women "simply transfer their experiences to the page." The effect of this stereotype, as Mills astutely observes, is to downgrade women's texts to "a less creative status."

Although *Lark Rise to Candleford* is the subject of Mills's study, she does not discriminate between the novels in the trilogy, but lumps them all together in her discussion. As a result, her statements about the trilogy are sometimes too broad and, in other cases, inaccurate. For example, in pointing out an apparent conflict in Thompson's portrayal of a hard-working but happy rural community, Mills says "this idyllic description is *constantly* juxtaposed with Laura's family's concern to escape from the community and move to the town" (emphasis added).[114] In *Lark Rise,* the narrator does devote several paragraphs to discussing the sometimes "daily" discussions that Laura's mother and father once had about moving away from Lark Rise, but it is a minor point in a complex narrative. Mills also states that Laura "only found out about the festivals, religion, etc. because she talked to the older women" of the community. While Laura does credit the older residents of Lark Rise for telling her about some of the older traditions, Laura is represented as participating in or observing the majority of these events in all three novels. Mills observes, correctly, that the first book of the trilogy, *Lark Rise*, is "little focused" on Laura, the book's protagonist. However, in the subsequent books of the trilogy, *Over to Candleford* and *Candleford Green*, Thompson focuses primarily on Laura and devotes less attention to documenting rural life.

Juliet Dusinberre and Sandra A. Zagarell, while accepting the trilogy as an autobiographical account, move toward a more nuanced literary appreciation of Thompson's work in their respective studies. Dusinberre, in "The Child's Eye and the Adult's Voice: Flora Thompson's *Lark Rise to Candleford*," variously identifies *Lark Rise to Candleford* as a "trilogy of recollections" about the author's childhood, a "third- person autobiography," and part of "the literature of childhood memories."[115] It is "a true story," Dusinberre says, in which Thompson "adheres resolutely to her conviction that she records facts unadulterated by fiction."[116] Dusinberre's study is focused on the creative power of memory and on Thompson's use of "the child's eye and the adult's voice" in the novels' narrative. Dusinberre states, "The picture is the child's, but the adult writing in the present is still the child watching in the past."[117] Dusinberre notes Thompson's artistry, comparing her to Proust, Virginia Woolf, and Dorothy Richardson, writers who share her "fascination with how memory works."[118] Dusinberre's sensitive analysis attests to the creative power of Thompson's memory and to her creation of that "special area where writer and child always meet, where the imagination roams freely."[119]

Identifying a new literary genre is the focus of Sandra A. Zagarell's treatment of *Lark Rise* in "Narratives of Community: The Identification of a Genre." Zagarell places Thompson in the company of women writers such as Sarah Orne Jewett, whose "narratives of community" present "a coherent response to the social, economic, cultural, and demographic changes caused by industrialism, urbanization, and the spread of capitalism."[120] Zagarell defines a "narrative of community" as a type of literature that focuses on "the minute and quite ordinary processes through which the community maintains itself as an entity." Noting that *Lark Rise* has generally been classified as a "source of historical or anthropological information," Zagarell says that approaching it as a narrative of community highlights its "literary distinction."[121]

Zagarell makes several interesting observations about characterization and plot in *Lark Rise*. She observes that Thompson is more concerned about community identity and community process than in delineating individual characters or plotting the course of individual lives. She also notes that the narrator of *Lark Rise* "often refers to the characters collectively" as "country people," "husbands," or "wives."[122] Even when the narrator presents individual characters such as "Old Sally and her husband," Zagarell says, their stories are generally used "to illustrate an aspect of the community's history, customs, or circumstances." As Zagarell points out, like other narratives of community, *Lark Rise* does not rely on a linear plot but proceeds by episodes that immerse the reader in "virtually every facet of community life," thus revealing community dynamics.[123] By identifying these differences between *Lark Rise* and more traditional novels, Zagarell provides valuable insight into the reason why *Lark Rise* continues to be read as a work of social history rather than fiction.

Conclusion

A thread that runs through the past sixty years of critical response to Flora Thompson is the difficulty of separating fact from fiction in her work. This is especially true of the books of her trilogy, but it is also true of Thompson's nature essays, *The Peverel Papers*. To legitimize or qualify their use of Thompson's work as a primary source, scholars in different disciplines have classified her books in various ways: as social history, fictionalized autobiography, third-person autobiography, and ethnography. And even though many critics and scholars have made note of Thompson's literary artistry, none has identified *Lark Rise*, *Over to Candleford*, or *Candleford Green* as novels. Too often, the three books are lumped together, even though *Over to Candleford* and *Candleford Green* are noticeably more fictionalized than *Lark Rise*. Another noticeable aspect of the scholarly response to Thompson has been the almost exclusive focus on the first book of her trilogy, *Lark Rise*. The subsequent books of the trilogy and Thompson's other published novels, *Still Glides the Stream* and *Heatherley,* have not been studied and are rarely mentioned in scholarly studies of the author. Thompson's poetry, short stories, and essays are also not discussed, unless to be dismissed as hack work.

Close study of Thompson's published work reveals that she was not a simple apprentice or hack writer before she penned *Lark Rise*. The nature essays that she wrote for *The Peverel Papers* are distinguished by a lyricism and sophistication that place them among Thompson's finest writing. These nature essays, as well as the literary essays that she wrote for *The Fireside Reading Circle*, reveal the author's impressive knowledge of English literature, history, and folklore. Even Thompson's formulaic short fiction has a charm born of her penchant for rural settings and literary-minded protagonists. *Lark Rise to Candleford*, *Heatherley*, and *Still Glides the Stream*, do more than document the minutiae of daily life in the countryside. They are sources of characters, themes, and settings whose interest is more than autobiographical. In addition, *Lark Rise to Candleford* and the posthumously published *Heatherley* provide a fascinating account of the reading habits and oral tradition of the agricultural working classes during the late Victorian era, a full fifteen years before Richard Altick published his groundbreaking study of the mass reading public, *The English Common Reader.*

To fully appreciate Thompson's significance as an early twentieth-century woman writer, it is necessary to consider the whole of her *oeuvre*, most of which has never been studied. What has been lost in the emphasis on *Lark Rise to Candleford* is a real sense of Thompson's career as a working writer. The novels that comprise *Lark Rise to Candleford* were published during the last seven years of Thompson's life. They are the culmination of Thompson's thirty-five-year career as a poet, essayist, short fiction writer, and freelance journalist, rather than the late flowering of a frustrated and repressed working woman.

2
The Peverel Papers

IN 1957, WHEN JOURNALIST AND BIOGRAPHER MARGARET LANE PUBLISHED the first biographical sketch of Thompson in the *Cornhill*, she described Thompson as a happy illustration of "the unquenchable vigour of those strange gifts which are sometimes bestowed in the most unlikely place."[1] In Lane's words, Thompson's "strange" gift "blossomed into fulfillment in old age" and did so "without education or encouragement."[2] The nature essays that Thompson published in the *Catholic Fireside* between 1921 and 1927 reveal, however, that she was an accomplished writer long before the publication of *Lark Rise*. These monthly nature essays, known as *The Peverel Papers*, also reveal that Thompson was an ambitious autodidact who acquired an impressive knowledge of nature and literature despite the inadequacies of her formal education.

The Peverel Papers is critical to an accurate assessment of Thompson's career as a working writer. The nature essays that she published in the *Catholic Fireside* form a complex body of work that reflects her passionate love for nature, her acute powers of observation, and her fascination with specific geographical locations. Individual essays focus on seasonal changes in the natural landscape near Thompson's home in Hampshire and combine evocative descriptions of the English countryside with detailed information on subjects such as the growth and development of familiar plants and animals.[3] Many of the essays also include brief commentary on human affairs, from the plight of World War I veterans to the lives of simple country folk. In addition to their merits as skillfully written nature notes, these essays feature Thompson's early experiments with representing herself through a fictional persona, a doctor's daughter who has retreated to the countryside seeking the healing power of nature in the aftermath of World War I. The nature essays also contain the seeds of stories and characters that would later blossom (to use Lane's metaphor) on the pages of *Lark Rise to Candleford*: stories of harvest suppers, May Day celebrations, and old Queenie the beekeeper.

Thompson was forty-four years old and the mother of three children when she published her first nature essay in *Out of Doors*, a nature series that debuted in the *Catholic Fireside* in January 1921.[4] The *Catholic Fireside*, a weekly publication for Catholic women, sold for the modest price of 3 pence an issue. Its subscribers were served traditional women's magazine fare (short fiction and articles on fashion, cooking, and gardening) along with decidedly more feminist articles on women's education, finances, and insurance, a combination that particularly appealed to Thompson.[5] During the first year of the series, the essays that Thompson wrote for *Out of Doors* averaged one page (three closely printed columns or approximately 1,200 words) in length. Over the next six years, Thompson's nature essays gradually grew in length, reaching an average of three to four pages (or approximately 2,500 words) by the end of the series. Renamed *The Peverel Papers* in 1922, Thompson's nature series proved to be a success. At least one admirer wrote to the *Catholic Fireside*, asking if past essays were available in book form.[6] Twenty-one years later, the Oxford University Press expressed an interest in publishing a book version of *The Peverel Papers*. In a letter dated March 5, 1943, Geoffrey Cumberlege wrote to Thompson, "The Peverel Papers are full of good things and I am sure you can do such a book as you describe extremely well."[7] Although handwritten notes on copies of the essays published in June and December of 1921 show that Thompson had begun to edit her published nature essays, the book never materialized.[8] Two collections of excerpts from *Out of Doors* and *The Peverel Papers* were eventually published after Thompson's death. The first collection was published in 1979 by Lane in *A Country Calendar*. Julian Shuckburgh selected, edited, and introduced a further selection of excerpts in *The Peverel Papers: A Yearbook of the Countryside*, published in 1986.[9]

Lane selected and arranged fifty-seven excerpts from the nature essays that Thompson published between 1921 and 1926 for *A Country Calendar*. She grouped her selection of excerpts by month without identifying the exact date of publication or arranging the excerpts within each month chronologically.[10] Inexplicably, Lane also eliminated Thompson's references to "Peverel" in several excerpts, despite acknowledging that the original essays were published as *The Peverel Papers* in her introduction to this book. In the excerpt from "January" 1925, for example, Lane changed Thompson's "Peverel" to "the hill."[11] In an excerpt from "October" 1923, Lane altered another reference to "Peverel" by substituting "this place."[12] Surprisingly, Lane also misidentified the month of publication for ten of the fifty-seven excerpts she selected.[13] Despite these alterations and errors, Lane made an important contribution to Thompson's literary legacy when she published *A Country Calendar*. Thanks to Lane, a new generation of readers was able to read samples of Thompson's work for the *Catholic Fireside* as well as her previously unpublished novel, *Heatherley*. However, Lane's selection of excerpts from *Out of Doors* and *The Peverel Papers* does have its limitations. Lane did not publish full essays but chose excerpts that reflected her personal taste for the more picturesque passages in Thompson's work. And, although Lane grouped the excerpts by month, her selection of excerpts lacks focus, particularly because she does not identify the year of publication or provide any context for the excerpts. Lane's approach might be more suited to the tastes of a general audience, but the full flavor and complexity of the original essays is lost in the process.

Julian Shuckburgh's *The Peverel Papers: A Yearbook of the Countryside* is devoted solely to Thompson's nature essays. Like Lane, Shuckburgh selected excerpts from the original essays and grouped them by month without identifying the exact date of publication. Unlike Lane, he included excerpts from 1927, the last year of the series. Shuckburgh's selection and arrangement of the excerpts is artful. Because he used ellipses between excerpts from the same essay or to indicate breaks between excerpts from different years, his arrangement creates the appearance of a continuous narrative for each month. This arrangement, although skillfully done, creates the impression that the original essays were more polished and unified than they sometimes were. However, because Shuckburgh's excerpts are longer and represent a wider range of the topics that Thompson covered in the original essays, his selection conveys more of the content and spirit of the originals.

Thompson's Fictional Persona

The Peverel Papers provides an intriguing glimpse of Thompson's first experiments with using a semifictional persona to represent her life experience. During the seven years that she published monthly nature essays in the *Catholic Fireside*, Thompson never revealed her true identity to her readers, despite publishing the essays under her own name. Rather than concealing her identity by adopting a pseudonym, she created a persona: a Flora Thompson who was unmarried, childless, and living in a cottage at the edge of the New Forest. The real Flora Thompson was a wife and the mother of three children. She lived approximately sixty miles from the New Forest and wrote her monthly essays at her kitchen table, amid the distractions of a busy household. Nearly twenty years later, Thompson would once again represent her personal experience through another semi-fictional figure, Laura, the protagonist of *Lark Rise to Candleford*.

The fictional "Flora" whom Thompson created for *Out of Doors* was a woman whose family, class, education, and religion were quite different from her own.[14] In the nature essays, "Flora" is a cultured doctor's daughter, presumably Catholic, who has come to the New Forest to seek spiritual healing in the aftermath of World War I. She is a solitary figure, living in a secluded cottage with her dog, Boojie. Apart from a few odd jobs correcting proofs and collecting botanical specimens, "Flora" lives with no visible means of support. She roams the English countryside, free of the daily demands of the real Thompson's husband and children. The most detailed information about "Flora" is found in the nature essays published between March 1921 and January 1922. In the essay for March 1921, "Flora" remarks, rather offhandedly, that she "had been working all the day before and far into the night correcting proofs." She is happy that Boojie is finally "back from the Vet's, his poor, trap-torn paw quite healed and strong again."[15]

Thompson provides far more detail about "Flora's" middle-class upbringing, genteel lifestyle, and personal relationships in the essay for April 1921. This essay opens with a poem entitled "April," which "Flora" says was written the previous spring when her Scottish friend Fiona was staying at her cottage.[16] The poem, "April," sets the tone for Thompson's depiction of "Flora," the aspiring poet and cultured nature lover. "Flora" recalls a childhood memory of stumbling across a nest of pheasant eggs while "playing truant" from her governess.[17] This incident establishes "Flora's" middle-class upbringing, as well as her independence and sense of adventure. "Flora" describes herself as "a prodigal daughter" who has returned to her "native heath." She lives in a cottage surrounded by a "wilderness" of overgrown plants that she has transformed into a garden of her "own making." Her cottage is bordered by an orchard full of trees that are "old, grotesquely, Japanesely so!" Despite her neighbors' advice to prune or replace its ancient, gnarled trees, the orchard remains untouched. It is her "shrine to Beauty." "Flora's" daily life is idyllic; she stays "at home for whole days together" or dawdles "through the woodland ways," filling a "primrose basket for the Bermondsey school-children." Despite her generosity toward school-children, "Flora" is mildly antisocial. After several encounters with her neighbors, she concludes that they have nothing to offer but an "arid desert of small talk." She also resents these neighbors for forcing her to fight "many a wordy battle" to justify keeping her orchard "inviolate." "Luckily," she reports with satisfaction, "my visitors soon found me out as an utterly impractical person, who was certainly not 'doing her bit' and left me to myself."

In "June" 1921, "Flora" describes the interior of her cottage and its middle-class accoutrements: the pictures, the overflowing bookcases, the "jars and bowls and vases of flowers," and the old writing table at which her father "wrote out his prescriptions."[18] More importantly, Thompson uses the "June" essay to establish "Flora's" cultural credentials and to represent the real Flora Thompson's literary accomplishments and ambitions. "Flora" announces that she has spent the morning wandering alone in the New Forest with a book of poetry in her coat pocket. Although she does not "greatly care for out-of-door reading," she always takes along "old, quiet soothing things" such as *The Excursion*, *The Faerie Queene*, or her "old battered, dog-eared book of sonnets." Although "Flora" believes that "the words of man, even the words of the greatest, always seem pale and inadequate before the vivid, spontaneous joy of Nature," she plans to "compile an anthology for out-of-door reading." Bound in a "serviceable, weatherproof cover" and priced at one shilling, her anthology would include "Shelley's 'Skylark' and the less known but equally beautiful 'Skylark' of Frederick Tennyson; Thomas Hardy's 'February Thrush'; and the 'Nightingale' of Keats."

When "Flora" discusses future literary projects, such as the anthology for "out-of-door reading," it is sometimes difficult to distinguish between Thompson and her persona. Because Thompson published a book of her own poetry, *Bog Myrtle and Peat*, the same year that she began publishing nature essays in the *Catholic Fireside*, she may have used "Flora" to voice her dream of publishing such an anthology in the future. Or, like the overflowing bookcases and vases of flowers described in this essay, the anthology may have only been one more fictional detail about "Flora." The discussion of poetry in the "June" essay certainly implies that her knowledge of English poetry is extensive. She is so familiar with Spenser's sixteenth-century masterpiece, *The Faerie Queene*, and Wordsworth's lengthy philosophical poem, *The Excursion*, that she turns to both works when she needs to read something that is "quiet" and "soothing." In the "June" essay, "Flora" also includes a stanza of poetry written, she says, by a "great living poet." She asks her readers, rather coyly, "I wonder if you know it?"[19] Thompson did not routinely challenge her readers to identify the poetry excerpts in her nature essays, even though she frequently incorporated unidentified lines or stanzas of poetry into these essays. The implication was that "Flora" is so familiar with the whole of English poetry that she can quote single lines or entire stanzas of poetry effortlessly. Thompson had a deep love for English poetry, and the expertise that "Flora" displays is Thompson's genuine expertise.

In the essay for July 1921, "Flora" reports that Father Conlan is bringing "the Poet" to tea.[20] In Thompson's nature essays, there are many individuals, like "the Poet," who are identified by their professions rather than by their names. Like the "overflowing bookcases" of the "June" essay, some of these nameless individuals are evidence that "Flora" is a cultivated woman with artistic and intellectual connections to the outside world. In this case, the unidentified poet has a literary purpose in coming to her cottage. He is writing the biography of a previous tenant, a "famous woman writer" who had lived in "Flora's" cottage "for a few tragic months." In the "July" essay, "Flora" also introduces a very different set of acquaintances: the gypsy companions of her youth. Gypsies play a recurring role in the nature essays. They are not only a part of her past, but they are also a part of her present life. In the nature essays, "Flora" has warm personal relationships with individual gypsies.

The nature essays for August through December 1921 add few new details to the portrait of "Flora." In "August" another anonymous professional, a "London naturalist," commissions her to collect flower specimens.[21] In "October," she prepares for winter by placing her Dante and an Italian dictionary "upon the little table by the hearth."[22] In "November" 1921, "Flora" meets a gypsy woman who reads her palm and predicts that she will be loved "by a lot o' folks—strangers shall become friends—people all over."[23] Thompson later reused this encounter with a gypsy woman (believed to be an actual event in Thompson's life) in *Candleford Green*, in the chapter entitled "At the Post Office." Over the years, this passage has been quoted in various books and articles about Thompson. This incident is found, for example, in Margaret Lane's introduction to *A Country Calendar* and in Gillian Lindsay's *Flora Thompson: The Story of the Lark Rise Writer.* The "November" essay also includes some unflattering criticism from one of Thompson's readers. The reader, she reports, "suggested, rather sardonically" that she should "write a book called *Gardening without Tears*" because her flowers "seemed to spring and blow without any pains or trouble" on her part. Apparently, the anonymous critic had touched a nerve, for Thompson uses this essay to defend "Flora" (and probably herself) from this type of criticism. "Flora" first disavows any claim to being an expert gardener. She then says, "I get my full share of disappointments, although I do not mention them, being, by nature, more inclined to dwell upon the successes than the failures." It is impossible to know whether Thompson had been describing a cottage garden that was real, remembered, or imagined in her essays for *Out of Doors*. An experienced gardener would have recognized "Flora's" rather flimsy defense for what it really was: an admission that she had been describing an ideal garden.

The nature essay for January 1922, published under the series's new title, *The Peverel Papers*, is the last essay to fully maintain the fiction of "Flora." A set of asterisks divides the essay into two sections. The first section provides a belated raison d'être for the essays Thompson had written during the previous year. The second section is composed of Thompson's nature notes for January. The first half of "January" is both a spiritual diary and a letter to the readers of *Out of Doors* in which "Flora" describes the series of events that brought her to the New Forest. At the end of World War I, after a period of being "in the press of things, getting and spending," "Flora" says that she decided to travel to Peverel Downs to research the life of a "holy hermit" who, according to local legend, had once lived by a lake known as "Hermit's Pool."[24] Once she set foot on Peverel Downs, however, she felt like "a homing bird after a stormy flight." She desired nothing more than to rest her "war-worn nerves" and to steep her "tired soul" in the beauty of nature. Within days, she chose to embrace a new way of life. Henceforth, she would be a "modern hermit," living alone in a cottage "tucked away amongst pine and holly at the foot of the Peverel Downs."

In the essay for January 1922, "Flora" describes the monastic simplicity of her current life. Her cottage, a "mere snail-shell of a place," has become a monastic "cell."[25] She has no human companions. Her dog, Boojie, and her books are her only "company." Like a hermit, "Flora" is self-sufficient; her cottage garden supplies her "frugal table," and her "pen" supplies her "simple luxuries." Despite the monastic simplicity of her daily life, "Flora's" retreat from the world is not overtly religious. The spiritual struggle and eventual healing that Thompson describes in "January" 1922 is more Wordsworthian than Christian. Like Wordsworth, who found in nature "that blessed mood . . . In which the heavy and the weary weight / Of all this unintelligible world is lighten'd," "Flora" also finds "the comfort and healing nature holds in store" for those who have been "stripped" by suffering.[26] In the two years [27] since her arrival on Peverel Downs, "Flora" has submitted herself to the healing power of nature: "I have steeped my whole being in the rain and dew, have rejoiced in the sun, exulted in the shrilling of the wind. The song of birds, the stirring of insects, the murmuring of bees in the heath-bells, of wandering winds in the tree-tops, the crackling of snow and frost, the plashing of summer rain—every one of nature's myriad voices has struck an answering chord in me." Despite the Franciscan undertones in this passage (including the use of the mildly religious "exulted" and "rejoiced"), "Flora's" spiritual testimony is actually an account of the healing power of nature. No doubt, Thompson's readers supplied the missing connection between the mystical love of God and the mystical love of nature that "Flora" describes in this passage.

In "January" 1922, "Flora" continues to assert her right to seclusion. Despite her claims to be a "modern hermit," "Flora's" lack of interest in her neighbors is not based on spiritual principles. As she does in the essay for April 1921, "Flora" rejects her neighbors because they do not share her interests or sensibilities. "They have their interests, I have mine," she comments tersely in the January essay.[28] "Flora's" true friends are her readers. They are the men and women who love the things she loves: "the small, beautiful, simple things in nature and in life." She writes her monthly essays in order to share "all I see and hear and read which I think will interest them, hoping that, before very long, they will come to think of the Hermit of the Peverel Downs as a friend."

Most of the detail that Thompson supplies about "Flora's" search for a simpler way of life in "January" 1922 is clearly fictional; however,

"Flora's" spiritual struggle and feelings of anguish are undoubtedly real. Thompson was heartbroken when her beloved brother Edwin Timms died in combat during World War I.[29] In this essay, when "Flora" says "that which I had, excepting a bare subsistence, the war took from me," she could be expressing the pain that Thompson experienced after losing Edwin. Thompson's readers would have found it easy to identify with the personal struggle she describes in "January" 1922. Like Thompson, her readers had also endured the privations of wartime and had lost beloved brothers, husbands, and sons on the battlefield.

Family Members

The "Flora" of *Out of Doors* and *The Peverel Papers* is a solitary figure, with few family members and few close friends. Apart from one brief mention of her father and a few memories of a brother named Edmund, there are very few references to "Flora's" family in the nature essays. The essay for June 1921 mentions a father, a grandmother, and several aunts, but only as the original owners of family heirlooms. In her cottage, "Flora" has "the old writing table" at which her father "wrote out his prescriptions."[30] She also has her grandmother's blue-and-white china and the samplers stitched by her aunts. In "November" 1921, "Flora" also refers to a grandmother who handed down a recipe for cowslip mead.

"Flora" introduces her brother Edmund in "July" 1921. She remembers the sight of Edmund hanging "suspended by his clothes" from the bough of a tree "for one terrible moment" after attempting to rifle a bird's nest.[31] "Flora" also describes the time she hurt Edmund's feelings by smearing her legs with peat and pretending that a gypsy boy was her real brother. Edmund had "walked aloof in outraged dignity" after this insult, even though the gypsy boy was his "sworn blood brother." In "October" 1922, "Flora" also recalls when she and a brother (this time unnamed) had stopped to play with a lonely boy who was scaring rooks away from a field freshly sown with winter wheat. Was this brother Edmund as well? Margaret Lane, Gillian Lindsay, John Owen Smith, and Christine Bloxham have all identified Edwin Timms as the Edmund of *Lark Rise to Candleford.* Should the reader assume that the Edmund of *Out of Doors* and *The Peverel Papers* is also based on Edwin Timms?

Thompson used the name Edmund in her first published short story, "The Toft Cup" (1912). In this story, Edmund Varney is a journalist who falls in love at first sight with the beautiful orphan Grace Coombe. There is no obvious connection between the Edmund of "The Toft Cup" and the Edmund of Thompson's nature essays. Although the Edmund in *Out of Doors* and *The Peverel Papers* is "Flora's" brother, it is not clear whether he is also the Edmund of *Lark Rise to Candleford.* Did the young Flora

Timms and her brother Edwin have a gypsy friend? If so, did Flora pretend that she was the gypsy boy's sister? The events described in *Lark Rise to Candleford* and *Heatherley* are often assumed (by Thompson's readers) to be true events in her life. Since none of the exciting stories about Edmund and "Flora" in the nature essays appear in *Lark Rise to Candleford*, does that mean that the stories in the nature essays are probably not true? Such questions underscore the difficulty of separating fact from fiction in Thompson's work. Because there are relatively few records of her life, Margaret Lane, Gillian Lindsay, John Owen Smith, and Christine Bloxham, the authors who have written the most important accounts of Thompson's life, have all used the novels of *Lark Rise to Candleford* and *Heatherley* as the starting point for their biographical research. Using public records, the letters exchanged between Thompson and her various correspondents, and the testimony of a few individuals who knew Thompson, each of these writers has identified the similarities and noted the discrepancies between what is known of the author's life and the events, settings, and characters that she describes in her novels. Without independent documentation it is impossible to know which of the events described in the nature essays or in the novels are factually true.

Friends

In *Out of Doors* and *The Peverel Papers,* "Flora" has few close acquaintances, apart from two friends introduced in the first year of the nature series. These two friends, Fiona and Father Conlan, visit "Flora" regularly in the *Out of Doors* essays. Father Conlan drops out of sight after 1921, but Fiona appears three more times: in "April" and "September" 1923 and in "August" 1924. Thompson first introduces Fiona in "April" 1921. Fiona's dancing "profession" keeps her in London for most of the year, but she visits the self-proclaimed Hermit of Peverel Downs when she needs a rest from her life on the stage. The free-spirited Fiona is always in motion. In the essay for "April" 1921, "Flora" describes Fiona "racing between wet sweet sweetbriar hedges, her green smock billowing, April incarnate, or practicing her dance steps beneath the orchard trees, flinging short, bright locks back from eyes the colour of dim, distant hills, as she looked up to throw a smile and a kiss to me at the bedroom window."[32] During a later visit, described in "April" 1923, "Flora's" "usually neat and orderly home" is "bewitched" when Fiona arrives.[33] Fiona makes coconut ice, places a wreath of white violets on a terracotta bust of Dante, and replaces the typewriter on "Flora's" writing desk with a sewing machine. "Flora" is "reduced to scribbling" this very essay on her knee as she sits "in the window seat." No matter how bewitching these visits from Fiona are meant to be, to the reader they appear to be invasions. And, when

Fiona insists that "Flora" change the color scheme in her garden ("May" 1921) or promise to never eat mushrooms again ("September" 1923), she sounds as much a petulant child as a free-spirited artist.

Although Thompson refers repeatedly to Fiona's Scottish heritage, Scotland and Scottish identity are not significant issues in *Out of Doors* or *The Peverel Papers*. Fiona's Scottish heritage is linked primarily to her eye color and to her first name. In "April" 1921, Thompson says Fiona's eyes are the "bluey-mauve" of the "bonny bluebells" of "her own beloved Scotland."[34] In "April" of 1923, Thompson tells her readers that Fiona was named after the "old Highland spaewife" who was "her great-great-great- grandmother."[35] Because Thompson was a lifelong reader of Sir Walter Scott's poetry and novels, she may have associated Scotland with all that is romantic and adventurous. Perhaps Thompson intended Fiona to be the embodiment of Scotland or even of romance itself. Unfortunately, the Fiona of Thompson's nature essays is so highly romanticized and so stereotypically artistic and bohemian that it is difficult to take her seriously. She is more of a caricature than a character.

Father Conlan, although an idealized figure, is more believable than Fiona, probably because he is shown performing the ordinary duties of a country priest. Thompson introduces Father Conlan in "May" 1921, briefly mentioning that he sometimes "walks over from Boldrewood" to take tea with her.[36] In this essay, Father Conlan is a fellow gardener who teases "Flora" for not knowing the nurseryman's names for the roses in her garden. Perhaps Thompson introduced Father Conlan in May, the month traditionally associated with the Virgin Mary, in order to connect with her Catholic audience. Thompson's first "May" essay also ends with two verses from a "May Carol" celebrating "the Queen of Heaven."[37]

In "June" 1921, the reader discovers that Father Conlan is writing a biography of St. Francis of Assisi and that he sometimes walks over to read a new chapter of this book to "Flora." The subject of the "Little Poor Man of Assisi" provokes an uncharacteristically bitter outburst in the "June" essay.[38] Having grown up in a poor rural community, Thompson knew that there is a profound difference between spiritual and material poverty. "Flora" tells Father Conlan that "poverty, real poverty, is mean and ugly." "All the saints and sages who have professed themselves her lovers," she adds, "had mistaken her identity and worshipped her sister, the pure and beautiful Lady Simplicity, under her name!" Father Conlan practices spiritual poverty by giving up sugar. The poor children "in all Europe" for whom he makes this sacrifice have no sugar. In this essay, "Flora" reveals that she is practicing a few austerities of her own. As she prepares her tea, she tells her readers, "I will bring out brown bread—no butter, for I too would be a humble follower of St. Francis and his lovely lady, call her Poverty or Simplicity, whichever you will!"

Apart from bringing his former student, "the Poet," to tea in "June" 1921, Father Conlan appears only one more time in *Out of Doors*. In "November" 1921, he pays "Flora" a visit after his "tramp across the forest to baptize a sick baby."[39] The reader learns that this self-sacrificing priest has sold his tulip bulbs to raise money for starving Russian children who have no bread. Because Father Conlan is still a "total abstainer from the simplest luxuries," such as sugar, "Flora" offers him a glass of cowslip mead, made from her grandmother's recipe. Since it is made with honey, not sugar, he gratefully accepts this glass of "bottled sunshine."

Thompson's sympathetic portrayal of Father Conlan in *Out of Doors* went beyond her professional association with the *Catholic Fireside*. Although Thompson remained a lifelong member of the Church of England, she was deeply attracted to the Catholic Church and may have even considered converting to Catholicism. When Thompson's sister May converted from Anglicanism to Catholicism in 1932, she wrote to congratulate her, saying, "I have always had a great love for the Catholic religion from a child and during the eight years I was writing for *The Catholic Fireside* I found many Catholic friends amongst my readers, including several nuns. I am fairly well instructed in the faith, as I have read many books on it, and of course have attended many services at different times, but I do not suppose I shall ever take the great step you have taken as there are family and other obstacles."[40] Although Father Conlan and Catholicism in general do not play a major role in *Out of Doors* or *The Peverel Papers*, Thompson's Catholic sympathies led her to criticize the Protestant Reformation in two nature essays published in 1922. In "January" 1922, she deplores the "so-called Reformation" for destroying the sanctity of marriage.[41] Her criticism of the Protestant Reformation is more indirect in "July" 1922. In this essay, she recommends a book to those of her readers who "cherish the faith of their fathers as a priceless jewel."[42] The book she recommends is *The Noble Army* by Christine Campbell Thomson.[43] Thompson describes *The Noble Army* as the story of a heroic priest who lived during "those dark days of Elizabeth when priests were hunted and outcast men, traveling the country in disguise to perform their sacred duties in secret." Based on the letter that Thompson wrote to her sister in May 1932, it seems possible that these statements were not mere window dressing for Thompson's Catholic audience.

The Literary Persona

Thompson's love for literature and her fascination with the lives of poets and writers is found in all of her published work, from her prize-winning essays in the *Lady's Companion* to the novels of *Lark Rise to Candleford*. In *Out of Doors* and *The Peverel Papers*, Thompson incorporates literary quotations, discusses literary topics, and even recommends specific poems or the works of particular poets to her readers in her monthly essays.[44] In "March" 1922, for example, she recommends the work of poet Robert Browning and identifies "The Last Ride Together," "Evelyn Hope," and "Prospice" as the "veins of pure gold" in his *oeuvre* (224).[45] Thompson also encourages her readers to cultivate their own taste for poetry. In "July" 1922, she suggests that her readers begin by borrowing *Palgrave's Golden Treasury* or *The Oxford Book of English Verse* from their local libraries. Occasionally, Thompson recommends a novel or an autobiography that she has recently read. In "October" 1921, she praises Walter de la Mare's *Memoirs of a Midget* (1921) in which "familiar, everyday objects become strange and new and wondrous" when seen through the eyes of his "infinitesimal heroine."[46] Thompson recommends *The Autobiography of Margot Asquith* (1920) to her readers in "May" 1922, telling her readers that, despite the "newspaper gossip about it," Asquith's book is a portrait of a "noble and generous nature."[47] In addition to recommending the work of specific poets, essayists, novelists, and autobiographers, Thompson discusses the value of literature in ordinary life. In "January" 1922, for example, she recommends "the works of the mighty dead" for consolation in "moments of exultation and despair."[48] Contemporary writers are particularly valuable, Thompson says in the same essay, for identifying "exactly where this old twentieth-century shoe of ours pinches."

Thompson's frequent use of literary quotations in *Out of Doors* and *The Peverel Papers* reveals her impressive knowledge of English literature, particularly English poetry. Thompson uses quotations from the works of over forty different literary figures in her nature essays. Although English poets of the nineteenth century are the figures she quotes most frequently, Thompson draws from sources as diverse as the Anglo-Saxon "elum which hateth man" to the twentieth-century poem "To a Fat Lady Seen from a Train" by Frances Cornford. She also draws several quotations from sacred texts, such as the Bible and the Koran. Gilbert White, the eighteenth-century naturalist, and John Gerard, the seventeenth-century herbalist, provide two additional sources of quotations. Thompson also refers to other poets, essayists, and novelists without quoting directly from their work. For example, she refers to Milton's use of cormorants in *Paradise Lost* when describing these birds in "August" 1923. In "February" 1924, she contrasts Sairey Gamp, from Charles Dickens's *Martin Chuzzlewit,* with the modern field nurse when discussing improvements in the status of women.

The plays and sonnets of William Shakespeare provide another source of quotations in Thompson's nature essays. "Now is the winter of our discontent" opens "April" 1922 (*The Tragedy of King Richard the Third,*

1.1.1). In "April" 1925, Thompson quotes from line 2 of Shakespeare's Sonnet 98 when referring to "proud pied April." In "July" 1922, Thompson identifies burnet saxifrage as Shakespeare's "ladysmock all silvery white," the flower mentioned in Spring's song in *Love's Labour's Lost* (5.2.885). The essay for "July" 1927 opens with four lines of a song from *The Winter's Tale.* The song that begins "Jog on, jog on, the footpath way" is a subtle reference to Thompson's discussion of footpaths later in the essay (4.3.121–24). Thompson quotes from two different Shakespearean plays in her discussion of owls in "September" 1926. Quoting from *Love's Labour's Lost*, Thompson refers to the owl's call as "too whoo! too whit! a merry note," slightly altering the original "tu-whit, tu-whoo! A merry note" (366; *Love's Labour's Lost* 5.2.908). Discussing the owl's reputation for being a bird of ill omen, Thompson quotes a line from King Henry's penultimate speech in *The Third Part of King Henry the Sixth:* "The owl shrieked at my birth an evil sign" (5.6.44).

Thompson frequently incorporates phrases, lines, or even entire stanzas of poetry into her nature essays, usually without identifying the poet or the poem by name. The poetry Thompson chooses is always related to her text in some way. Sometimes, an essay will start with a stanza of poetry related to the month or the season. At the beginning of "June" 1922, for example, she opens with two lines from James Russell Lowell's *The Vision of Sir Launfal:*

> What is so fair as a day in June?
> Then, if ever, come perfect days![49]

A stanza from William Morris's "August," which begins, "Now came fulfillment of the year's desire / The tall wheat, coloured by the August fire / Grew heavy-headed, dreading its decay," opens "August" 1926.[50] Many times, Thompson embeds lines of poetry in her text to enhance a description or to comment on her subject. In "November" 1921, Thompson uses the line "Where are the songs of spring; ay, where are they?" from John Keats's "To Autumn" to emphasize the silence in the woods after birds have departed for their winter homes.[51] In "November" 1924, the same line follows Thompson's description of thrusting her hand into a pile of cold damp leaves on a chill autumn day.[52] Thompson repeatedly uses the poetic phrase "a green thought in a green shade" from Andrew Marvell's "The Garden" to comment on the "all pervading green" she sees in the landscape.[53]

Thompson was fascinated by artistic vision, particularly the visionary gifts of poets. "Artists and dreamers, poets and mystics" are nearer the truth than the rest of the "matter-of-fact world," Thompson states in "September" 1922.[54] In "December" 1923, quoting from *Prometheus*

Unbound, Thompson endorses Shelley's vision of the poet as one who watches "from dawn to gloom" to create "forms more real than living man."[55] Thompson associates the poet's visionary gift with nobility of spirit. In "August" 1924, Thompson's description of poppies leads to a discussion of the "opium habit" and its terrible effects on "some of our best and noblest by nature."[56] Visionary poets who suffered the torment of opium addiction, Thompson says, "learned in suffering what they taught in song."[57] In "July" 1922, Thompson's perception of Mary Shelley as a woman of noble spirit inspires her to make a pilgrimage to her grave in Bournemouth. Thompson is impressed by the deep scarlet of the geraniums blooming on Shelley's grave and says, "It seemed so exquisitely appropriate that such living flame should spring from the mortal dust of the once-passionate heart."[58]

Thompson turns her attention to the dearth of female artists and poets in "August" 1922. The "era when everything, down to soap and candles had to be made at home," Thompson exclaims, "lost to us who knows how many women poets and painters!"[59] After reading reviews of a new anthology of women's poetry, Thompson reflects on the difference between the poetry written by men and the poetry written by women in "April" 1922. Surveying the works of poets such as Christina Rossetti, Elizabeth Barrett Browning, Joanna Baillie, Jean Ingelow, Alice Meynell, and Augusta Webster, Thompson concludes that "the work of women, saturated, as it often is, with beauty, rises very seldom indeed to greatness."[60] She has come to this conclusion, Thompson says, "rather in spite of myself, for I am an ardent supporter of my own sex." She ends this essay by quoting two praiseworthy stanzas from the work of an unidentified female poet. The poet is Emily Brontë, and the poem from which the two stanzas are taken is "No Coward Soul is Mine." It is curious that Thompson does not identify the poet or the poem that she so admires, particularly since her essay criticizes female poets for seldom rising to "greatness."

When Thompson wrote her nature essays for the *Catholic Fireside,* she was an aspiring poet herself. Her book of poems, *Bog Myrtle and Peat,* had been published in January 1921, the same month and year that she published her first nature essay in the *Catholic Fireside*. In addition to "April," the poem that Thompson used to open her essay for April 1921, another of her poems, "To a Poet," was printed at the end of the essay for "February" 1921.[61] Thompson's interest in literature, however, went beyond her personal dream of being a poet. She was genuinely fascinated by the life and works of various poets, novelists, and essayists. Her passion for literature, which began to emerge in her published nature essays, would find its next expression in the purely literary essays that she wrote for the *Catholic Fireside* in *The Fireside Reading Circle.* [62]

"Flora" and the End of The Peverel Papers

After "January" 1922, Thompson dropped most of the superficial details that she had built up around her persona. "Flora" remained a single woman, living in a cottage with her beloved books and dog, Boojie, until the very end of the nature series, but her doctor father and Father Conlan dropped completely out of sight after 1921. Thompson now expanded her monthly nature essays to include more information on specific plants and animals, as well as references to English history and folklore. At this point, Thompson may have decided that further development of "Flora" was no longer necessary.

"Flora" is best understood as an embodiment of Thompson's inner world. She shares Thompson's acute powers of observation, as well as her passionate love for nature and literature, even though she represents a privileged way of life that the author could only imagine. Thompson ended *The Peverel Papers* without explanation in December 1927. "Flora," who had described the spiritual quest that brought her to Peverel Downs in "January" 1922, did not inform her readers that "December" 1927 would be her last essay. "Flora" and *The Peverel Papers* simply disappeared. It is possible that unwelcome changes in her personal life impelled Thompson to end her nature series without comment. In 1927 Thompson's husband had applied for and then received an appointment to be the postmaster of Dartmouth, Devon. John Thompson's new position required the family to leave their home in Liphook, Hampshire, a prospect that disheartened his wife. According to Thompson's biographer, Gillian Lindsay, Thompson "found it hard to forgive her husband for uprooting the family" at this time.[63]

THE NATURAL LANDSCAPE

Just as Thompson later used her intimate knowledge of rural Oxfordshire to write *Lark Rise to Candleford*, she used her knowledge of Hampshire to accurately represent the natural landscape in and around two specific locations in the Hampshire countryside: the New Forest and Weaver's Down. In her very first nature essay for the *Catholic Fireside*, published in January 1921, Thompson describes standing at her garden gate and witnessing the "unearthly splendor" of a frosty winter morning in the New Forest.[64] Because Thompson wrote this essay when she was living with her husband and three children in Liphook, Hampshire, a location approximately sixty miles from the New Forest, her very first description of a natural landscape was, technically, a fiction. This description was based on her memory of the New Forest, where she had often walked during the fourteen years (1903–16) she and her family lived in Winton, a suburb of Bournemouth.[65] Thompson continued to use the New Forest as the setting for her nature essays throughout 1921. Occasionally she would slip, as she did in "February" 1921 when she described her walk to Forestmere in search of a washerwoman. Forestmere, approximately one mile from Thompson's Liphook home, was certainly not within walking distance of the New Forest. Thompson finally dropped the pretense of living near the New Forest in 1922, when she changed the name of her series from *Out of Doors* to *The Peverel Papers.* Her new setting was Peverel Downs, the fictional name she gave to Weaver's Down near her Liphook home. Peverel Downs remained the focus of Thompson's nature essays thereafter.

Thompson never revealed why she chose the name "Peverel" for her nature series. According to Lindsay, there were several places, such as Peveril Down and the village of Bradford Peverel, that may have suggested the name to her. There had also been a Peverell family living in Juniper Hill when Thompson was a child. Like Thompson's brother Edwin Timms, two members of this family died during World War I. Their names, along with Edwin's, were recorded on the World War I memorial tablet in Cottisford Church. Thompson's "Peverel" might have even been inspired by Sir Walter Scott's novel, *Peveril of the Peak* (1823). As Lindsay points out, Flora and Edwin Timms both loved the work of Sir Walter Scott; Edwin had even carried a book of Scott's verse into battle.[66] Perhaps Thompson used the name "Peverel" to honor her brother's memory. Whatever the reason for Thompson's choice, the nature essays that she wrote for *The Peverel Papers* were based on the observations that she made during her frequent walks to Weaver's Down, Woolmer Forest, Bramshott Common, Waggoners Wells, and Forestmere, locations within a five-mile radius of her Liphook home.

The Visual Landscape

Thompson's descriptions of the country landscape in *Out of Doors* and *The Peverel Papers* are complex and multilayered. They are guided by Thompson's observation of large and small changes on the heath, in the orchard, in the woods, and in her garden. Thompson draws the reader into her narrative landscape by creating a sense of immediacy. She often refers to events that took place "today," "last night," "this morning," or "as these last words are written." In "January" 1921, for example, Thompson writes of her "tramp into town to-day," adding later, "Today I met scarcely a soul."[67] She concludes her essay for "December" 1925 with "As these last words are written, the early December dusk descends upon Peverel."[68] By creating this sense of immediacy, Thompson invites her reader to imaginatively walk with her through the varying landscapes she describes, reminding them that she is describing events that have just happened.[69]

Thompson's descriptions of the landscapes she observes during her solitary walks are often visually lush. Thompson sometimes creates her visual effects by viewing a landscape from a unique perspective. In *Out of Doors* for "April" 1921, for example, she describes a view from the highest point of a village street, "where the Forest lies spread a sea of tree-tops, and farther out, tamed by distance, the real sea sleeps like a misty blue eye."[70] More often, Thompson creates a lush visual landscape by combining precise descriptions of environmental color with imagery that suggests the magnifying or intensifying effect of water, mist, or frost. In her nature essay for "March" 1922, Thompson recalls the enchantment she experienced while walking to Woolmer to find wild snowdrops. She describes her descent into a valley where she discovered the snowdrops in a landscape "not heathy and barren like mine, but emerald with water-meadows and threaded with streamlets—and there, in a copse by the waterside, I found the wild snowdrops. Pool after snowy pool, all down the slope; and, beyond and around, isolated clumps piercing the dark green of moss and ivy and overhanging and reflecting themselves in the bright brown water."[71]

In "October" 1924, Thompson notes the saturated color of bracken, trees, and heather one morning when "a curtain of mist hung over the heath": "Above the reddish brown of the bracken, young birch trees stood like fountains of pure gold; the heather, freshened by the wet, flushed to its last rose-colour; close at hand the line of the beechwood loomed, a dark and misty red."[72] In "January" 1924, Thompson notes how an overnight frost "had livened the bracken to a deep copper colour; mosses and lichens glowed beneath a sprinkling of ice. Against the rich dark hues of such things, leaf and fern and gossamer threaded stalk stood out crystallized."[73] Like Thompson's description of the snowdrops at Woolmer, these vivid descriptions of the heath owe much to Thompson's careful delineation of color and her description of the intensifying effects of water.

In addition to writing vivid descriptions of large landscapes, Thompson writes lush descriptions of small and hidden landscapes. Her descriptions focus on the multitude of small animals, insects, and plants that grow or move about in such places. Thompson conveys a childlike delight in the magical quality of these hidden worlds in miniature. In the "dim green underworld beneath the bracken fronds" that she describes in her essay for "September" 1923, she describes "the weird and elfin harvest of the different kinds of fungi": "Some are rounds of bright scarlet with greyish spots, like the toadstools in modern fairy pictures; others waxen yellow, honeycombed beneath or pearly white, shaped like umbrellas turned inside out by the wind. Out upon the open stretches of turf puff-balls are scattered like showers of giant pearls." [74] Thompson's reference to "modern fairy pictures" and to "puff-balls" that look like "giant pearls" encourages her readers to envision fairies, windswept blades of grass, moonlit nights, and other images associated with the work of popular fairy-tale illustrators of this period, such as Arthur Rackham and Cecily Mary Barker.

In "February" 1925, Thompson describes another magical landscape: the hidden world beneath an old double hedgerow. The hedgerow, "thickened with trees and twined about with creepers," is a perfect hideaway for children.[75] Under the hedgerow, children have made "small, well defined paths" that lead to "many a secret bower entwined with honeysuckle or wild hop." In this hidden world, "the earliest violets are always found, and later in the year there are primroses and bluebells, with nuts and blackberries to follow." In "July" 1923, Thompson describes another hidden landscape: a forest pool. The pool is "as populous as a great city":

> It is a dim, mysterious life, very alien to ours. Out in the cool depths below the water-lilies great blunt-nosed carp circle endlessly; in muddy caves beneath the bank lurk cruel pike, waiting to snap their shark-like jaws upon any unsuspecting swimmer by; frogs slip from the bank, rippling the calm surface; water rats, breasting the current, make business-like passages from shore to shore. Even the muddy margins where the water is shrinking are teeming with a myriad small and unconsidered living things—water-spiders, water-beetles, water-crickets.[76]

Thompson's forest pool is a landscape fit for a fairy tale or tale of terror. On the banks of the pool and on its surface, a multitude of creatures carry out their usual activities in the light of day. However, in the cool, dim world beneath the water lilies, predators "wait to snap upon any unsuspecting swimmer by." Dark and hidden worlds, like the forest pool, house unnamed horrors that defy rational thought. The fascination of Thompson's forest pool is akin to the fascination of the monastery pond in Ted Hughes's "Pike," which holds an ancient predator in its "stilled legendary depth."[77] Hughes's pike, like Thompson's, lurks beneath "heat struck lily pads" awaiting its next victim with an "ancient malevolent grin."

Sights, Sounds, and Scents

Thompson's descriptions of natural landscapes are not purely visual. Most of her essays are infused with the sounds and fragrances of each month. In *Out of Doors* in "January" 1921, Thompson describes the sights and sounds of a frosty winter morning: "This morning, every branch and twig bore a pearly burden of hoar-frost. Over the narrow lane which leads to my retreat, the morning star still glittered coldly; the silence of the winter dawn was only broken by the rumbling of wheels upon the frosty ruts, and the *crop, crop* of the forest ponies as they munched their scanty breakfast beside my garden hedge."[78] Characteristically, Thompson not only describes the sounds that she hears on this frosty winter morning, but she also uses the onomatopoetic "*crop, crop*" and "rumbling" to recreate the sounds of cart wheels and feeding ponies in her text.

Birdsong is a frequent element in Thompson's nature essays, whether it is the song of an individual bird or the collective sound of birds in a natural landscape. In "September" 1922, Thompson describes the "churring" of the nightjar as a "harsh, long-drawn-out note, something between a rattle and a saw."[79] In "June" 1923, she notes how the song of the cuckoo changes from "the clearly enunciated 'Cuckoo!' of a month before" to the "eager stammer—'Cuck-Cuck-oo!'" when the bird is eager to "depart overseas."[80] Thompson links the collective sound of birdsong or insect sounds to certain times of the year. In "April" 1924, she declares "the singing of birds" to be the "voice" of April.[81] Similarly, in "July" 1925, Thompson declares the sound of insects to be "the voice of full summer, just as birdsong is the voice of spring," and combines both in her essay for that month: "That steady booming of bees and other insects goes on all day long and everywhere; the air is full of murmuring and the brush of tiny wings. . . . Now and then, in the warm, still afternoons, the long-drawn "*Coo-Coo-oo-oo!*" of the wood pigeon may be heard in the pine-woods; the black bird utters its throaty chuckle of satisfaction among the raspberry canes; or a linnet flits with its plaintive '*Tweet! Tweet!*'" [82] Once again, Thompson's use of onomatopoeia allows the reader to hear the "steady booming bees," the "murmuring" and "brush" of insect wings, and the "throaty chuckle" of the blackbird in the raspberry canes in this passage.

In late summer and early autumn, Thompson adds the sounds of the harvest to her usual descriptions of bird and insect sound. In "August" 1922, for example, Thompson conveys a sense of the ripening heat of this month in her description of gorse and broom pods that "pop audibly in the hot sunshine, each tiny explosion scattering the seed within for yards."[83] In "September" 1924, the "the sound of laughter, mingled with the soft, leafy swishing of boughs released" coming from nearby apple orchards is accompanied by the "humming of innumerable bees in the heath bells."[84] In "September" 1923, among all the sounds of birds and insects, she notes "the distant booming of the thrashing machine at work in the farm rick yards."[85]

Thompson increased the sensual appeal of her nature essays by adding fragrance to her descriptions of seasonal sights and sounds in the Hampshire countryside. Each month of the year has its characteristic fragrance, and Thompson often analyzes the components of this fragrance as if the country air were a perfume. In "March" 1921, she describes the fragrance of the air as the "incense from the earth" composed of "the incense of flowering currant, or bog myrtle" and "hidden violets."[86] In "April" 1923, the "rich, damp earth scents" are a combination of "wet moss and springing herbage, the rosin of bursting larch-buds, and the soft breath of the primroses."[87] The scent of the primrose appears again in "April" 1924, when Thompson declares it "the very breath of April."[88] In the same essay, Thompson explores the connection between scent and memory, noting how "the scent of a flower in the hand of a passer-by" may be "potent to unlock the memory and transport the mind a hundred miles or a score of years." In "June" 1923, Thompson ponders "how many separate perfumes" make up the scent of new-mown hay:

> First and foremost, of course, is the scent of the hay itself, the sweet vernal grass, which forms the basis of most grass-seed mixtures. Then there are the clovers, white and red, the wild rose scent from the hedges which hem the fields in, and the scent of the earth with the heavy dews of June upon it, and perhaps a breath of cottage garden flowers, and a suspicion of the margin of the rapidly shrinking brook, and the breath of the cows in the neighboring field, forming altogether a compound of perfume which any exile would recognize immediately as "England in June."[89]

Autumn brings the mingled scents of ripeness and decay. In "September" 1921, the morning air is "ineffably sweet" with the fragrance of "heather and wild-thyme, peat and moss and pine."[90] In "September" 1923, Thompson declares that the "sharp scent" of fallen crab apples mixed with "the smell of wet clover, stubble, and pollen" is "the very essence of autumn."[91] In "November" 1922, when a "poet-friend" declares that he could identify any English county by its scent alone, Thompson replies that a genuine "observer" of nature could even "tell the *month of the year* by the sense of smell alone."[92] In the same "November" essay, Thompson describes the aftereffects of a heavy rainstorm that leaves the air filled with the combined fragrances of "wet bracken and decaying leaves, of crab-apples rotting amongst their leaves in the ditches, and, as always upon Peverel, the sharp, sweet rosin of the pine." In another "November" essay (1924), Thompson describes "the old elemental earth-scents": the "mossy odours of wet leaf-mould, the sharpness of wood-sap, and the spiciness of pine and peat."[93]

In *The Peverel Papers*, Thompson combines the sights, sounds, and scents of the English countryside in essays that have the power to "unlock the memory and transport the mind." With Thompson as a knowledgeable companion, the reader can pause, imaginatively, to listen to the "steady murmur of bees," to smell the "sweet, fresh, wholesome scent" of the primrose, or to study the delicate structure of the wood anemone "in its fragile prime, swaying and bending with every breath of air."[94]

Nature Education: Reptiles and Amphibians, Mammals, Insects, and Birds

After her first year of writing nature essays for *Out of Doors,* Thompson steadily increased the educational content of the essays she published under the series's new title, *The Peverel Papers*. Many of the essays contain detailed information about particular reptiles, amphibians, mammals, insects, and birds that she encounters during her solitary walks. The essays also contain detailed information about foraging, food hiding, hibernation, and migration. Thompson also urges her readers to put aside their unreasoning prejudice against creatures that have an unsavory reputation. In "March" 1923, for example, she describes two chance encounters with adders, reassuring her readers that the adder does not use "its poison fang unless attacked at close quarters" or unless it is "accidentally trodden upon."[95] In "August" 1923, she devotes five paragraphs to "the very emblem of evil": the cormorant.[96] While acknowledging that the bird's appearance is "sinister" and "primitive," she assures her readers that the cormorant is "of such a high order of intelligence and capable of such faithfulness and affection to man, as to be only comparable to a dog." She supports her assertion by informing her readers that in the Orient, cormorants "have been trained from remotest times to fish for their masters."

Insects and insect activity play a prominent role in the monthly essays, although Thompson does not usually discuss a particular type of insect at great length. Butterflies, wasps, ants, and bees are typically described in more detail than other insects in *The Peverel Papers*, and they also provide several interesting anecdotes. In "March" 1924, Thompson describes sighting "one white butterfly–the first of the season" and then recounts the memory of seeing a group of elderly men and women trying to capture such a butterfly as they stood in line in a village street waiting to draw their old-age pensions.[97] Thompson writes a fascinating description of the gestation of wasps in her six- paragraph treatment of the queen wasp in "November" 1924. Her description of wasps hunting baby caterpillars in "September" 1926, though gruesome, is equally fascinating. Thompson describes the wasp as a "self invited guest" to the rolled leaf that forms the "caterpillar's abode."[98] After a "buzzing inquiry" at both ends of the leaf, Thompson observes, the wasp "dispenses with farther formality by eating its own way through the leafy wall and proceeding to dine on its host."[99] The social hierarchy and cooperative behavior of ants inspires several essays. In "November" 1922, Thompson devotes a full eight paragraphs to describing the nest, the hierarchy, and the cooperative behavior of the red wood ant. In this essay, Thompson also describes the "very touching" behavior of the female ant that nips off her own wings "lest she should be tempted to disport herself in the sunshine to the detriment of her maternal duties."[100]

Bees and bee lore are the focus of Thompson's essay for "September" 1922. In this essay, she describes the drone of the honey bee as "the living music of the moors."[101] She also tells a story that, slightly modified, would later appear in *Lark Rise.* When a child, she says, she once observed a young village blacksmith tapping on the family beehives after his father's death, saying, "Bees, Bees, your master's dead, so now you must work for your missus." When the story is told again in *Lark Rise*, it is old Queenie, the hamlet beekeeper, who taps on her beehives after her husband's death to deliver the same message. Thompson devotes a full seven paragraphs to honeybees in this particular essay.

At the end of her essay for "September" 1922, Thompson acknowledged a reader who had asked her to write "more about birds" in *The Peverel Papers*.[102] This request was certainly honored, for birds predominate over every other living creature in Thompson's nature essays. It is clear that Thompson found birds fascinating. In "March" 1923, even in the midst of expressing her frustration with starlings that are pulling up bulbs from her crocus beds, she asserts that she loves birds "better than gardens."[103] In many of her nature essays, Thompson devotes considerable space to describing current bird activity in great detail. Surveying the landscape before her, Thompson identifies the specific type and number of birds she sees, also noting where each type of bird is feeding, hopping, or flying. In some cases, bird activity is only a charming detail in her description of a large landscape. However, Thompson occasionally focuses on bird activity itself and uses the landscape as a mere setting. Such descriptions are surprisingly long, averaging from eight to twelve consecutive paragraphs. In "December" 1924, for example, Thompson devotes seven consecutive paragraphs to describing bird activity one frosty winter morning. As she observes the birds from early to midmorning, her focus shifts from place to place as she follows the birds' movements on the ground and in the air. In the early morning, "starlings, blackbirds, and chaffinches all crowd together in the rimey hedges, all alike reduced to shivering, cold puffed balls of misery."[104] Later in the morning, "in the sky, far above the circling lapwings, the starlings move in organized flight from one feeding ground to another." Thompson's focus later shifts from the sky to the meadow pools, where "a couple of magpies step daintily, their black and white smartly conspicuous against the green of the turf." Her attention is also drawn to a hedgerow where "the hawfinches are busily cracking the haw-stones."

In *The Peverel Papers*, Thompson uses the arrival and departure of birds as signposts in the year. April and May are marked by the song of the cuckoo. "Does anyone, I wonder, hear it for the first time of the season without a thrill?" she asks in "April" 1923.[105] May is also the month in which the swallows return. Thompson describes the swallow as her "best beloved among birds" in "May" 1921, and she devotes eight paragraphs to describing it in "September" 1923.[106] The nightingale inspires every "June" essay, primarily because of its association with English poetry. In "June" 1922, after citing two- to three- line excerpts from the mournful nightingale poetry of Robert Bridges, John Keats, and Matthew Arnold, Thompson asserts that "in spite of its long-drawn '*Jug, Jug tereu eu!*' many of its notes are exuberantly joyous. Its quieter commencing notes always seem to me to bubble like the rain of a golden fountain."[107] Thompson's description of the nightingale's song is only one example of the deep connection Thompson sees between birdsong and poetry.

Thompson provides a wide range of information about birds in her nature essays, covering everything from mating habits to migratory patterns. In her extended descriptions of particular birds, such as the kingfisher, the chiff chaff, and the bullfinch, Thompson not only provides a detailed description of every conceivable aspect of the bird's life but also includes historic events, popular wisdom, or folklore associated with it. Thompson also employs anthropomorphism, particularly when describing birds, to engage and entertain her readers. For example, she humorously compares a barn owl to an elderly lady taking a nap in "January" 1923, and she describes baby birds as "marauding hooligan bands" when she observes their furious activity in "July" 1924.[108] Although they rely on cultural cliché for their effect, such descriptions were suited to a general audience, such as the readers of the *Catholic Fireside*.

Nature Education: Plant Life

Thompson's descriptions of plant life are a testament to her artistic sensibilities as well as to her considerable powers of observation and precise description. Thompson's descriptions of the ever-changing colors of leaves, grasses, fruit, and berries are frequently painterly. She has an eye for beauty, whether it is found in the "great purple waves" of heather or in the exquisite beauty of a wood anemone in its "fragile prime."[109] Apart from reveling in the beauty of the various plants she describes, Thompson uses plants, even more than her beloved birds, to mark seasonal change. She also devotes many paragraphs in her nature essays to describing the specific plants she finds during her rambles. These descriptions become vehicles for brief lessons in botany, history, and folklore.

Thompson is attuned to the smallest signs of seasonal change, observing subtle signs such as the swelling of leaf buds or the first faint tinge of color in a ripening apple. In the chill of February, Thompson looks for signs of spring, finding a "rumour of her coming" where "the woods flush reddish-purple with thickening bud and rising sap."[110] In "March" 1923, signs of new life can be seen in "every sunny angle of the hedgerows" where "the buds are bursting into a light veil of green."[111] In "August" 1926, Thompson detects early signs of autumn in the "scent of ripe fruit" and in the "heavy clusters of orange berries just deepening to scarlet" on the rowan trees.[112] Even in winter, Thompson finds signs of life in the ivy plant that produces its flowers and fruit between "Michaelmas and Easter" and in the mosses that bloom into "fairy forests of emerald plumes" in January and February.[113] Even the most subtle alteration in the natural landscape is evidence of the eternal in nature. As Thompson observes in "August" 1924, regardless of "changes in man's outlook and circumstances," the rural landscape remains the same. Man's "ceaseless hewing and planting, draining and enclosing, result but in scratches upon the face of the earth."[114]

Thompson's extended treatment of specific plants is an occasion for lessons in botany, history, literature, and folklore. In "February" 1923, for example, after describing the "mystic loveliness" of the snowdrop, Thompson speculates on the introduction of this flower to England.[115] "Botanists have surmised" that the snowdrop was imported by the Romans, Thompson says, but she wonders whether it was really imported by a Franciscan "gardening friar." Perhaps this anonymous friar wished to plant a few bulbs in "the newly-made garden of the English monastery" as a memento of "the dearly-loved founder of his Order" and as a symbol of "Lady Poverty." In her extended treatment of poppies in "August" 1924, Thompson tells her readers that the poppy "has always been used as the symbol of sleep" in poetry and sculpture.[116] She retells the Greek legend of Persephone and comments that "the ancients valued the poppy so much that they used to twine its rounded seed-cases with wheat-ears to grace their thanksgiving festivals."

In her numerous descriptions of plants, Thompson devotes her most extensive descriptions to trees. She describes the trunk, bark, limbs, leaves, and growth habit of these trees and encourages her readers to recognize the unique qualities of each type of tree she describes. For example, in "January" 1926, she encourages her readers to take advantage of "this time of general overhead leaflessness" to observe tree shapes.[117] Thompson describes the form of the oak, elm, ash, beech, poplar, and silver birch in this essay to demonstrate that the "far-off forms" of leafless trees make identification easy. In "January" 1925, Thompson describes the "voices" of the oak, beech, birch, poplar, and aspen. "Every tree has its own characteristic voice" in wind and rain, Thompson says, and "that of the oak is a deep, dull roar—'the bull-voiced oak' Meredith called it-and, with that suggestion in mind, its sound has a ferocious wildness; at other times, or in other moods, its sound is the sound of the sea in tempest, or the cheering of immense crowds at a royal procession."[118]

In *The Peverel Papers*, trees are not only fascinating in themselves, but they are also important as physical landmarks and as symbols of English history and culture. In "January" 1925, Thompson says the oak "is still, as it has always been, the favourite tree of the English people, who like to persuade themselves they see in its rugged strength a symbol of their own national qualities."[119] From the "Saxon times" to the Middle Ages, Thompson continues, acorns were ground to make bread "for the lower classes," this practice being revived during "the late war" when acorn flour was used to make "war bread."[120] After observing an ancient oak being hauled through the streets of Oxford in "October" 1923, Thompson imagines how the oak must have looked down in "its saplinghood" on an Oxford that was only "a castle tower with a cluster of mud huts around."[121] As the centuries passed, "Shakespeare may have halted in its shade as he rode from Stratford to London, for it is a tradition that he always turned aside to sleep at the Davenant's hostelry. Shelley may have leaned against its trunk upon one of his country walks. Newman may have paced beneath, torn by inward questions. Who can tell?" In *The Peverel Papers* trees, such as the oak, and flowers, such as the snowdrop and the poppy, become potent symbols of English history and of the ancient cultures of Greece and Rome.

"The New Domesday Book" and Property Rights

When Thompson published *Lark Rise*, she not only wrote about Laura, the stonemason's daughter, but she also described daily life in rural Oxfordshire during the final decades of the nineteenth century. Thompson's passion for recording and preserving the past can also be seen in *The Peverel Papers*. Thompson viewed the English countryside as a fascinating historical artifact that should be respected and preserved for future generations. Acknowledging that change is inevitable, whether brought about by man or by natural forces, Thompson proposes a system of "school historians" to record all such changes in the country landscape in "November" 1923: "One finds, when we come to study a small stretch of country at all intensively, that every field and lane, every tree and clod, has a history. I wonder that no educationist has suggested that the school children of a parish should be appointed its historians. What a multitude of interesting, yet little regarded, facts, likely to be intensely interesting to future generations, those small, sharp eyes would note."[122] Thompson is dismayed when local newspapers do not report the felling of an ancient tree, once said to have "marked the verge of the Royal Forest of Woolmer." She comments: "If the school history had been in being, the disappearance of so ancient a landmark would certainly have been chronicled, with a description of the exact spot where it stood, and perhaps a snapshot to show to what a mere hollow tooth of a tree it had dwindled." In this essay, Thompson's ultimate vision is the creation of a system "linking all the country together in a network of parishes." This network of school historians would create a "New Domesday Book" in which future generations could find records "of climatic conditions, of rare bird visitors, of the making or draining of ponds," or the "planting and felling of woods." The "New Domesday Book" would also link famous men and women to the landscapes in which they lived or from which they drew their inspiration. As Thompson explains, "The well-known poet who stayed at the hotel, and spent hours gazing upon a certain view; the farmer's son, a native born, who became an engineer and patented a world-shaking invention—such facts as could be obtained without impertinence relating to such ones would be there, ready to the hand of future biographers." Thompson concludes, "It would make interesting reading for the people of the year 2,000, this 'New Domesday Book'; or 'Every Parish its own Historian!'"

Thompson was as interested in preserving the people's access to the English countryside as she was in preserving its history. She objected to the fencing of vast expanses of the countryside and to the enforcement of property rights by gamekeepers. In "May" 1923, she tells her readers, "When I first came here I had an idea that in the country one might wander where they would. I was soon disillusioned; nowhere are the rights of property held more sacred."[123] A note of defiance creeps into her essay of "October" 1923 where she asserts, "Crown land and common land is all the same to me. The War Department, since the end of the war, have made little use of their share, and I wander where I will."[124] In "March" 1924, Thompson expresses her particular frustration with the professional gamekeeper who "seems to lie constantly in wait" for innocent trespassers.[125] She says, "It is vain to insinuate to him that for one man to lay claim to a primrose wood or bluebell dell and to pay another man to watch it is an outrage upon the rest of humanity."

Popular resistance to strictly enforced property rights is seen most clearly in the battle over that "ancient right of way," the footpath. [126] In "March" 1924, Thompson describes the angry confrontation she once witnessed between a landowner and local villagers after the landowner attempted to close a footpath on his property. Thompson says, "The whole population of the heath assembled one Sunday after church, broke down the barriers," and even "trampled the corn." Thereafter, the landlord made no attempt to replace the barriers that had been destroyed by the angry crowd. For their part, the local men, women, and children continued to "assert their ancient right by going a little out of their way" to use that particular footpath. During the time that Thompson was writing her nature essays, many time-honored features of the English landscape, such as the footpath, were gradually disappearing, the victims of improved farming methods. In Thompson's last essay for *The Peverel Papers,* published in "December" 1927, she regretfully notes another "sure sign of the times": the sound of "the hedge-cutter's billock."[127] With his billock, the hedge-cutter removes the most appealing features of the hedgerow: the "hips and haws and the last cottony tassels of the traveller's joy" and "many a last year's nest." The result of the hedge-cutter's labors, Thompson notes, is "more pleasing to the farmer than the nature lover, for the tidy, uniform fence of interlaced stakes it leaves behind is a poor exchange for the wild luxuriance of the natural growth." Thompson takes comfort in the thought that with time the hedgerow "will bloom again" and "become once more the wild, luxuriant tangle it has been."

The Human Landscape

During the seven years that Thompson wrote monthly nature essays for the *Catholic Fireside*, she seldom wrote about villagers or the local gentry. Instead, she described the humble country laborers whom she encountered during her rambles through the Hampshire countryside. Thompson's focus on the men who worked as shepherds, farmers, and harvesters was not the result of gender bias but a response to the economic, social, and historical forces of her time. Thompson also wrote compassionately about the war veterans whose lives were devastated by World War I and about the homeless and the unemployed. Gypsies, male and female, play a unique role in *Out of Doors* and *The Peverel Papers*, appearing as fascinating individuals whose way of life is, in some respects, enviable. Seasonal work, such as hop picking, and seasonal celebrations, such as May Day and Harvest Home, are also depicted in the essays. Thompson's depiction of the English tradition of the hunt and pastimes, such as collecting nature specimens, reveals that she was an early proponent of animal rights.

Portraits of Working Men

In *The Peverel Papers*, Thompson expresses great respect for the hardworking men who plough the fields, harvest the grain, and shepherd the lambs in her little corner of Hampshire. These men are never identified by name. Instead, Thompson identifies them by their professions, treating them as noble types rather than flawed individuals. Thompson respected such men because they were highly skilled and attuned to the rhythms of nature. She also admired them because they demonstrated uncomplaining endurance under the harshest of conditions. Thompson describes "the harvester" in "August" 1922, saying, "His calling is so sure, his toil so immediately beneficial that no doubts of his use in life can ever assail him."[128] He works with "the dignity of one who knows himself indispensable." Thompson admires the skill of a particular hedger and ditcher whom she observes in "December" 1922. He is "a tall old man, apple-cheeked and direct of eye, one who knew his own worth, probably, and demanded his due, always taking care to give good value for it."[129] The shepherd Thompson describes in "December" 1923 is an almost cosmic figure. She says, "He will be up all night about his lambing duties, and see the marches of the stars over Peverel from dusk till dawn."[130] Such men are poor and obscure, but they possess true wisdom. Thompson recalls her encounter with this particular shepherd "one winter evening during the war," at a time when her heart "had been full of bitterness."[131] The shepherd had pointed to the moon saying, "They can't put that out . . . nor the sun, nor the stars, for all their mightiness."[132] The simple words of this shepherd influenced her "at a moment when the written word of poet or philosopher was mere paper and printer's ink to me," Thompson comments.

Although Thompson's portraits of working men are sometimes romantic or sentimental, she challenges several romantic myths about country life. In the nature essay published in "July" 1923, she points out that the picturesque, rose-covered country cottages with diamond-paned windows, so idealized by lovers of the English countryside, were actually miserable hovels. In such cottages, families were "herded like animals for lack of space" and "insufficiently nourished."[133] The "elders" were "crippled with rheumatism" and "the young stricken down with consumption." Thompson also challenges romantic notions about winter in the country. "Snowy roofs and hanging icicles look better upon a Christmas card than in actual life to one who has his living to find out of doors," she comments in "December" 1923.[134] In "October" 1922, Thompson gladly notes that the passage of time, along with improved education and increased wages, had gradually transformed the "village rustic" into a well-dressed modern farmer.[135] However, economic and social changes were also leading to the dissolution of many family farms. In "August" 1926, Thompson describes an "old commoner" who sells his herd and retires to "a fashionable seaside town to end his days" because "his sons are scattered to the ends of the earth—one a soldier in India, another at sea, two in Canada and one in Australia."[136]

World War I Veterans, Gypsies, the Homeless, and Tramps

The human landscape that Thompson describes in her nature essays includes those men, women, and children who live on the margins of rural society. Just as Thompson steps off a footpath to take a closer look at a patch of violets that others might pass without noticing, she also steps off a road, a village street, or a country lane to speak with individuals who are socially invisible. Chiefly, these are the war veterans, gypsies, homeless people, and tramps that she encounters during her nature walks. Thompson describes the distressing condition of those she meets in brief, sometimes adding a bit of mild social commentary before briskly moving on.

During the first two years of the series, Thompson documented the terrible aftereffects of World War I, chiefly through her quiet descriptions of injured veterans. In "February" 1921, "Flora" comes upon a Punch and Judy show in a village street and notes that the puppets are back after "five years' war rest."[137] Punch and Judy, she exclaims, are "a little dimmer as to paint, a little seedier as to raiment, a little less broad in their Hampshire dialect," but "otherwise unchanged!" This disarming description is followed by a more somber description of the puppeteer: "Not so this pair of human hands which manipulated them. Of these one was artificial entirely—a cleverly-joined thing of wax and steel; the other minus a finger. Pinned to the shabby green baize curtain was an envelope with "Woonded 5 times" [*sic*] scrawled upon it; underneath were a row of medals, including the Mons Star." The misspelled sign, the row of medals, and the cunningly constructed artificial hand are all poignant symbols of the bitter aftermath of war. Military service, however meritorious, does not provide the same advantages as education or social class. Regardless of the personal sacrifices that he has made for his country, this veteran must return to the village streets to make his living as a puppeteer. In "March" 1922, Thompson describes her encounter with a shell-shocked veteran, "ragged and poor looking to wretchedness," who is reduced to selling rabbit skins for a living.[138] Another veteran that she encounters in "August" 1922 sleeps out of doors and sells oranges to survive, despite his government pension. Thompson first mistakes this man for a tinker until she hears his "public school accent" and sees his "stiff mechanical leg."[139]

The tragedy of World War I is also etched on the rural landscape. Thompson continues to document these changes as late as September 1923. In "June" 1922, while describing the landscape around Peverel, Thompson notes "the half-filled trenches of Kitchener's Army."[140] In "March" 1921, Thompson describes a well that "military authorities" had dug "for a camp that never materialized."[141] It had come to be known as

Soldiers' Well because "one dark winter night a poor, war-worn world-weary soldier filled his haversack with stones and sunk himself in its icy depths." In "October" 1923, "Flora" eats her sandwiches "in the shelter of decaying notice-boards inscribed with terrifying warnings of bomb practice and gunfire."[142] These signs remind her of witnessing "a new make of tanks" being tested "upon the downs" years before. The tanks had looked like "huge reptilian monsters," and they moved "over hills and through woods, flattening the gorse and bearing young trees like straws before them." In "September" 1924, Thompson explains that the year's unusual abundance of blackberries is actually due to the "costly pruning" of World War I.[143] For five years, Canadian soldiers had lived and drilled upon the open spaces where there "had been nothing but briar and bracken." When the camp was finally dismantled after the war, "nature set to work to heal the scars; and almost the first growth was the long green shoots of the blackberry brambles." The blackberries that followed were of the finest quality but "cultivated at what tremendous cost!" Thompson exclaims.

Like other writers, artists, and scholars in Great Britain during the 1920s, Thompson was fascinated by gypsies. Writers such as Victoria Sackville-West, Sacheverell Sitwell, and D. H. Lawrence portrayed gypsies as either idealized children of nature or highly charged erotic figures in their works.[144] The gypsy's unique style of dress and way of life, which had fascinated Augustus John during the late nineteenth century, now inspired the paintings of the fashionable Alfred Munnings. The Gypsy Lore Society (originally founded in 1888) was revived in 1922 in response to a new generation of scholars who found gypsies a fascinating subject.[145] Thompson was fascinated by the very things that made gypsies marginal figures: their appearance, their mysterious origins, their language, and their domestic instability. Unlike the anonymous war veterans she describes in *Out of Doors* and *The Peverel Papers*, the gypsies whom Thompson describes are often fully realized as individuals and as families. Some of the gypsies not only have names but also a family history. Gypsies appear in Thompson's nature essays from the very beginning of the series. In her first nature essay, published in January 1921, Thompson mentions passing a gypsy woman "with a basket of pegs on her arm and a fat, brown, black-eyed baby astride her hip."[146]

Thompson is attracted by the very things that make gypsies outlandish, or at least exotic, in the eyes of country folk. In "November" 1921, she encounters an old gypsy woman searching for wood sage and is fascinated by her appearance. Although the woman claims to be eighty-nine, her hair is still black, and she is "gorgeously and uniquely clad in a man's crimson quilted dressing-gown, finished with hobnailed, steel tipped boots."[147] "Flora" is similarly fascinated by a gypsy girl who shelters in her cottage during a downpour in "February" 1922. She stops her work "for the sake of the pure pleasure" of looking at this beautiful girl and "listening to the soft, husky, caressing tones of her wholly gypsy voice."[148] However, "Flora" is not so dazzled by her exotic little visitor that she ignores the lies the girl tells. She notes with dismay: "Alas! More than half of the story she told me was pure fiction, for she told tale after tale, contradicting one with another, and weaving a web of deceit around her family and circumstances which, although tangled, was at least transparent." Thompson touches again on the gypsy's reputation for being a manipulative liar (what Thompson calls "the old guile of their race") in her final essay, published in December 1927. Despite their new respectability as owners of the land they camp on and their determination "to keep upon good terms with police and gamekeeper," the local gypsies use their outsider status to make a profit.[149] Whenever a new home is built on the heath, the gypsies immediately buy the plot next door, knowing that the new homeowners will not want gypsies for neighbors. If the homeowners refuse to buy the gypsy plot "at a greatly increased price," the gypsies will pitch a tent or erect a shed as near as possible to the homeowner's front door.[150] As Thompson observes, "A few weeks of squalling children, lines of dingy washing, piles of old iron, rags, bones" and "rabbit skins" result in a quick sale.

Thompson's essays confer a special dignity upon the gypsies she describes. She not only treats them as interesting individuals, but she also refers regularly to their royal lineage. In "July" 1921, "Flora" accepts a ride from a gypsy whom she had known as a child. He is "of royal blood, a descendant of the house of Lee, the old kings of the Romany tribe."[151] This "old friend" is the same "sworn blood brother" with whom she and Edmund had enjoyed so many childhood adventures. Now his daughter, a "gypsy princess," leaves baskets of whortleberries and mushrooms at her cottage door. In "May" 1922, a gypsy girl named Feena tells "Flora" "tales of the past grandeurs of her people."[152] Her great-grandfather, Thompson reports, "was known as 'King Stanley of Brokenhurst' and dealt out laws to the whole of the New Forest tribes." In "December" 1927, Thompson explains the history of the gypsies to her readers, describing how they arrived in medieval England, "a strange mysterious people, speaking an outlandish language, from no one knew where."[153]

Thompson implies that she has had personal relationships with gypsies all of her life. In "May" 1922, gypsy children are regular visitors to her cottage. They bring her little gifts, such as arrowheads and rush baskets filled with ferns. Feena gives her lessons "in the Romany" language that the gypsies speak.[154] In return, "Flora" helps Feena with her reading. "Flora" says that Feena is "a strange girl, not so vivid, perhaps, as some of the others, but interesting in quite another way." This is because Feena wants nothing more than to live in a house, "wear velvet dresses, and sit on the sofa and sew all day." Thompson returns to the subject of Feena in "July" 1925, reminding her readers that she had told the girl's story "a year or two ago in these papers."[155] However, Thompson changes some of the details from the previous essay. In 1925 Feena has been renamed Nancy, and she is now the daughter of "Flora's" childhood friend, the "gypsy princess" who used to leave whortleberries and mushrooms at her cottage door. In this second installment of Feena/Nancy's story, the reader discovers that the young woman has fulfilled her dream by marrying a Portsmouth shopkeeper. Now, however, Feena/Nancy's dream has totally changed. She tells "Flora" that her greatest desire is "to stop on the heath all my life and never to see a town again as long as I live!"[156]

For Thompson, the gypsy's freedom is full of romance. In "May" 1922, she describes a gypsy grandmother who refuses to go to an infirmary, even though she is seriously ill. "In the open she was born," Thompson says, "and in the open she meant to die, with her cup of tea and her old black cutty-pipe beside her."[157] In "July" 1925, after she describes Feena/Nancy's change of heart, Thompson notes: "It is seldom, indeed, that one of pure Gipsy [*sic*] blood can be prevailed upon to sleep beneath a roof for more than a night or two together. They say they cannot breathe properly indoors, that the four walls seem to press inwards upon them, and that, after a night 'cooped up,' they feel positively ill."[158]

Although Thompson admires, and perhaps even envies, the enterprise and freedom of the gypsies, she looks quite differently on the plight of the homeless and unemployed. Unlike the gypsies, these individuals are not part of a romantic alternative culture. Instead, they are the emblems of human tragedy. In "March" 1922, "Flora" encounters an unemployed couple pushing "a perambulator piled with dingy bundles," with a "kettle and frying-pan slung behind."[159] Like many "upon the road this winter," she notes, the man is thin, poor, and "ill-clad." When his wife stops to gaze at a shop window, her face is full of "such longing" that "Flora" wishes that she could "tap her upon the shoulder" and say, "Choose whatever you will, and it shall be yours!" In "June" 1922, "Flora" describes a distressing sight she had recently seen on the streets of Bournemouth. Standing in front of a toy shop window was a family carrying "a few poor bundles," apparently "on the tramp."[160] The mother had "that waxen, sallow sharpness of feature which comes from a long course of insufficient nourishment." Her little boy of "three or four" whimpered when he walked because "the front part of the soles of the tiny shoes was worn completely away; the tender feet were torn and bleeding." After this encounter, "Flora" says she stood in the street, "haunted by the feeling that all the gaiety and well-being were but surface qualities; that beneath it all swept a sinister undercurrent."

A few of the homeless people whom "Flora" encounters have adapted to their circumstances and have managed to create a tolerable life for themselves. In "October" 1925, "Flora" describes a tinker and his wife who have made their home in a thicket of holly and pine for forty years. Their makeshift home is neatly arranged, and the couple appears to live happily. Because the man and his wife are nature lovers, "Flora" romanticizes their plight, saying: "Poor and ignorant in some things as these people were, they were no common people. They were both of them, the man especially, true nature-lovers, knowing and loving every bird that visited the heath and pointing out anything out of the ordinary in tree, bush, or flower with a proprietary pride akin to that of an estate owner taking a visitor over the Home Farm."[161] In this passage, Thompson challenges the stereotypes associated with "common people." This couple is "poor and ignorant" and yet, Thompson asserts, they are not "common people." If knowledge and love of nature (rather than social standing) determined an individual's worth, then the tinker and his wife would be members of the landed gentry: "estate owners" with "proprietary pride" in the heath that constitutes their "Home Farm." Unfortunately, the tinker and his wife lose their home due to a "secret flaw": alcoholism. When they come home drunk one night, the couple accidentally set fire to their rustic retreat. "Flora" moralizes, "Poor old things! Their fate is a humble illustration of Meredith's line, 'We are betrayed by what is false within.'"

"Flora" is excited when she meets a tramp in "September" 1926. The "professional tramp," once a "familiar type has almost disappeared from country life," she explains.[162] The tramp had been "changed to something new and strange—drilling in barrack squares, dozing over nightwatchmen's braziers, rolling lawns and digging up pet flowers in mistake for weeds, or even, in extreme cases, breaking the habit of a lifetime by serious work." The tramp she meets on an August Bank Holiday is a "perfect specimen" of the original type. At first, "Flora" seems to find the tramp picturesque, describing his boiling tea kettle and his cheery rejoinder to her greeting. Even though this tramp seems perfectly happy, she wonders, "But what about his life in wet and cold, and upon the tea and tobaccoless days, not to mention the almost certain probing of past regrets and future fears?" The sad truth, she concludes, is that the tramp is "a scrap of human wreckage flung up upon that particular roadside by who can say what circumstances."

Seasonal Work and Celebrations

In addition to describing the work of farmers, ploughmen, and shepherds in her nature essays, Thompson describes seasonal work and seasonal celebrations that serve a more social function in rural society. Seasonal work such as picking hops, harvesting chestnuts, cutting ferns, and making bracken ricks is often done in a holiday mood. Other activities such as flower, nut, and berry picking are outright sources of entertainment, particularly for children. In "March" 1924, Thompson describes the children who go "violetting" on weekends in March, "straggling along the hedgerows, searching the leaves and hailing each discovery with shouts of joy."[163] October is the month for nutting. In "October" 1922, "On half-holiday the cracking of twigs, clashing of carelessly released boughs, and shouts of happy schoolboy laughter proclaim the nutting season in full swing."[164]

One of the most memorable aspects of Thompson's first published novel, *Lark Rise*, is her description of the traditional celebrations of Harvest Home and May Day. Thompson first wrote about these two celebrations in *Out of Doors* and *The Peverel Papers*. In "August" 1924, she assumes her middle-class persona and describes a childhood memory of "staying at a farm in the Midlands" to enjoy the fun of a harvest supper.[165] Anyone familiar with the "Harvest Home" chapter of *Lark Rise* would easily recognize much of what "Flora" describes in this essay. In "May" 1921, Thompson describes a famous artist who "attempted a revival of Merrie England" complete with a "maypole and dancing on the green."[166] This story does not appear in *Lark Rise*, but Thompson's description of a bedraggled group of children who come to her door on May Day offers a glimpse of a future chapter in *Lark Rise* entitled "May Day." Although their May garland is trailing in the dust and the children look tired and dusty, they sing a May carol that they had learned from their grandmother. Thompson describes herself and these children as "survivals," a term she would later use in *Lark Rise* to describe old customs that were rapidly disappearing.

Animal Rights

Thompson was by instinct a conservationist, and her passionate love for nature made her exquisitely sensitive to alterations in the natural landscape. Whenever a tract of trees, or even a single tree, is cut down, Thompson notes which animals and birds have been displaced by this event. She also notes when tree clearing has had a positive effect. In "November" 1923, for example, she notes that "immense natural gardens" of wildflowers spring up whenever the Chestnut Fencing Company clears acres of chestnuts to make fencing stakes and barrel hoops.[167] However, Thompson always objects to the senseless destruction of living creatures, particularly when done for trivial pursuits like collecting and hunting.

"Flora" is distressed whenever she comes upon a creature that has been killed unnecessarily. In "March" 1921, she is saddened to find a slain grass snake hung "upon the prickles of a gorse bush," with "all its golden lustres dulled."[168] She says, "It seemed a shame" that this "poor, harmless thing" should be killed while trying to warm his body after his "long winter sleep." In "July" 1921, she encounters a clergyman who proudly shows her a recent catch. "Flora" is appalled by what she sees, saying: "I could have wept. In a stoppered glass poison-jar he had immured a lordly red-admiral, king of all the butterflies. At first I thought it was alive, for its crimson wings were outspread, poised as though for flight. But no, it was dead, 'Quite dead!' he repeated triumphantly. I suppose he would take the lovely lifeless thing home, pin it down in a case and make a show of it. Already he alluded to it as a 'specimen.'"[169] In "February" 1922, when "Flora" hears that "the landlord of the village inn" has preserved a stuffed kingfisher in a glass case in his bar parlor, she has a similar reaction.[170] She says, "I do not think I should care to meet the man who could find it in his heart to slay so much beauty and to keep the stuffed body in an atmosphere of stale beer and bad tobacco." In "October" 1922, "Flora" happens upon a "human heron" fishing for salmon.[171] After the fisherman proudly shows her the salmon in his basket, she reflects, "I stood for a long time looking at the torn mouth and spasmodically-convulsed form, and wondered how anyone could find pleasure in drawing a happy living thing from the cool, clear water to perish so miserably."

Thompson is also disturbed by the fashion for caging wild birds as house pets. In "April" 1922, Thompson stops by a cottage to buy eggs. The woman of the house, knowing that she is a nature lover, proudly shows Thompson her caged cuckoo. "This was a sight she was sure I had never seen," Thompson explains.[172] She continues, "I had not and was glad of it." The caged cuckoo is "a puffed-up shivering ball of misery," but its proud owner seems unaware of its suffering. In "August" 1926 Thompson expresses gratitude that "the cage bird fashion seems to have died out," noting that the goldfinch had once been "an object of merchandise, with a definite price set upon its tiny head."[173] In "August" 1922, Thompson notes another distressing practice: the repeated rifling of lapwing nests to supply plover eggs for hotel and cottage breakfasts. Thompson comments that she found it "very discouraging" to hear that a local laborer had consumed an omelet made of fifteen plover eggs.[174]

Thompson also voices her opposition to hunting in *The Peverel Papers*. "December" 1924 contains the most complete statement of her position. She begins by commenting that pheasants are "constantly harried by shooting parties" during December, and she expresses her sympathy for the pheasants that "escape wounded."[175] The fate of these birds, she says, "is piteous in the extreme." She continues: "It is one of the saddest woodland sights to see a cock pheasant, his eyes glazed and his golden plumage dabbled with blood, swaying backwards and forwards upon a bough waiting for the slow death which is to release him from his sufferings." In the same essay, Thompson remembers meeting a party returning from an otter hunt. "One of them," she recalls, "a young and pretty girl had evidently been in at her first 'kill' and honoured on that account with the ceremony of 'blooding,' for her fair if somewhat insipid face was smeared with gore."[176] Thompson concludes, "The destruction of the lesser beasts of prey does not rise to the dignity of 'sport.'"

Thompson's view of hunting, collecting, and displaying wild creatures was ahead of its time. Her descriptions of the clergyman who delights in the death of a butterfly, the laborer who eats fifteen plover eggs for breakfast, and the young woman who returns from the hunt with her face "smeared with gore" reveal such acts to be cruel and insensitive. It is not nature, but human beings who are brutal and violent, Thompson implies. Far from viewing nature as a commodity, Thompson argues for a deeper reverence for all living creatures in *The Peverel Papers.*

The Peverel Papers and Thompson's Literary Legacy

When Margaret Lane published her biographical sketch of Flora Thompson in the *Cornhill* in 1957, she not only celebrated *Lark Rise to Candleford,* but she also celebrated Thompson's life. Thompson was a woman who, without the usual advantages of birth and education, had defied the odds and had become a respected author. Lane viewed the trilogy as the culmination of the author's long apprenticeship. Thompson's entire life, Lane said, "was a preparation, instinctive at first but eventually perfectly conscious and directed to this one end."[177] Lane's view of Thompson is unfortunate, for it reduces her literary legacy to the novels of *Lark Rise to Candleford* and implies that her earlier work was merely "instinctive." The nature essays that Thompson wrote for the *Catholic Fireside* prove, however, that she was a "perfectly conscious" working writer long before she wrote the novels of *Lark Rise to Candleford*. The essays not only attest to her lifelong passion for nature and competence as an amateur naturalist, but they also showcase what is arguably some of Thompson's best writing—her lyrical descriptions of nature. Thompson's impressive knowledge of nature was neither "instinctive" nor acquired in a classroom; it was the product of her intellectual curiosity and determined research.

In "Were There No Women? British Working Class Writing in the Inter-War Period," Rebecca O'Rourke makes several assertions about Thompson's life and writing career that, in the light of *Out of Doors* and *The Peverel Papers,* have proven to be inaccurate. O'Rourke characterized

Thompson as "the proper model of a working-class woman writer" who "comes late to writing and produces little."[178] Thompson's early freelance work, especially the prize-winning literary essays published in the *Lady's Companion* in 1911, prove that Thompson did not, in fact, "come late" to writing. In addition, Thompson enjoyed immediate success, albeit on a small scale, a full twenty-eight years before *Lark Rise* was published. The sheer volume of the nature essays that Thompson wrote for the *Catholic Fireside* disprove O'Rourke's assertion that Thompson produced "little" in her writing career. In the light of O'Rourke's statements, it is, however, important to make a distinction between the short fiction Thompson published in various women's magazines and the nature essays that she wrote for *Out of Doors* and *The Peverel Papers.* Thompson may have been "simply writing what would sell" when she wrote her short fiction, but when she wrote the nature essays for *Out of Doors* and *The Peverel Papers*, as well as her literary essays for *The Fireside Reading Circle*, she was writing about her two great passions: nature and literature.

Despite the fact that Thompson's nature essays appeared in monthly installments and conveyed much factual information about the flora and fauna of Hampshire, *The Peverel Papers* is more than just a long series of individual nature notes. *The Peverel Papers* is also an aesthetic creation, the product of Thompson's memory and imagination. Her nature series is best understood as an extended narrative in which "Flora," the amateur naturalist and lover of literature, shares her nature observations, her love of literature, and the stories of her encounters with country folk with her faithful readers. Thompson created her narrative by combining fact and fiction (just as she would later combine fact and fiction in *Lark Rise*, *Over to Candleford*, *Candleford Green*, and *Heatherley*) in ways that suited her narrative purpose. Thompson was a writer who knew her audience, and the conscious decisions she made to conceal or reveal aspects of her personal life were made with her narrative purpose in mind. Thompson's nature essays demand a reassessment of her entire literary career, not only to correct previous inaccuracies about her early writing, but also to shed new light on the relationship between fact and fiction in *Lark Rise, Over to Candleford, Candleford Green,* and *Heatherley.*

3

The Major Works: *Lark Rise to Candleford, Heatherley,* and *Still Glides the Stream*

Flora Thompson is known almost exclusively for three novels she published between 1939 and 1943: *Lark Rise* (1939), *Over to Candleford* (1941), and *Candleford Green* (1943).[1] Since 1945, these three novels have been published together as the trilogy *Lark Rise to Candleford.* In the last year of her life Thompson wrote of her Oxfordshire childhood, which had been the inspiration for her popular trilogy:[2] "It happened that at Lark Rise in the 1880's a child was growing up who was a born observer. Nothing which happened around her escaped her notice and, about past times in the hamlet she asked so many questions that the neighbours called her 'a fair werrit.' They little thought that she was the 'chiel among them takin' notes,' and would one day print them."[3]

In *Lark Rise to Candleford* and in the posthumously published novel, *Heatherley,* Thompson used her childhood memories to create a working-class heroine, Laura the stonemason's daughter. Each of the novels is named for a rural community in which Laura lives, and because Laura is portrayed as a keen observer of village life, each novel provides a rich portrait of rural life during the last two decades of the nineteenth century. Laura is a solitary young girl, whose passion for reading and deep love for nature set her apart from the men and women of the communities in which she lives. Each book marks a stage in Laura's intellectual development, and as Laura moves further and further from her childhood home, her life becomes, quite literally, a journey of self-discovery.

Thompson completed two additional novels before her death in 1947: *Gates of Eden* and *Still Glides the Stream.* Although *Gates of Eden* was completed before Thompson began to write *Lark Rise,* she never submitted the manuscript to a publisher.[4] After completing *Over to Candleford,* Thompson began writing a new novel that she entitled *Dashpers.* She submitted the first chapter and a plot outline of *Dashpers* to the Oxford University Press in 1941 but abandoned this novel after receiving a lukewarm response from her editor.[5] In 1945 Thompson began to write another novel, tentatively entitled *These Too Were Victorians.* Renamed *Still Glides the Stream,* this book was completed in 1946, but it was not published until 1948 due to postwar shortages.[6] Although *Still Glides the Stream* is set in rural Oxfordshire in the 1880s and 1890s, it is not a continuation of Laura's story. The protagonist is Charity Finch, a retired schoolteacher who returns to her childhood home, the village of Restharrow, to revisit the scenes of her youth and to reminisce about her family and childhood.

The Novels of *Lark Rise to Candleford* and *Heatherley*

In March of 1947, when the Readers Union offered a 7 shilling edition of *Lark Rise to Candleford* as an optional book to its members, Thompson wrote an article for its publication, *The Readers News*, entitled "A Country Child Taking Notes." In this article, Thompson revealed that, while writing a series of "nature and country-life articles" for "one of the Catholic weeklies" in the 1920s, she discovered "the feature most liked in the articles were my sketches of old country life and characters, remembered from my childhood, and I determined that in some future time I would describe them more fully."[7] Thompson eventually described the "old country life and characters" in three separate articles published during the 1930s: "Old Queenie," "An Oxfordshire Hamlet in the 'Eighties," and "May Day in the 'Eighties." "Old Queenie," subtitled "A 'Memory' by Flora Thompson," was published in the *Lady* in 1937. In this article, Thompson describes an elderly beekeeper and lacemaker, known as Queenie (first described in *The Peverel Papers* in August 1924), whom she had known during her childhood in Juniper Hill. She also returned to the subject of "telling the bees," a country tradition that she had previously described in her short story "The Toft Cup" and in a nature essay published in *The Peverel Papers* in September 1922. In 1937 Thompson published her second article, "An Oxfordshire Hamlet in the 'Eighties," in the *National Review*. In this article, Thompson describes the Oxfordshire hamlet of Juniper Hill, where she was born and where she lived until the age of fourteen. "May Day in the 'Eighties," an article describing the celebration of May Day during Thompson's Oxfordshire childhood, was published in the *National Review* in May of 1938. When *Lark Rise* was published in 1939, a revised version of "An Oxfordshire Hamlet in the 'Eighties" became the first chapter ("Poor People's Houses") of this novel. A revised version of "Old Queenie" became the book's fifth chapter ("Survivals"), and "May Day in the 'Eighties" became the thirteenth chapter ("May Day"). Although there is a vague reference to "the children" in "Old Queenie," Laura and the field full of larks that gives *Lark Rise* its title did not appear in these three articles.

When Thompson submitted an early manuscript of *Lark Rise* to the Oxford University Press in 1938, Sir Humphrey Milford (publisher to the university) recognized the manuscript's importance and encouraged her to develop it into a book.[8] Because the Oxford University Press did not publish works of fiction in 1939, Thompson's editor was faced with the immediate problem of classifying the book for publication. Geoffrey Cumberlege's decision was to publish *Lark Rise* as an autobiography, a decision that was to have a profound effect on the reception of *Lark Rise* and of Thompson's subsequent novels, *Over to Candleford*, *Candleford Green*, and *Heatherley*.[9] Book reviews, biographies, scholarly articles, and even introductions to the subsequent editions of Thompson's novels have all been shaped by the perception of *Lark Rise* as a work of nonfiction. Cumberlege's classification preserved *Lark Rise to Candleford* as a source of valuable information about rural life in the 1880s and 1890s, thereby legitimizing scholars' later use of the trilogy as a source of evidence.[10] Unfortunately, this classification has also limited the critical conversation about these novels. At present, studies of *Lark Rise to Candleford* either explore the grounds for treating the trilogy as a quasi-historical document or debate the degree to which Thompson disguised, revealed, or modified her personal experience in writing these books. Although *Lark Rise*, *Over to Candleford*, *Candleford Green*, and *Heatherley* provide a wealth of settings, characters, and themes, these books have never been studied as works of fiction.

Lark Rise

When Thompson was in her sixties, she turned her attention from Hampshire, which had been the inspiration for her short fiction, poetry, and nature essays during the 1910s and 1920s, to her native county of Oxfordshire. Drawing on memories of her birthplace, Juniper Hill, Thompson created a portrait of daily life in the fictional hamlet of Lark Rise during the 1880s and of Laura, the stonemason's daughter. The popular appeal of this novel was historical in part. England was on the verge of war at the time of *Lark Rise*'s publication, and readers were attracted to the novel's depiction of a more stable time in English history and its portrayal of rural characters who survived grinding poverty with dignity rather than self-pity.[11] After its first appearance in 1939, *Lark Rise* steadily grew in popularity and was reprinted in 1941, 1943, and 1944.

In the first chapter, "Poor People's Houses," Thompson introduces the reader to the hamlet of Lark Rise. The oft-quoted first paragraph of this chapter reveals the sensitivity to natural beauty that characterizes her prose: "The Hamlet stood on a gentle rise in the flat, wheat-growing north-east corner of Oxfordshire. We will call it Lark Rise because of the great number of skylarks which made the surrounding fields their springboard and nested on the bare earth between the rows of green corn."[12] In this chapter, Thompson also introduces Laura, her working-class heroine, and Laura's family. Laura's father is a stonemason who earns a slightly higher wage than the farm laborers who live in the hamlet.

Laura's mother, Emma, who is better educated than the other hamlet women, is also distinguished from the other residents of Lark Rise by having been a nursemaid for a prosperous family.[13] Because Laura's parents have a slightly higher social status than the other residents of Lark Rise, Laura and her younger brother Edmund are "more fortunate than their neighbors" because there are a few more refinements in the "end house" where they live.[14]

Although the narrative focus of *Lark Rise* is divided between Laura and life in the hamlet, Laura is the most important character in this work. Like her mother and father, Laura is distinguished from the other residents of Lark Rise. Unlike the village children, Laura has an inquiring mind, a love of reading, and a sensitive response to the beauty of nature. Laura's position in the narrative is reflected symbolically by the physical location of her family's home, which stands "a little apart, and turning its back on its neighbours, as though about to run away into the fields."[15] Although an active participant in village activities, Laura maintains a certain psychological distance from her community. She finds the rough, or even cruel, pastimes of the local children distasteful. Her closest companion and kindred spirit is her brother Edmund. Although the narrator of *Lark Rise* portrays Laura and Edmund as "observers of and commentators upon the country scene of their birth and early years," it is important to note that they never provide direct commentary. Laura and Edmund function only as characters in this text.[16]

Although Laura and her family are important figures in *Lark Rise,* Thompson focuses much of her attention on documenting the daily lives of poor agricultural workers and their families in the 1880s. Except for her treatment of the elderly residents of Lark Rise in the chapter entitled "Survivals," Thompson refers to most of the residents of the hamlet as *men, women, mothers, fathers,* and *children,* thereby creating a portrait of a community rather than a portrait of individuals. Thompson describes in detail how the hamlet women attended to their housework, how the men farmed, and what the children learned in school. She also describes the social life of the men, women, and children of Lark Rise, from the singing of the men at the Wagon and Horses and the gossiping and tea drinking of the women to the popular games that hamlet children played. She also describes how the community celebrated Christmas, Easter, May Day, Harvest Home, and Guy Fawkes Day.

Lark Rise is a rich source of information about the attitudes, values, and prejudices of the agricultural working classes. The residents are not a pious, church-going people, but they do prize virtues such as endurance. "Not to flinch from pain or hardship" is their "ideal."[17] Their prejudices mirror the prejudices of their nation and social class. Like other English men and women, they are suspicious of gypsies, the Irish, and Catholics.

The men's low wages and low social standing guarantee a lifetime of poverty for themselves and their families. Consequently, the men and women of Lark Rise focus their energies on survival rather than on education, exquisite sensitivities, and cultural refinement. The narrator observes the adults of Lark Rise and admires them for knowing "the now lost secret of being happy on little" but also recognizes that the villagers are "poor fallible human beings" and does not indulge in much sentimentality when describing their behavior.[18] As Laura's mother observes, "There's nothing the matter with Lark Rise folks but poverty, and that's no crime."[19]

In the final chapter of *Lark Rise*, the celebration of Queen Victoria's Jubilee in 1887 stands as a symbol of the end of the old way of life and the beginning of a new era, for "after the Jubilee nothing ever seemed quite the same."[20] Mechanical reapers begin to appear in the fields, and in the not too distant future, the narrator informs us, the elderly would have an old-age pension to keep them from sinking into abject poverty and dying in the workhouse. In the last chapter of *Lark Rise*, the narrator expresses regret over the loss of simple pleasures from that bygone era but also notes the improved living conditions that would eventually result from higher wages and better sanitary conditions in the hamlet. *Lark Rise* concludes by alluding to the horrors of war that the unsuspecting hamlet boys would face in the coming years: "Gallipoli? Kut? Vimy Ridge? Ypres? What did they know of such places? But they were to know them, and when the time came they did not flinch."[21]

Over to Candleford

Thompson began working on a sequel to *Lark Rise* in 1939. The new novel, *Over to Candleford,* was written during the early years of World War II. While Thompson was writing this novel, she was also attending to the daily necessities of life in wartime England and coping with her declining health.[22] Although Flora and John Thompson moved from their home in the port town of Dartmouth to a safer location in Brixham in March 1940, she managed to have the finished proofs of her new novel ready by February 1941. *Over to Candleford* was published by the Oxford University Press later that same year.[23] *Over to Candleford* was reprinted in 1942, 1943, and again in 1944, before being reprinted in *Lark Rise to Candleford* in 1945.

Thompson clearly establishes the significance of her title in the first paragraph of this new novel: "'Come the summer, we'll borrow old Polly and the spring cart from the 'Wagon and Horses' and all go over to Candleford,' their father said, for the ten-millionth time, thought Laura. Although he had said it so often they had never been. They had not been anywhere farther than the market town for the Saturday shopping."[24] In

Over to Candleford, Lark Rise and Candleford are portrayed as two communities with different financial, social, and educational opportunities. The promised trip to Candleford, which finally occurs in the sixth chapter, is highly significant because Candleford is Laura's first experience of the "outerworld": "In the outerworld men were running up tall factory chimneys and covering the green fields for miles with rows of mean little houses to house the workers. Towns which were already towns were throwing out roads and roads of suburban villas. . . . But the hamlet people saw none of these changes. They were far from the industrial districts and their surroundings remained as they had been from the time of their birth.[25]" Although Thompson describes the social and economic milieu of Candleford, contrasting it with the impoverished Lark Rise, the long passages of documentary information about life in the 1880s that form such a central part of *Lark Rise* are not present in *Over to Candleford*. In this work, Thompson concentrates more on plot development and characterization rather than on recording social history.

Over to Candleford sees the residents of Lark Rise emerging from their anonymous positions as *mothers*, *fathers,* and *children* to become fully developed characters. The older women of Lark Rise, such as Old Queenie, Old Sally, and Old Mrs. Prout, are described in loving detail, along with their stories of life in early Victorian England. Thompson uses anecdotes to reveal the true character of several hamlet residents, such as Miss Shepherd (the school mistress), Mr. and Mrs. Herring (the owners of Laura's cottage), and Mr. Marley (a saintly curate). Thompson also reintroduces Laura and her family, providing far more detail about Laura, her younger brother Edmund, and the children's parents, Emma and Robert.

Thompson's portraits of Laura's family members illustrate the restricting influence of poverty. Laura's mother is an important presence in *Over to Candleford*, telling stories, giving practical advice, and worrying over Laura's getting a place. Laura's mother does not understand how her daughter can bury her nose in a book when there are babies to be cuddled at home. When Laura shows no interest in or aptitude for being a nursemaid, her mother expresses her disappointment with brutal honesty. Laura is crushed by her mother's criticism and feels a "sense of defeat, of having been tried and found wanting."[26] Like the other residents of Lark Rise, the narrator explains, Laura's mother "was kind and sensible and loved her children dearly, but she did not believe in showing too much tenderness towards them or in 'giving herself away' to the world at large."[27]

Laura's father, Robert, although an elusive figure in *Lark Rise*, is described in more detail in this novel. Laura first remembers him as a "slim, upright young man in the late twenties, with dark, fiery eyes and raven-black hair, but fair, fresh-coloured complexion": "Even in darkness his step could be distinguished, for it was lighter and sharper than that of the other men. His mind moved more quickly, too, and his tongue was readier, for he belonged to another breed and had been brought up in another environment."[28] The limited opportunities in the hamlet of Lark Rise play a part in Robert's degeneration from a young and vibrant man to the "lost and thwarted man" that he becomes in later life. Robert, the narrator informs the reader, "had strayed into a life to which he did not belong," and his "own weakness would keep him there for the rest of his days." Laura's father dies an "old and embittered man," the narrator informs us, finally defeated by his "weakness": alcoholism.

Laura's Uncle Tom and Aunt Ann, who live with their children in Candleford town, provide a significant contrast to Laura's parents. The summers that Laura spends with this family expose her to a world where parents freely express affection for their children and reading books is considered a worthwhile pastime. It is Laura's Uncle Tom, not Laura's father, who is the most fully developed male character in this book. He encourages Laura's love of reading and gives her full access to his attic full of books. Laura describes her uncle as "one of the most liberal-minded men she was ever to know and one of the wisest."[29] An entire chapter of *Over to Candleford* is dedicated to describing Uncle Tom's "queer fish," those customers and village eccentrics who always stop by Uncle Tom's shop to ask for his opinion or to talk over important matters. Uncle Tom's wisdom and Aunt Ann's warmth provide an atmosphere of love and acceptance in which Laura is given free rein to read and to develop her imaginative life. It is an atmosphere in which she flourishes emotionally and intellectually.

Laura, the sensitive young girl, considered rather odd by her neighbors, is clearly the protagonist of *Over to Candleford*. Her individuality is established on the day of her birth: "Laura arrived on this scene on a cold December morning when snow lay in deep drifts over the fields and blocked the roads. . . . 'Oh, we were so cold, so cold,' her mother would say when telling the story, and Laura liked that "we." It showed that even a tiny baby who had never been outside the room in which she was born was already a person."[30] As a young schoolgirl, Laura is teased by the other children because something about her looks, clothes, or voice does not conform to the "accepted school pattern."[31] Laura is "bent on improvement," and her earliest attempts consist of dying her hair with ink to improve her "cross-grained" combination of "dark eyes and pale yellow hair."[32] However, what really distinguishes Laura from her childhood companions is her active imagination, thirst for knowledge, and love for books. As a young child, Laura's imaginative life is fed by her mother's exciting bedtime stories and by the few books available to her in Lark Rise. Laura loves to read stories in the Old Testament and is fascinated by the poetic beauty of the Psalms. She is also familiar with popular literature such as *Froggy's Little Brother*, *Christie's Old Organ*, *Ministering Children*, and *Old Saint Paul's*. When a neighbor loans the family several of Sir Walter Scott's Waverley novels, *The Bride of Lammermoor* becomes "one of the first books" Laura reads "with absorbed interest."[33] Laura and her brother are both "voracious readers," and their shared love of literature and imaginative recreation of scenes from their favorite books and poetry create a special bond between them. After Laura and Edmund are introduced to Scott's poetry, the two children even try their hands at "writing a little verse."[34] Laura's literary horizons expand when she spends summers at her Uncle Tom's home in Candleford. She is delighted to be called a bookworm by her cousins, especially when it means being compared to her beloved Uncle Tom. Laura spends many summers reading to her uncle as he works in his shop, the first of the books being *Cranford*, Elizabeth Gaskell's tale of village life.

Like *Lark Rise*, *Over to Candleford* is full of sensitive descriptions of nature. When Laura's family takes its first trip to Candleford, they stop in a field and drink milk out of bottles while they listen "to the skylarks overhead" and smell "the wild thyme at their feet."[35] For Laura, nature is the source of "her life's deepest joys."[36] Thompson's descriptions of nature, as seen through Laura's observant eyes, reflect the changing of the seasons as well as details of plant life. When spring comes, Laura not only notices the bluebells blooming in the fields but also the unrolling of chestnut candles and young bracken fronds.[37] Just like Thompson's narrative persona in *The Peverel Papers*, the fourteen-year-old Laura turns to nature for healing and consolation. Laura becomes depressed when she contemplates her future and worries that the world has "no use for her."[38] Laura's depression finally lifts on a "dull November day" when she runs "out into the fields" and feels at one with nature: "The fresh green moss, the glistening ivy, and the reddish twigs with their sparkling drops seemed to have been made for her alone and the hurrying, foam-flecked water seemed to have some message for her. She felt suddenly uplifted. The things that had troubled her troubled her no more."

It is in *Over to Candleford* that Laura's progressive moves away from her childhood home begin to develop into the plot of a *bildungsroman*. At the end of this novel, Laura leaves the hamlet of Lark Rise in a horse-drawn cart to take a position as an assistant to the postmistress of Candleford Green, Dorcas Lane. Laura's move to Candleford Green marks the end of her life of rural isolation as well as the end of her childhood. As Laura departs from Lark Rise, she moves into a wider world where "new churches and chapels and railway stations and schools and public houses" are being built "to meet the needs of a fast-growing population."[39]

Candleford Green

Thompson began writing the last novel of her trilogy in the spring of 1942 amid the devastation of wartime England. Since the Thompson family lived within five miles of strategic naval targets in Dartmouth and Brixham, she and her family suffered through the heavy bombing raids in that area. At times, Thompson was forced to work on the manuscript of *Candleford Green* in the Morrison shelter in her cellar.[40] Despite the fact that she was nearing sixty-six and in ill health, Thompson managed to complete *Candleford Green* in less than a year.[41] *Candleford Green* was published in January 1943 and proved to be so popular that it was reprinted twice in 1943 and once again in 1944.

Candleford Green opens quite literally where *Over to Candleford* ends, with Laura sitting with her father on the high front seat of a spring cart as they begin their journey to the post office in Candleford Green. It is the beginning of the 1890s in rural Oxfordshire, and Laura is now fourteen and a half. She leaves her birthplace, Lark Rise, with a precious gift from her brother stowed away in her trunk: a penny exercise book he has inscribed "*Laura's Journal*."[42] As the title of this first chapter proclaims, Laura is moving "From One Small World to Another." When Laura's father leaves her with Dorcas Lane, the postmistress of Candleford Green, Laura watches him drive away "with the sinking feeling of one whose last link with a known world is vanishing."[43] Laura starts her new life in Candleford Green with only a few assets: "the contents of the trunk, the clothes she was wearing, youth and health, and a meager education."[44] Like most young people of her age, the narrator comments, Laura "had no idea of the slenderness of her equipment for life and no fears for the distant future which stretched before her."

Thompson makes a careful distinction between hamlet, village, and town in *Candleford Green*. Candleford Green is identified by the "large irregular square of turf" that gives the village its name.[45] Candleford Green is "still a village" and the life lived there is "still village life."[46] In a hamlet like Lark Rise, "there lived only one class of people; all did similar work, all were poor and all were equal." However, in Candleford Green "the population . . . was more varied. It had a clergyman of its own and a doctor and independent gentlewomen who lived in superior cottages with stabling attached, and artisans and labourers who lived in smaller and poorer ones, though none so small and poor as those of the hamlet. . . . The village was a little world in itself; the hamlet was but a segment." Laura's new home and place of employment is the "long, low white house" located on the "farther, less-populated side of the green."[47]

The green is the center of village life for all social classes in Candleford Green. Members of the working classes gather on the green to celebrate

Feast Mondays with hurdy gurdy music, naphtha flares, and "shouting [themselves] hoarse in swingboats."[48] On Meet Morning, the first Saturday in January, members of the gentry gather on the green on horseback, clad in scarlet riding habits and surrounded by barking dogs. The green is also the center of village commerce. The shops that line the green display the latest merchandise in their windows, celebrating "the march of progress" in an increasingly commercial England.[49] In *Candleford Green*, Thompson presents a rich and varied portrait of village life that is sensitive but not sentimental. Candleford Green is "a pleasant and peaceful place," but it is "no second Garden of Eden."[50] The darker side of village life is revealed in short character sketches of wife beaters, poachers, and malicious gossips. Yet, the narrator assures the reader, "the majority of Candleford Green dwellers were kindly, as majorities always are."[51]

When Laura arrives in Candleford Green, she is still the thin, plain girl of *Lark Rise* and *Over to Candleford.* Now a "tall, lanky fourteen," she judges herself "ignorant" because she has only the "country born" girl's minimal education.[52] Laura chooses to imagine herself "interesting-looking," despite her mother's harsh comments about her personal appearance: "*You'll* never be annoyed by people turning round in the street to have another look at you. . . . But that cuts both ways: if you're no beauty, be thankful you're not a freak."[53] Although she likes to imagine herself in a scarlet coat riding "to hounds across fields and over streams," Laura acknowledges she is "not of the stuff of which heroines are made."[54] In *Candleford Green*, Laura is the quiet but shrewd observer of village life, a "born looker-on" who prefers to "watch from her window."[55]

Despite doubts about her personal appearance, Laura still prides herself on her individuality. She turns down an invitation to join the Primrose League because "she never did wish to do what everybody else was doing . . . because her thoughts and tastes ran upon different lines than the majority."[56] Her independence keeps her from settling on an early marriage. She resists the romantic advances of a self-absorbed gamekeeper, Philip White, even though she finds it flattering to be courted. Philip is far too self-satisfied for Laura's tastes. Likewise, she is not content to remain at Candleford Green for the rest of her life. She resists pressure from her formidable employer, Miss Lane, who tells her, "I don't see why you should ever leave here. You and I get on very well together, and perhaps, after my time you might take my place in the office."[57] Laura's mother tells her, "You're not cut out for a pleasant, easy life. You think too much!" but Laura takes pride in her independence and is sustained by her deep love of nature and her passion for reading.

Although her position as assistant to the postmistress gives Laura "leisure for human contacts" and the post office window provides an excellent view of the village green, Laura pines for "her old freedom of the fields."[58] She longs "to smell things and touch things, warm earth and flowers and grasses, and to stand and gaze where no one could see her, drinking it all in." Eventually, Laura takes over a country delivery and comes to know "every tree, flower-patch and fern clump beside her path, as well as the gardens, houses, and faces of the people on her round."[59] *Candleford Green* abounds in lyrical descriptions of nature, as Laura drinks in the beauty of local flora and fauna and notes the changing of the seasons. Symbolically, when Laura gives up the "stout waterproof shoes" she had worn while delivering mail in the country, she gives them to a gypsy woman in exchange for a "basket of plaited twigs filled with moss and ferns."[60]

As in *Lark Rise* and *Over to Candleford*, Laura is fascinated by books and reads everything that comes into her hands. Laura's life at Candleford Green provides her leisure time to discover great works of literature: "Those were the days for Laura when almost everything in literature was new to her and every fresh discovery was like one of Keats's own *Magic casements opening on the foam*."[61] When Miss Lane is engrossed in private conversation with a customer, Laura slips away quietly and heads for the bookcase in the parlor where Miss Lane keeps her best books. During this period, Laura discovers *Barchester Towers* and *Pride and Prejudice*, which give her "a taste for the work of Trollope and Jane Austen which was to be a precious possession for life."[62] Miss Lane allows Laura to borrow all of her books, except for Byron's *Don Juan*. Since Miss Lane thinks it a "terrible book," Laura is forced to read *Don Juan* on the sly: "She felt she simply had to know what came next, and the blue skies and seas of those foreign shores and the seaside caves and golden sands and the wit of the author and the felicity of his language and the dexterity of his rhymes enchanted her. She was shocked by some of the hero's adventures, but more often thrilled. Laura learned quite a lot by reading *Don Juan*."[63] After Laura reads most of the books in Miss Lane's parlor, she obtains a library card from the mechanics' institute in Candleford and continues the process of educating herself.

Literature is so important to Laura that she forms her closest relationships with those who share this love. Laura's friendships with two young men, Godfrey Parrish and William Stokes, are both based on a shared interest in literature, particularly poetry. Laura shares more with these young men than she does with the young girls of the village, who are content to read popular religious novels such as Susan Bogert Warner's *Queechy* and *The Wide Wide World*. Thompson provides a detailed picture of reading tastes in the 1890s in *Candleford Green*. The narrator comments on the popular works frequently found in middle-class parlors of the period and the classic works of English literature Laura favors, as well as on more controversial works, such as Darwin's *On the Origin of Species* and the works of Oscar Wilde. Thompson's depiction of reading habits in *Candleford Green* is fascinating for what it reveals about social class and the cultural values of this period.

Life in Candleford Green suits Laura. After she first settles into her new home, she is "happier, or at least gayer than she had been since early childhood": "Because of her age, or the overflowing abundance of Miss Lane's table, or because something in the air or the life suited her, her thin figure filled out, a brighter colour appeared in her cheeks, and such an inrush of energy and high spirits took hold of her that she would dance, rather than walk, about the house and garden, and she felt she could never tire."[64] For the first time in her life, Laura is free from the daily cares of life in a large, poor family. She is a child again, living in a houseful of adults. The kind attention and affection she receives from Miss Lane and the other members of the household help her to feel cherished in a different way than she had felt in her loving but less demonstrative family. After living in Candleford Green for seven months, Laura goes home to visit her family in Lark Rise and discovers that nothing has changed during her absence. The inhabitants of Lark Rise are "just as they had been from the day of her birth," yet to Laura they seem "rougher and cruder than formerly."[65] Laura finally realizes that it is she who has changed since leaving home.

The years that Laura spends in Candleford Green not only mark a transitional period in her life, but they also mark a transitional period in the life of the village itself. Candleford Green is in the process of turning from a "quiet and secluded village" into a "suburb of a small country town."[66] When Laura becomes friends with a local girl, Doreen Green, it is her first contact with a new social class that is "on the borderline between the working and middle classes."[67] The narrator of *Candleford Green* expresses mixed emotions about the forces of economic and social change in Candleford Green and about the new social class that these changes have produced. Although the members of this new social class are mainly "frugal and home-loving," they have spiritually "lost ground, rather than gained it" by substituting the new "creed" of "keeping up appearances" for the old religious and political ideals.[68] The members of this class were "the kind of people among whom much of [Laura's] life was to be spent," the narrator notes.[69]

After two years of living in Candleford Green, Laura decides to leave her position with Dorcas Lane, "driven on by well-meant advice from without and from within by the restless longing of youth to see and experience the whole of life."[70] The novel ends as Laura walks away from Candleford Green, savoring her last impressions of the village and the surrounding countryside. Laura breaks through the final barricades in her life, symbolized by the "gossamer threads, spun from bush to bush" that seem to be blocking her path.[71] As Laura breaks through "one after another of these fairy barricades," she reflects that "the threads which were to bind her to her native county were more enduring than gossamer. They were spun of love and kinship and cherished memories."[72]

Candleford Green is a complex text that, despite its descriptions of village life and social and economic changes during the 1890s, is essentially a *bildungsroman.* The novel continues the story of Laura, following her as she moves from her home in the hamlet of Lark Rise to take her first post office position in the village of Candleford Green. Laura is a sensitive and observant child from the ranks of the rural poor. When she moves to Candleford Green, she follows the village tradition of getting a position to reduce the financial strain at home. However, as this novel develops, it is clear that Laura is embarked on a journey of self-discovery. Living in Candleford Green frees Laura from the restrictions of poverty in her native Lark Rise and allows her to develop a rich inner life.

Heatherley

Heatherley, Thompson's final novel about Laura, was not published until 1979, thirty-two years after the author's death. Based on existing records, it appears that Thompson never submitted the manuscript of *Heatherley* to the Oxford University Press.[73] Thanks to Margaret Lane, this novel was finally published in *A Country Calendar. Heatherley* is a novel of particular interest to fans of the earlier trilogy because it continues Laura's story. Like the novels of *Lark Rise to Candleford, Heatherley* is named for the village in which Laura comes to live several years after her departure from Candleford Green. Laura comes to Heatherley seeking a more permanent position in the post office, even though she has had to move far from family and friends for the first time in her life. As in the novels of *Lark Rise to Candleford*, a sense of place is extraordinarily important in *Heatherley.* As the novel opens, Laura approaches Heatherley on foot and catches her first glimpse of the heath. For the first time in her life, Laura sees a field of heather, a plant that she had imagined since reading Sir Walter Scott as a child. Laura is overwhelmed by the beauty of the landscape before her: "Her preconceived idea seemed crude and cold before the living reality.Pale purple as the bloom on a ripe plum, veined with the gold of late flowering gorse, set with small slender birches just turning yellow, with red-berried rowans and thickets of bracken, the heath lay steeped in sunshine."[74]

Although Laura's love for the Oxfordshire countryside is a notable feature of *Lark Rise to Candleford*, her response to the landscape of Hampshire is far more intense. For Laura, the countryside around Heatherley is the expression of her poetic soul, and her greatest pleasure is "to roam on the heather-clad hills or to linger in one of the valley woods."[75] When she walks alone on the heath, Laura experiences a happiness that she has never before experienced: "It was then, when she let the heather brush the hem of her skirt and breathed the honey-scented moorland air, that she was filled with a sense of freedom and detachment from ordinary life such as she was never to know elsewhere."[76] Laura recognizes that being in tune with nature is essential to her "bodily and spiritual well being," and she experiences the heath as "an enveloping atmosphere from which she drew strength and delight."[77] Laura's love for Oxfordshire, the county in which she was born, is that "of a child for its parent, a love which takes all for granted, instinctive rather than inspiring."[78] Her love for the countryside around Heatherley is of a different nature: "more a falling in love on her part than of merely loving."[79] *Heatherley* provides a clear textual link back to Thompson's early writing career, when she wrote short stories, poetry, and nature essays that celebrated the Hampshire countryside. It is ironic that Thompson's reputation has been built upon her description of Oxfordshire when, in reality, her greatest love and source of inspiration was the Hampshire landscape.

The village of Heatherley is very different from the hamlet, town, and village of Laura's childhood. Laura discovers that Heatherley is not "strictly speaking" a village at all, but "a settlement of recent growth consisting of a couple of roads with shops, a new model inn with an artistic signboard and a few modern cottages and villas."[80] Heatherley had recently come into existence as a health resort after a famous scientist had settled in the region to enjoy "the virtues of moorland air." Heatherley is a prosperous and leisured world, a village that serves the various literary and artistic celebrities who live in the surrounding countryside. In Laura's eyes, however, Heatherley is "a less kindly, solid, and permanent world than that of her birth" because it is a community of people who have "broken with their own personal past" to live "chiefly for the passing moment" in a place without traditions.[81]

Thompson based *Heatherley* on the period that she spent working in the post office in Grayshott, Hampshire, from 1898 to 1901. During this period, a number of famous literary figures, who lived in nearby Hindhead, relied on the Grayshott post office to send telegrams and to conduct their business.[82] Consequently, Thompson was given a unique opportunity to encounter famous living authors, if only over the post office counter. In *Heatherley*, Laura also has the thrilling experience of serving famous living authors, such as Sir Arthur Conan Doyle, in the post office. Laura also attends readings given in a local church hall by famous authors such as George Bernard Shaw and even makes a "pious pilgrimage" to the cottage of George Meredith, content to merely gaze at the home of the author who had written of a new world "where women existed in their own right, not merely loved or unloved, as the complement of man."[83] Laura loves the heroines of Meredith's novels, even though "she had herself never come into contact with any woman half as delightful, and thought of their world as a paradise of the well-born and well-educated from which she was barred by her birth."[84]

The chief interest of *Heatherley* is the continuing evolution of Laura, from a sensitive young woman to an aspiring author. At twenty, Laura is still recognizable as the poor young girl of the *Lark Rise* trilogy, the child with a deep love of nature and an insatiable appetite for reading. Laura still delights in simple pleasures, and "quiet and solitude" are her "spiritual meat and drink."[85] Despite her poverty and humble social standing, Laura is not bothered by feelings of self-pity, for "it was, to her, the individual who counted, not his or her place in society." Being an individual is of paramount importance to Laura. The two loves that define her as an individual continue to be her love of literature and her love of nature.

In the pages of *Heatherley*, Laura admits to a lifelong ambition to become a writer. She imagines writing a novel and naming it after the local variety of a parasitic plant called dodder. Laura explains her idea to her friends, the Brownlows: "It would be the story of a man or woman—she thought a woman—of fine, sensitive nature, bound by some tie—probably marriage—to one of a nature which was strong, coarse, and encroaching, and would tell how, in time, the heather person shrank and withered, while the dodder one fattened and prospered."[86] In the final chapter of *Heatherley,* the narrator informs the reader that Laura "had not entirely neglected to cultivate her one small gift of self-expression": "Short stories and articles of hers had been appearing occasionally for the past ten years in newspapers and women's weeklies. The remuneration for these had been a welcome addition to the family exchequer, but otherwise they amounted to little. . . . [S]he had sometimes told herself with a somewhat wry smile, though not without enjoyment of the humor of the situation, that the pen she had taken for a sword had turned in her hands into a darning needle."[87] Such passages offer tantalizing glimpses of Thompson's attitude toward her early writing career and the short stories and essays that she published in women's magazines during the 1910s and 1920s.

As in *Candleford Green*, the friends whom Laura makes in Heatherley are those who share her love for literature. Mr. Foreshaw, a retired big-game hunter with a reputation for being a woman hater, becomes Laura's friend, in part because of their shared love of literature. Alma Steadman, who works with Laura behind the post office counter, becomes another friend because she shares Laura's love for poetry. For a time, Laura enjoys a close friendship with Mavis and Richard Brownlow, a brother and sister who are "modern" and thoroughly "fin de siècle."[88] Laura enjoys the

Brownlows because they "had read and could discuss new books by new authors whose names, to Laura, were but vaguely familiar." Walking at night with the Brownlows, Laura often joins the brother and sister as they chant "in unison the quatrains of Omar Khayyám, or a chorus from Swinburne." Laura's affection for Mavis and Richard is so great that she even shares some of "her moorland and woodland haunts" with them.[89] Initially, Laura is intrigued by a local character named Bob Pikesley, whom she observes sitting silently on the heath. At first, Laura imagines Pikesley to be a peasant poet or philosopher, but her romantic notions are quickly dispelled when she discovers that he is not only a man of "limited ideas" but is also totally "devoid of human feeling."[90]

Laura's experience of living with the sinister postmaster, Mr. Hertford, and his family provides several dramatic episodes in *Heatherley*. The sinister atmosphere in the Hertfords' home, and the peculiar events that transpire while Laura is living with the family, provide a gothic element in the novel's plot. When she first arrives, Laura detects something "strange and gloomy, even a little sinister" about the postmaster's parlor.[91] Laura finds Mrs. Hertford to be a silent and melancholy woman, with a face that is "the saddest [Laura] had ever seen."[92] Mr. Hertford is a man with a "strange wild light in his eyes" who has several "disquieting" habits, such as quoting biblical texts in a "hissing whisper" and laughing silently in a "pantomime of hilarious laughter."[93] When Laura works behind the post office counter, she often hears a "deep hissing of abuse" and "heartbroken weeping" coming from the Hertfords' parlor.[94] After Mrs. Hertford informs Laura that her husband often prowls the house at night looking for an "unnamed enemy he believed was lying in wait for him," Laura immediately understands why she sometimes wakes at night feeling that someone has been standing by her bed.[95] After Mr. Hertford fires a revolver on the upstairs landing to scare away imaginary burglars, Laura immediately moves into new lodgings. Several years after leaving Heatherley, Laura learns that the postmaster had murdered his wife. The characters of Mr. and Mrs. Hertford and the events that occur in the Hertford home are based on actual events that occurred while Thompson lived with William Chapman, the Grayshott postmaster.

In the last three chapters of *Heatherley*, Thompson turns her attention to historical events at the turn of the twentieth century. It is as if she is discharging her responsibility to record a changing era, much as she had already done in the novels of *Lark Rise to Candleford*. In the chapter entitled "The Village in Wartime," Thompson describes the impact of the Boer War on Laura and the other residents of Heatherley. Laura's brother Edmund reappears, this time as a solider fighting in the Boer War. The penultimate chapter of the novel, "The New Century," ushers out the nineteenth century by describing the death of Queen Victoria (in 1901) and the end of the Boer War, when "prosperity returned" and it seemed "the long-looked-for new era had begun," even though conditions in the London slums "were very much worse."[96] Heatherley itself is a victim of the changing times. After a telegraph machine is installed in a neighboring village, Heatherley loses its local importance and begins a period of decline. Laura would leave Heatherley to take a position "in a distant part of the county," the narrator informs the reader, before beginning the new phase in her life as a married woman.[97]

For Laura, life in Heatherley is happy, "with work she enjoyed, a new countryside to explore, plenty of books to read, and some interesting people to observe."[98] In the final chapter of the novel, "A Post War Pilgrimage," a middle-aged Laura returns to Heatherley. She experiences a sense of healing when she "beholds her life as one whose youth had long ago fled and been followed by the better years of mature life."[99] This last chapter is Thompson's poignant farewell to Laura and to the bygone era that she had so lovingly evoked in the pages of *Lark Rise*, *Over to Candleford*, *Candleford Green*, and *Heatherley.*

Still Glides the Stream

Although Thompson completed *Still Glides the Stream* in August 1946, this novel was not published until 1948, the year following her death. Like *Lark Rise to Candleford*, *Still Glides the Stream* is set in rural Oxfordshire in the 1880s and 1890s. The protagonist, Charity Finch, is a retired schoolteacher living in post–World War II England. She has returned to her birthplace, the agricultural community of Restharrow, for the first time in twenty-four years, hoping to find "in a changed world . . . one beloved thing unchanged."[100] With the exception of the first and the last chapter of this novel, *Still Glides the Stream* is based on Charity Finch's memories of her Restharrow childhood, as told through a third-person narrator.

Still Glides the Stream takes its title from William Wordsworth's *Valedictory Sonnet to the River Duddon.* Lines four and five of this poem are printed opposite the title page:

> I see what was, and is, and will abide;
> Still glides the stream, and shall not cease to glide.

From her early childhood, the sound of a running stream had been a part of Charity Finch's consciousness. The stream that "ran below the garden hedge" in front of Charity's childhood home had filled the house with "the sound of running water" during all seasons of the year.[101] Thompson uses the gliding or running stream as a metaphor for the passing of time and the passing of generations of men and women.[102] She returns to this metaphor in the final paragraph of the novel when Charity stands before her childhood home, now fallen into decay, musing: "We come, we go, and, as individuals, we are forgotten. But the stream of human life goes on, ever changing, but ever the same. . . . And as she once more trod the old footpath way with the sound of running water in her ears, these thoughts gave her an extraordinary sense of comfort and reassurance.[103]

When the now elderly Charity Finch returns to Restharrow, her "neat grey suit, smart hat, and good shoes" announce that she is not an "ordinary countrywoman."[104] Charity, once a simple country girl, is now a retired schoolteacher. When she first walks through Restharrow, Charity has "a feeling of unreality, of herself walking like a ghost" because she is the "one living survivor" of her family.[105] However, once standing before the derelict cottage that had once been her home, Charity finds that she can still hear the voices of her family members and see them "in their accustomed haunts." (12) As she gazes at a nearby footpath, "before her inward eye" it becomes "once more a well-beaten track," and Charity sees "two tall girls in their teens, her cousins, Bess and Mercy," and their little sister, Polly, walking toward her.[106] Thus begins the narrative that traces the early life of Charity and her family.

Although Charity Finch is the protagonist of *Still Glides the Stream*, the most significant events in this novel occur in the lives of Charity's relatives, the Truman family. Reuben Truman, a widowed farm bailiff and Charity's uncle, lives with his three daughters at the nearby, and appropriately named, Waterside Farm. Also living at Waterside Farm are Mrs. Pocock, the widow of the previous farm bailiff, and her beautiful daughter, Stella. Stella, a cold and devious beauty, plays a small but significant role in the novel. The plot of *Still Glides the Stream* is based on Charity's memory of significant events in the Truman family over a period of approximately ten years. It is a simple plot that is built around a handful of dramatic events: a secret romance, poison-pen letters, two marriages, and a fire at Waterside Farm.

Reuben's oldest daughter, Bess, becomes the subject of village gossip when she begins to meet secretly with Roger Maitland, the son of the "tall, tight-lipped, aristocratic-looking" Mrs. Maitland, who lives in the local manor house.[107] The developing relationship between Bess and Roger triggers a series of poison-pen letters that not only expose Bess and Roger's secret romance but also lead to a dramatic confrontation between Bess's father and Mrs. Maitland. Reuben Truman and Mrs. Maitland both share the conventional view that the young couple's differing social classes make their romance impossible. However, Reuben acts unconventionally when he refuses to comply with Mrs. Maitland's demand that he end the romance by sending Bess away from home. It is Roger who is finally sent from home to live at a family estate in the West Indies.

The two marriage plots in *Still Glides the Stream* are centered on Bess's marriage to a schoolmaster, Arnold Milton, and on Stella Pocock's marriage to Charity's Cousin Oliver. Unlike Bess's earlier romance with Roger Maitland, the romances that develop between the two young couples do not violate any class boundaries. Both matches are advantageous for the brides because Bess and Stella both marry men with a slightly higher social status than their own. Although both marriage plots contain elements of surprise, the most dramatic event in *Still Glides the Stream* is the fire at Waterside Farm that leads to Reuben Truman's tragic death. Reuben's death is particularly significant because it marks the passing of a generation of humble and honorable country men. Reuben, the narrator informs the reader, "was one of the last of the old country breed, poor in this world's goods, obscure in position, not gifted with speech or any intellectual attainment, but for all that a man who stood out from his fellows in his complete mastery of all that pertains to the land, and in his tolerance, sympathy, and sturdy independence."[108] With Reuben's passing, the Truman family is dispersed. One by one, Reuben's daughters leave the village, and the Truman family, once a vital part of life in Restharrow, completely disappears from the village scene.

Unlike the novels of *Lark Rise to Candleford* and *Heatherley*, *Still Glides the Stream* describes more of the dark side of village life. In Restharrow's dark and violent past, "the village families had intermarried for generations," producing "a wild, lawless race of sheep-stealers, poachers, and fighting and drinking men": "Stories were still told of pitched battles with gamekeepers, or the men of neighbouring villages, in which knives and bludgeons had figured. There were stories of murder, almost openly committed, for which no one had been brought to trial, for none would give information lest by doing so they brought down upon themselves and their families the vengeance of the murderer's relatives."[109] One of the most horrific events in the village's not too distant past was the murder of a five-year-old boy, whose "charred remains" were discovered in the bread baking oven of his mother's cottage.[110] The boy's stepfather, who "had been known to dislike the child and to have treated him badly," is immediately suspected but never charged with the crime.[111] This story is one of the most gruesome events described in Thompson's novels.

The poison-pen letters that circulate in Restharrow during Charity's childhood reveal another ugly side of village life. The letters, which begin by exposing the romance between Bess Truman and Roger Maitland, soon start arriving at homes throughout the village, accusing the villagers of infidelity, illegitimacy, and theft. The letters, always signed by "Well Wisher," also mock those with physical deformities such as "splay feet, a red nose, or an impediment in the speech."[112] The poison- pen letters wreak havoc in many village families and eventually turn the residents of Restharrow against each other. Village outrage finally erupts in an assault on Mrs. Burdett, a defenseless old woman who is often observed writing in her cottage. One evening, an enraged mob of "youths and young men" force their way into Mrs. Burdett's cottage and wrench a ledger from her grasp as she sits writing.[113] Mrs. Burdett falls in the scuffle and has to be sent to the local hospital to recover from her injuries. What the young men discover when they read the ledger is that Mrs. Burdett had been writing in her nature journal, rather than writing poison pen letters. Charity finally discovers the identity of the poison pen when she is writing out valentines with her cousins at Waterside Farm. When she picks up a valentine written by Stella Pocock, she immediately recognizes the careful printing of the poison-pen writer.

In *Still Glides the Stream,* Thompson also describes the tragedies of everyday village life: the death of children, the mistreatment of the handicapped, the suffering of disappointed lovers, and the decline and senility of the elderly. Little Johnny Tuffrey, so vibrant at age seven, dies several years later when he is "flung, face foremost, from a loaded wagon in the harvest field."[114] Clem Moss, born with a cleft palate, is mocked by the village children, who call him a "looney" because he cannot speak clearly.[115] Luke Atwell, who works as a carter for Reuben Truman, falls desperately in love with Bess Truman and is devastated when she marries Arnold Milton. Charity encounters Luke in a field after Bess's wedding and observes "a look of real suffering in his china-blue eyes."[116] Another resident of Restharrow, an elderly stonemason named Tom Hearne, falls from his position as a well-respected member of the community to become "poor old Tom Hearne" that "tiresome old fool."[117] Hearne finds it difficult to accept that his days as a master craftsman are over. A younger generation of stonemasons, who know "all the latest dodges for saving time and materials," are being given the important jobs that were once his.[118] After a younger stonemason is given Hearne's bench at the firm where he works, Hearne quits in a fit of temper. Advancing in age and unemployed, Hearne grows "thin as a rake," and a "fire of fanaticism" begins to burn in "his fine dark eyes."[119] Agricultural workers, walking to their fields in the early morning, often see Hearne returning from a night of guarding church buildings against mysterious foes, looking "wild-eyed and wild-haired and dew-soaked." In his last days, Hearne is a needy and garrulous old man, whom all the villagers are eager to avoid.

There are obvious similarities between the novels of *Lark Rise to Candleford* and *Still Glides the Stream.* All are set in rural Oxfordshire during the 1880s and 1890s, and their respective protagonists, Laura and Charity, are portrayed as solitary figures who are quiet observers of village life.[120]

Charity serves as a pupil teacher during her last years in school, as Laura does in *Over to Candleford.* In *Still Glides the Stream*, it is Charity's Uncle Reuben (like Laura's Uncle Tom) who appears to be the most significant male figure in her life. But, although Charity's childhood (like Laura's) is spent among "simple people whose lives had been restricted by poverty and other hardships and deprivations," her family is fortunate to be among the "comfortable poor" in Restharrow because Charity's father is the village carpenter.[121] In *Lark Rise to Candleford*, despite the advantages of having a father who is a stonemason and a refined mother, Laura's family is truly impoverished. Unlike Laura, Charity expresses neither an extraordinary love of nature and literature nor any ambitions to become a writer. Charity leaves home to attend a teachers college in preparation for her eventual career, not to take a post office position to relieve the strain on family finances like Laura does in *Over to Candleford.*

When Charity returns to Restharrow in old age, her loss is absolute. She is the last living member of a once-vibrant country family. Her childhood home and her Uncle Reuben's home, Waterside Farm, once so full of life, have both fallen into ruin. Thompson wrote *Still Glides the Stream* during the last two years of her life. She was still mourning the loss her beloved son, Peter, who had perished during World War II, and she was elderly and in ill health. Knowing this adds a special poignancy to Thompson's depiction of Charity Finch at the end of *Still Glides the Stream*, as she stands alone before the ruins of her childhood home, pondering life, death, and the survival of families.

Reclassifying the Trilogy

Despite the sixty-year tradition of viewing *Lark Rise to Candleford* as Thompson's autobiography, there are important grounds for reclassifying the trilogy and treating it as a work of fiction. Reclassifying *Lark Rise to Candleford* and its posthumously published sequel, *Heatherley*, would open a variety of new critical approaches to these works since they are not only rich in themes, settings, and characters, but they also contain elements of the *bildungsroman* and *künstlerromane*. The basic similarities between *Lark Rise to Candleford* and other works of rural and regional fiction provide one source of support for reclassifying the trilogy. Thompson's handling of literary conventions, particularly narration, provides yet another. Additional support for reclassifying the trilogy comes from Thompson herself. In several private statements that she made near the end of her life, Thompson revealed that she considered her books to be literary creations that required both painstaking revision and the creation of characters.

Rural and Regional Fiction

During the first half of the twentieth century, popular interest in rural and regional fiction tended to intensify during periods of political and cultural instability. In the 1890s, cultural anxieties arising from the rapid social changes witnessed in *fin de siècle* Britain revived interest in traditional English country life. This interest further intensified in the years leading up to World War I and World War II.[122] Nostalgia for an idealized "organic community rooted in the seasonal round"[123] led to various social phenomena, from the formation of local antiquarian societies to the growing popularity of novels about rural life.[124] The reading public's renewed interest in "a suppositious pastoral world of peace and plenty in times of insecurity and change" did not, however, recommend rural and regional novels to literary scholars during the 1930s.[125] In a book review published in *Scrutiny* in 1936, Q. D. Leavis dismissed the regional novel as a "commercially profitable line of goods" promoted by the "professional fiction monger."[126] The regional novel was unworthy of academic consideration, according to Leavis, because it was either a vehicle for "left-wing propaganda" or a "commonplace work of fiction" made interesting only by the "painstaking application of rural local colour." The popular appeal of rural and regional fiction, Leavis implied, was a symptom of a new literary degeneracy, encouraged by "reviewers, Book Society committees and popular lecturers."[127]

Fortunately, during the 1970s, works such as Raymond Williams's *The Country and the City* (1973) and Glen Cavaliero's *The Rural Tradition in the English Novel* (1977) acknowledged rural and regional fiction as a subject worthy of scholarly consideration. Interestingly, both Williams and Cavaliero recognized the significance of *Lark Rise to Candleford* and praised the trilogy for its realistic depiction of country life in their respective studies. However, neither classified the trilogy as a work of fiction, even though *Lark Rise to Candleford* resembles the rural novels they describe. *Lark Rise to Candleford* is not mentioned in a more recent study of the regional novel edited by Keith D. M. Snell, professor of rural and cultural history at the University of Leicester. In his introductory chapter to *The Regional Novel in Britain and Ireland, 1800–1990* (1998), Snell provides a definition of the regional novel that closely corresponds to the trilogy's most distinctive features. Like the regional novels that Snell describes, *Lark Rise to Candleford* is set in a "recognizable region" of Britain and describes the distinctive features of that region, such as "social relations, customs, language," and dialect use.[128] Thompson's novels also convey a "strong sense of local geography, topography [and] landscape" and portray the effects of "particular" environments on characters of "working- or middle-class origin." Describing the regional novelist's "loyalty to a region," Snell notes the "recurring phenomenon" of "the regional novelist as outside witness, in some cases almost as anthropological visitor, participant-observer and investigator, in others as having been displaced by education and mobility from the people and landscape the fiction describes, experiencing a sense of dislodged or multiple belonging."[129] In *Lark Rise to Candleford,* one recognizes qualities that Snell ascribes to regional novelists in Thompson's narrator and in her working-class heroine, Laura. Thompson's narrator functions as an "outside witness" and "anthropological visitor"; Laura is a "participant-observer" in the novel's narrative, who experiences "a sense of dislodged or multiple belonging" due to being "displaced by education and mobility" from her native hamlet. Snell's identification of R. L. Stevenson, Thomas Hardy, D. H. Lawrence, Arnold Bennett, and H. E. Bates as regional novelists underscores the crucial role that literary classification and reception history play in the scholarly response to individual works. Despite the fact that *Lark Rise to Candleford* and *Heatherley* revolve around four specific rural communities and share many of the characteristics that Cavaliero and Snell attribute to rural and regional fiction, these books continue to be excluded from scholarly studies of these subgenres. This is primarily because the Oxford University Press, for the sake of expediency, classified *Lark Rise* as an autobiography in 1939.

Narrative Conventions

Thompson's narrative choices in *Lark Rise to Candleford* provide another rationale for reclassifying the trilogy. In the standard autobiographical reading of *Lark Rise to Candleford*, the third-person narrator is understood to have two voices: the voice of the child named Laura and the voice of an adult narrator. Because *Lark Rise to Candleford* is classified as an autobiography, the reader instinctively identifies the third-person narrator as the adult Thompson, who tells the story of her childhood through the eyes of Laura, her fictional alter ego. In this reading, *Lark Rise to Candleford* becomes both a source of biographical information about Thompson and an eyewitness account of life in rural Oxfordshire during the 1880s and 1890s. Scholars in various disciplines have found *Lark Rise to Candleford* to be a useful source of information about country life, but as Margaret Lane, Julian Shuckburgh, and Barbara English have all observed, Thompson's trilogy is more questionable when used as a source of information about the author's life.[130]

To resist the strictly autobiographical reading of *Lark Rise*, *Over to Candleford*, *Candleford Green*, and *Heatherley*, one must look more closely at Thompson's handling of specific literary conventions in these novels, particularly narration. Suzanne Keen's study of authorial and figural narrative situations and overt and covert narrators are particularly useful for examining the third-person narrator in the novels of *Lark Rise to Candleford* and *Heatherley*.[131] Peter J. Rabinowitz's analysis of literary conventions and the ways in which they shape reader interpretation provides further insight into the reasons why critics and scholars still debate whether *Lark Rise to Candleford* is a work of fiction or nonfiction.

The Narrative Situation

In *Narrative Form* (2003), Suzanne Keen describes an *authorial* narrative situation as one in which the narrator "functions above or outside his creations, like an author, employing an external perspective."[132] In a figural narrative situation, Keen explains, the narrator reflects "internally upon individual figures" who are "inside the story world." The concept of overt and covert narrators provides additional insight into what Keen calls the "degree of personification of the narrator."[133] Overt narrators, Keen explains, project a "distinct personality." She adds: "They can identify characters with capsule descriptions of their traits, pasts, appearance, and what they think, as well as what they do not think or say. Overt narrators can offer commentary, including interpretations of the action, judgments about characters or events, generalizations, and even self-conscious remarks about the narration." In contrast, a covert narrator is a "scarcely noticeable functionary who provides speech tags and indications of setting and temporal movements, identifies characters, and narrates actions, all untinged with personality." The degree to which a narrative situation is authorial or figural and the degree to which a narrator is overt or covert can shift within a single text. Such shifts can be found in all four of Thompson's novels about Laura; however, the most significant narrative shift occurs in Thompson's second novel, *Over to Candleford*. Although *Over to Candleford, Candleford Green,* and *Heatherley* all employ a third-person narrator, the narration in these novels differs considerably from the narration of *Lark Rise*.

In *Lark Rise*, an overt third-person narrator functions in a narrative situation that is primarily authorial. The narrator in *Lark Rise* is an authoritative figure who describes, explains, and interprets daily life in the hamlet of Lark Rise as well as the life of Laura and her family. As Keen points out in *Narrative Form*, an overt narrator in an authorial narrative situation is often mistaken for the author. Since *Lark Rise* is classified as an autobiography and Laura is, therefore, understood to be Thompson's fictional alter ego, the reader readily assumes that both Thompson and Laura have a narrative role in *Lark Rise*. However, Laura does not narrate any passage in *Lark Rise*; rather, she functions as a character in the text. In Thompson's second novel about Laura, *Over to Candleford*, the narrative voice undergoes a change. In the first chapter of the novel, the overt narrator of *Lark Rise* once again describes the hamlet of Lark Rise from the perspective of an authoritative outsider. Beginning in the second chapter, however, the narrative begins a process of transformation, as the narrative focus shifts from life in the hamlet of Lark Rise to the life of Laura and her family. As specific characters and a discernable plot begin to emerge, the overt narrator and authorial narrative situation of *Over to Candleford* become increasingly covert and figural. In short, *Over to Candleford* evolves into a novel. *Candleford Green* and *Heatherley* continue the trend that begins in *Over to Candleford*. In both novels, the narrative focus is on Laura, the narrator is primarily covert, and the narrative situation is primarily figural. Although Thompson never submitted *Heatherley* to her publisher, this final novel supplies a satisfying conclusion to Laura's story, especially because her personal story does not begin in earnest until *Over to Candleford*. Because *Over to Candleford*, *Candleford Green,* and *Heatherley* are more like each other than they are like *Lark Rise*, these three books could be read together as an alternative trilogy or as a *bildungsroman*, providing a new critical approach to all four novels. Thompson's four novels about Laura also contain a fascinating record of the reading habits of the rural working classes at just the time when these men and women were beginning to gain access to printed material through the cheap presses and public libraries. *Lark Rise to Candleford* and *Heatherley* also trace Laura's intellectual and artistic development by focusing on the books and periodicals she reads, the cultural experiences she enjoys, and her growing desire to become a writer. Consequently, these novels could also be studied as *künstlerromane*.

The "Rules of Reading"

In *Before Reading: Narrative Conventions and the Politics of Interpretation*, Peter J. Rabinowitz identifies key narrative conventions that guide readers' understanding and interpretation of literary texts. Rabinowitz articulates a system for classifying these conventions based on four "rules of reading": rules of notice, rules of signification, rules of configuration, and rules of coherence.[134] These rules "serve as a kind of assumed contract between author and reader—they specify the grounds on which the intended reading should take place."[135] Genre, for example, is a narrative convention that permits a reader to treat a text "conveniently as a whole."[136] Genre makes a complex narrative more manageable and increases its "apparent coherence by stressing some features and downplaying others."[137] Readers recognize a work's genre based on their prior knowledge of specific textual features. If the reader finds that a "reasonable number of textual features" match a work to the "textual pattern" of a known genre, then that genre can be treated as an appropriate label for the work at hand.[138] Some narratives, Rabinowitz observes, "provide insufficient guidance for their own proper decoding" and therefore "offer themselves up to contradictory interpretive keys."[139] Rabinowitz's "rules of reading," specifically his rules of notice, rules of signification, and rules of coherence, explain why Thompson's handling of particular narrative conventions continues to send confusing signals to her readers, thereby creating an "ambiguity of genre" in *Lark Rise to Candleford* and *Heatherley*.[140]

Rules of notice "give priority to certain kinds of details in a text."[141] The resulting "hierarchy of importance" is crucial, Rabinowitz states, because readers cannot "attend to everything equally" in a complex narrative.[142] Two of Rabinowitz's rules of notice shed light on several sources of genre confusion in Thompson's trilogy. The first of these rules states that a narrative is read against an "intertextual grid" that encompasses both the norms of the work's perceived genre and the writer's background.[143] The intertextual grid not only shapes a reader's interpretation, but it also provides a basis for evaluating the narrative itself. The second rule of notice states that certain textual elements, such as titles, occupy privileged positions in complex narratives.[144] The details a writer places in such privileged positions are understood to be more important than other details and suggest an appropriate interpretation for the text as a whole.

Clearly, the intertextual grid that forms the interpretive background for *Lark Rise to Candleford* was first established by the Oxford University Press when it decided to publish *Lark Rise* as an autobiography. This interpretive background was further reinforced by critics and scholars who either compared the trilogy to specific nonfiction works about the English countryside or interpreted the trilogy within the context of nonfiction genres such as agricultural history, social history, and ethnography. As Rabinowitz observes, a writer's previous work also provides an "appropriate background" for the interpretation of subsequent texts.[145] Since *Lark Rise* has continued to be celebrated as the first and most significant book in Thompson's trilogy, it is not surprising that it continues to shape the interpretation of *Over to Candleford*, *Candleford Green*, and *Heatherley,* even though these books differ in important ways from *Lark Rise*. Clearly, the ongoing classification of *Lark Rise to Candleford* as a work of autobiography and the existing scholarship on the trilogy would tend to discourage reading it as a work of fiction.

Titles, Rabinowitz observes, occupy privileged positions in nineteenth- and twentieth- century narratives.[146] They influence the reader's "sense of the text's meaning" and encourage the reader "to end up with an interpretation that could account more fully" for the information that is conveyed in the title.[147] Thompson's choice of titles for her books about Laura has shaped the interpretation of these works in important ways.

The title of the first book, *Lark Rise*, carries important weight because it is the first title in a series. This title is also significant because it identifies the specific rural community in which the narrative is set and the subject of the book itself: daily life in a specific rural hamlet during the 1880s. The subsequent books of Thompson's trilogy, *Over to Candleford* and *Candleford Green*, are also named for specific rural communities; however, daily life in the communities of Candleford town and Candleford Green is not the subject of these sequels. The true subject of these two books is Thompson's working-class heroine, Laura. When these three books were published as a one-volume trilogy in 1945, under the composite title *Lark Rise to Candleford*, it further reinforced the notion that *Lark Rise*, *Over to Candleford*, and *Candleford Green* were narratives of the same type. In reality, the titles of these books convey different types of information. The title of *Lark Rise* is a literal statement of the book's setting and subject. However, the titles of *Over to Candleford*, *Candleford Green,* and *Heatherley* are primarily metaphoric, reflecting successive stages in Laura's journey of self-discovery. *Heatherley,* Thompson's final novel about Laura, suffered from being published posthumously. Because it was not published during Thompson's lifetime and has never been published in one volume with *Lark Rise*, *Over to Candleford*, and *Candleford Green*, the reader assumes that *Heatherley* is either an inferior work or only tenuously related to the trilogy. Although such discrepancies are subtle, they send confusing signals to the reader and, therefore, contribute to the ambiguity of the trilogy's genre.

Rabinowitz's rules of configuration and rules of coherence provide additional insight into Thompson's use of literary conventions in *Lark Rise to Candleford* and *Heatherley.* Rabinowitz's rules of configuration describe the ways in which readers recognize "clumps of literary features" and use them to identify "plot patterns" and literary formulas.[148] According to Rabinowitz, one "metarule of configuration" is that "whether or not the author is striving for formal elegance as an end in itself," most narratives "are balanced in one way or another."[149] One way that balance is achieved is through consistency in point of view and focus on a general subject. The fundamental principle of Rabinowitz's rules of coherence is simply that readers assume that texts *are* coherent.[150] Typically, readers experience coherence by attending to a narrative's "universal theme—central metaphor."[151] Reading a narrative against its intertextual grid provides another source of coherence, since it allows readers to focus on textual details that link the narrative to works of the same type. Literary parallels (ranging from characters and plot lines to settings and titles) provide another source of coherence because readers understand that any elements that "*can* be treated as parallel *should* [*sic*] be treated in that way."[152]

In *Lark Rise, Over to Candleford, Candleford Green*, and *Heatherley*, the general shift in point of view and subject between *Lark Rise* and its sequels creates a subtle imbalance in Thompson's overarching narrative. *Lark Rise*, with its overt narrator and authorial narrative situation, focuses primarily on community life in a rural hamlet. However, the sequels to *Lark Rise* feature a covert narrator and figural narrative situation and focus primarily on Laura. Some readers experience *Lark Rise to Candleford* and *Heatherley* as a coherent narrative by focusing on Laura as the unifying figure in these books. Others, reading against the intertextual grid established by *Lark Rise*, focus on the novels' perceived status as Thompson's autobiography. The author's detailed descriptions of community life and chronicling of social change also reinforce the coherence of the series, although such details play a relatively minor role in the sequels to *Lark Rise*. Despite the fact that they convey different types of information, the parallel titles of *Lark Rise, Over to Candleford, Candleford Green*, and *Heatherley* also create a sense of coherence. Depending on the reader, these titles can be interpreted as significant settings or as metaphors for Laura's journey through life.

Flora Thompson the Novelist

Nineteen years before she wrote *Lark Rise*, Thompson experimented with representing herself and her personal experience through a fictional persona in *The Peverel Papers*. These nature essays demonstrate that Thompson was not an unsophisticated countrywoman who simply transferred her childhood memories to the page when she wrote *Lark Rise*.[153] Instead, Thompson was an experienced writer, fully capable of constructing a narrator, a plot, and characters (however autobiographical) to suit her narrative purpose. The question still remains: How did Thompson view her trilogy? Because Thompson left few personal letters and even fewer public statements about her work, it is impossible to arrive at a definitive conclusion. When *Lark Rise to Candleford* was published in 1945, Thompson wrote to H. J. Massingham, "No one but you has recognized my aims and intentions in writing of that more excellent way of life of our forefathers."[154] This statement is essentially ambiguous, since it could be used to support reading the trilogy as a work of nonfiction or as a work of realistic fiction. Thompson is also recorded as saying of *Lark Rise*, "Every one of the characters lived at Juniper and were just as described, with only the names altered."[155] However, she also stated, "In *Over to Candleford* and *Candleford Green* I wrote more freely than in *Lark Rise*, and do not think I described any house or place exactly as it actually existed, excepting 'Miss Lane's' post-office forge, and Shelswell Park, where I used to carry the letters." A letter Thompson wrote three years before her death reveals the rigorous artistic process that lay behind her seemingly simple account of childhood in *Lark Rise to Candleford*:

> All arts are similar, there is a good deal of time and patience needed for writing, if it is to turn out a success. I write my books several times over, revising every paragraph and entirely remoulding many until I get them, not as good as I should like them to be but the best it is in me to do. The final object being, of course, the simplicity which shall appear spontaneous. It was Byron, I think, who said "easy writing makes damned hard reading" and the same rule applies to all the arts. Leave the reader or the beholder to think the book or picture is dashed off in a moment of inspiration, it is a compliment to the writer or artist when they think so as it shows the book or picture shows no sign of effort or strain, but there is always, as you know by this time much hard drudgery behind such an effect.[156]

In the same letter, Thompson also wrote, "In writing you give yourself a certain latitude, you know a character well and can think in that character and know by instinct what he or she would say in the circumstances." These statements reveal that Thompson approached writing her novels as an artistic process and even thought of the persons she described as *characters*. Such personal statements provide further support for treating *Lark Rise to Candleford* and *Heatherley* as artistic creations and, more specifically, as novels.

In years to come, when the historical, social, and biographical context of *Lark Rise to Candleford* becomes increasingly remote, will the trilogy become a mere curiosity, drawing only those who wish to learn about late Victorian country life? Or, will the trilogy survive because of the enduring appeal of Laura? Reclassifying *Lark Rise to Candleford* and *Heatherley* as works of fiction has important implications, both for the survival of these texts and for their interpretation by future scholars and critics.

Conclusion

Thompson's significance as a woman writer should no longer be based solely on her famous trilogy, *Lark Rise to Candleford*. The frequently overlooked *Heatherley* and *Still Glides the Stream* deserve to be fully considered in studies of this author's literary legacy. *Heatherley* is not only as fine a novel as *Lark Rise*, *Over to Candleford*, and *Candleford Green*, but it also provides a satisfying conclusion to Laura's story. *Still Glides the Stream* is clearly a rural novel. There are no confusing connections between this book and Thompson's life or the life of her heroine, Laura. *Still Glides the Stream* can be simply enjoyed for what it is: a quiet and moving rural novel. Like the nature essays that Thompson wrote for *The Peverel Papers*, *Heatherley* and *Still Glides the Stream* stand on their own as significant works in Thompson's *oeuvre.*

The time has come to move the critical conversation about *Lark Rise to Candleford* beyond stagnant debates over its reliability as a work of nonfiction. Although Thompson's personal statements and handling of literary conventions may not convince some critics and scholars that *Lark Rise to Candleford* should be studied as a work of fiction, a more nuanced approach to the trilogy, one that recognizes that it combines elements of various fiction and nonfiction genres and subgenres, would make it possible to view *Lark Rise to Candleford* within a larger context. Chapter 6 explores important connections between the trilogy and several of these genres, thereby suggesting a variety of new critical approaches to Thompson's most famous work.

4
The Minor Works: Short Fiction, Poetry, and Literary Essays

THOMPSON'S CAREER AS A WORKING WRITER BEGAN IN 1911, WHEN HER prize-winning essay on Jane Austen was published in the pages of the *Lady's Companion*. From 1911 until the publication of *Lark Rise* in 1939, she published a variety of minor works, including short stories, a book of poetry, and a series of literary essays. Thompson's short stories and literary essays are not as well known as *Lark Rise to Candleford* because they were published in women's magazines during the 1910s and 1920s. Unlike *The Peverel Papers*, none of these works has been published in book form.[1] Thompson's book of poetry, *Bog Myrtle and Peat,* never achieved wide circulation, although individual poems have been published on websites devoted to preserving the author's memory.

Those who admire *Lark Rise to Candleford* often find Thompson's work in these genres to be disappointing. Certainly, the short fiction Thompson published in various women's magazines, the poetry she published in *Bog Myrtle and Peat*, and the literary essays she published in a series entitled *The Fireside Reading Circle* are uneven in quality. Nevertheless, these minor works are important because they provide a more accurate picture of Thompson's career as a working writer and provide intriguing glimpses of the creative process that eventually led to the creation of *Lark Rise to Candleford.*

EARLY FREELANCE JOURNALISM

Between 1911 and the publication of *Lark Rise* in 1939, Thompson published essays and short stories in a variety of women's periodicals, including the *Lady's Companion,* the *Literary Monthly,* the *Catholic Fireside,* the *Lady*, and the *National Review.* On the letterhead of the Peverel Society, which she cofounded with Mildred Humble-Smith in 1925, Thompson also listed herself as a contributor to *Countryman*, *Queen*, and "other periodicals."[2] Thompson's biographer, Gillian Lindsay, reports that Thompson was, briefly, a ghost writer for an unidentified big-game hunter. Perhaps the "other periodicals" were the *Scottish Field*, *Chamber's Journal*, and the African newspapers in which the ghost written articles were reportedly published.[3] Thompson also published at least one article under the penname Francis Stuart Thompson. "Homes Afloat," an article describing design innovations in small coasting vessels, was published on June 22, 1936, in the *Farmer's Home*, a supplement to the *Farmer and Stock-Breeder.*

Thompson began her writing career by submitting three hundred-word literary essays to a competition run by the *Lady's Companion*, a weekly magazine for lower middle-class women.[4] As Jonathan Rose observes in *The Intellectual Life of the British Working Classes,* the essay contests sponsored by many popular periodicals during the late nineteenth century provided "the first rung up the ladder of literary success" to "slum children with some writing talent."[5] In 1911 the *Lady's Companion* provided such a "first rung up the ladder" to Thompson as well.

Founded in 1900, the *Lady's Companion* offered its readers short fiction, articles on self-improvement, and a literary feature entitled *Our Book Club* for the modest price of 1 pence per issue. *Our Book Club* encouraged its readers to improve their knowledge of literature by reading the English classics and the works of contemporary writers such as G. K. Chesterton, Hilaire Belloc, and Rudyard Kipling.[6] "Dorothea," the author of *Our Book Club* and the judge of its literary competitions, announced the topic for each competition and published excerpts from the winning essays in this column. In 1911 Thompson's very first submission, an essay on Jane Austen, was awarded first prize. At this time, Thompson was thirty-four years old and the mother of two young children, Winifred Grace (age seven) and Henry Basil (age thirteen months). Thompson continued to submit literary essays to *Our Book Club* throughout 1911. In July she won another first prize when she entered an essay in the "Shakespeare's Heroines" competition. *Our Book Club* acknowledged another four essays written by Thompson during 1911. Her essay on the Brontës received a second prize, and four additional essays received mentions in the column.

Thompson's prize-winning essay on Jane Austen was published in *Our Book Club* in February 1911. In her essay, Thompson praises the novelist's "quiet, gentle stories" for their treatment of everyday people and events, noting the contrast between Austen's work and the novels of her day that depended on "involved plot, sensational incident and the long arm of coincidence."[7] Noting that Austen compared herself to "a painter on ivory," Thompson likens the enjoyment of reading an Austen novel to the pleasure of possessing "an exquisite miniature." While acknowledging that many find Austen's novels "dull" and "tame," Thompson echoes Shakespeare's *Hamlet* in proclaiming them "*caviare* [*sic*] to the general." She concludes her essay with the statement "No one loves Jane Austen moderately." In her essay, Thompson refers to Austen's contemporary admirers, Sir Walter Scott, Sydney Smith, the Countess of Morley, and the Prince Regent. This may indicate that she had read *A Memoir of Jane Austen* (1870) by J. E. Austen-Leigh, a book in which these particular Austen admirers are discussed in detail.[8] Thompson, it appears, was already researching the topics she wrote about, just as she would later research the topics she discussed in the nature and literary essays she published in the *Catholic Fireside.*

In July 1911 *Our Book Club* announced its "Shakespeare's Heroines" competition. Once again, Thompson's essay won first prize. In her essay, Thompson writes of Shakespeare's Juliet, describing her as a young woman "throbbing with passionate humanity."[9] Thompson traces Juliet's development from "a simple child, standing on the threshold of maidenhood," to the "brave and resolute woman" she becomes. Through her judicious use of quotations from *Romeo and Juliet,* she illustrates the "maternal protecting element" in Juliet's love for Romeo and the "gross and vulgar spirit" of the nurse who "fails her in her hour of need."

Although Thompson's essay on Emily Brontë did not win first prize in "The Brontës" competition, it was published in *Our Book Club* in April 1911. In this essay, Thompson describes Emily Brontë as a "shy, reserved girl" whose "icy manner" concealed a "heart of fire."[10] Brontë's novel, *Wuthering Heights*, is a poignant reminder of "*what might have been*" [*sic*] had Brontë not "died her hard, unwilling death," Thompson declares. Thompson's description of Brontë's love for the moors, "clad in the rustling heather, brown and somber," provides an early glimpse of her gift for writing sensitive descriptions of natural landscapes, a gift that would be displayed to full advantage in the nature articles that she would write for the *Catholic Fireside* ten years later.

Thompson received a mention in *Our Book Club* for her entries in four other competitions: the "Gallery of Heroines" competition, the "Finest Passage from Thackeray" competition, the "Poetry or Prose" competition, and the "Favorite Poet" competition. "Dorothea" wrote a one-sentence acknowledgement of Thompson's "excellent paper" on "Queen Katherine of Aragon" when she announced the winner of the "Gallery of Heroines" competition in April 1911.[11] Thompson's entries for the "Finest Passage from Thackeray" and the "Poetry or Prose: Which Do You Prefer and Why?" competitions both received mentions in *Our Book Club* in September 1911. "Dorothea" published the passage that Thompson had selected from chapter 32 of *Vanity Fair,* in which Thackeray describes George Osborne's death at Waterloo. "Dorothea" refers to Thompson's entry in the "Poetry or Prose: Which Do You Prefer and Why?" competition as a "charming paper" with "quotes from Omar Kháyyám."[12] Thompson wrote another essay on Shakespeare for the "Favorite Poet" competition in *Our Book Club.* In October 1911, "Dorothea" mentioned

Flora Thompson and the authors of several other essays on Shakespeare only to dismiss them all, stating, "I think most readers will prefer quotations about poets of whom they have read less."[13]

Thompson achieved another modest success in 1912 when she published a prize-winning essay in the *Literary Monthly.* Her critical essay on Dr. Ronald Campbell Macfie's ode on the sinking of the *Titanic* so impressed the Scottish physician and poet that he traveled to Bournemouth to pay her an unannounced visit that same year.[14] Ronald Campbell Macfie (1867–1931) was the published author of books of poetry, fairy tales, and popular medicine.[15] He became Thompson's friend, literary mentor, and source of encouragement until his death in 1931.

Short Fiction

From the mid-nineteenth century, serialized novels and short stories had been a staple in women's magazines, but by the end of the century, the market for serialized fiction was declining in favor of the short story complete in one issue.[16] Thompson responded to this new market by writing her own short, sentimental stories about love, marriage, and family life. Although she was not particularly proud of these "small sugared love tales,"[17] her reason for writing them was pragmatic; the money she earned from publishing these stories, as well as her later nature and literary essays, enabled Thompson to send her children to good schools.[18]

Thompson published her first short story, a romantic tale entitled "The Toft Cup," in the *Lady's Companion* on January 6, 1912. "The Toft Cup" was the first of five short stories that she would publish in the *Lady's Companion* before it ceased publication in 1915. Two additional stories, "The Nut Brown Maid" and "The Education of a Genius," were also published in 1912. "The Mistress of Boldre Farm" followed in 1913. Thompson published her last short story in the *Lady's Companion*, "His Lady of the Lilac," in May 1914, only four months before the beginning of World War I. In 1913 Thompson also published a short story entitled "The Leper" in the *Literary Monthly*, a more prestigious publication than the *Lady's Companion*, as it was a literary paper rather than a women's weekly.[19] "The Leper" is a story of religious faith, married love, and self-sacrifice set in medieval England, a striking departure from the contemporary love stories that Thompson published in the *Lady's Companion* during this same period. The popularity of medieval romances, such as Michael Fairless's *The Gathering of Brother Hilarius,* may have inspired Thompson to write her own romantic medieval tale.[20]

Short Fiction before World War I

The early twentieth century was a boom time for aspiring short story writers. As Cynthia L. White observes in *Women's Magazines, 1693–1968*, the short fiction published in women's magazines during the nineteenth century was often viewed as a pernicious source of escapism. However, by the beginning of the twentieth century such stories were increasingly viewed as harmless, or even therapeutic, entertainment for careworn housewives. By 1910 an extensive market for short stories of two thousand to two thousand five hundred words, especially stories complete in one issue, developed in periodicals for middle- and lower middle-class women. The sentimental love stories published in such magazines typically centered on the lives of two or three main characters and dealt with the problems of everyday life. Writers sometimes added a touch of mystery or suspense to their stories to provide their readers with an additional thrill.[21]

The short fiction that Thompson published in the *Lady's Companion* between 1912 and 1914 conformed to this new market standard. In each of her short stories, the plot revolves around two to three main characters. In addition, each is labeled "a complete story." Three of Thompson's short stories are romantic. In "The Toft Cup" and in "His Lady of the Lilac," a young man and woman meet and fall in love, but they must conquer a host of personal and financial difficulties that threaten their romance. In "The Nut Brown Maid," a young artist sketching in the New Forest meets and falls in love with a beautiful gypsy girl. He eventually proposes to her, despite the difference in their social status. Marital infidelity is the subject of "The Mistress of Boldre Farm." In this story, a farm wife fears her husband of ten years has fallen in love with another woman after she hears a bit of local gossip. "The Education of a Genius," a story of maternal love, describes the personal sacrifices a blacksmith's wife makes to send her twelve-year-old son to a prestigious school in a nearby market town. All of these stories are grounded in the financial difficulties, misunderstandings, and romantic dilemmas of everyday life, and each provides a touch of suspense and a happy ending. "The Toft Cup" is a particularly good example of Thompson's prewar fiction since it is thematically linked to the other stories that she published before World War I and to the novels of *Lark Rise to Candleford*.

"The Toft Cup" opens in the midst of a family crisis. Unable to pay the annual rent on their family home, Grace Coombe, the heroine, and her elderly grandmother are on the verge of being evicted. Grace and her grandmother have scheduled an appraiser to inventory their belongings, but at the last moment, the appraiser falls sick and sends his handsome young son in his place. The appearance of the appraiser's son,

Edmund Varney, is the first of a series of fortunate events in this story. Edmund Varney not only falls in love at first sight with Grace, but he also recognizes a valuable antique among the family possessions: the Toft cup, a three-handled loving cup made by Thomas Toft in 1693. Edmund offers to find a buyer for the antique cup, but he is initially unsuccessful. However, when Edmund stops to rest at a tea shop, his luck changes. A museum director, who is taking his tea in the same shop, recognizes the Toft cup as a valuable antique and is eager to purchase it for his museum. By the end of the story, the sale of the Toft cup not only strengthens the relationship between the young lovers, but it also saves Grace and her grandmother from being evicted.

The beautiful heroine, handsome hero, fortunate series of events, and romantic conclusion to this story are all conventional. However, to this conventional framework Thompson adds her distinctive touch. In these first short stories, the reader finds a number of elements that would appear in Thompson's later short fiction as well as in her essays and novels. "The Toft Cup" and the other four stories that Thompson published in the *Lady's Companion* are all set in the same rural community near the New Forest in Hampshire. Thompson's choice of a New Forest setting is early evidence of her propensity for writing about specific rural communities. "The Toft Cup" and "His Lady of the Lilac" are set in romantically derelict country homes located in the New Forest. "The Nut Brown Maid," "The Mistress of Boldre Farm," and "The Education of a Genius" are set in communities near the New Forest, in landscapes that feature the pine, peat, and heather associated with this region of Hampshire.

In the 1910s and the 1920s, rural communities in Hampshire are the most frequent settings for Thompson's stories and nature essays. It wasn't until the 1930s that Thompson returned to the scene of her Oxfordshire childhood to write "Old Queenie," "An Oxfordshire Hamlet in the 'Eighties," "May Day in the 'Eighties," and the novels of *Lark Rise to Candleford*. In the short stories that Thompson published in the *Lady's Companion*, she conveys a sense of the rural communities in which these stories are set through working-class characters who speak the local dialect. The coach driver in "The Toft Cup," the blacksmith and his wife in "The Education of a Genius," Lucy the milkmaid in "The Mistress of Boldre Farm," and Jane the housemaid in "His Lady of the Lilac" all speak in dialect. In "The Nut Brown Maid," the men and women at a public house speak the local dialect, and a gypsy woman speaks several lines of Romany. In the later novels of *Lark Rise to Candleford*, *Heatherley*, and *Still Glides the Stream*, Thompson also uses dialect when portraying working-class characters.

Literature, which plays a central role in all of Thompson's published work, appears in her first published short stories as well, usually as an indication of a character's refinement. Sometimes, a shared love for literature creates a special bond between young lovers. In "The Toft Cup," Grace Coombe comes from a family of book lovers. Grace's father and her three uncles had all been "delicate, studious men" before their untimely deaths.[22] Grace's most prized possession is the library of books left to her by her father, which fills the walls of the parlor at Ashbies, her family home. When Grace meets Edmund Varney, she describes herself as "a real bookworm." Edmund confides in return, "I am a book lover too." Grace's cultural refinement is further revealed when Edmund discovers her sitting by the parlor fire with a copy of John Ruskin's *Sesame and Lilies* lying open in her lap.

Reading and books also play a significant role in "The Education of a Genius." In this story, the proof of twelve-year-old Arthur Wellstead's genius is his ability to write poetry and his interest in reading Shakespeare and Robert Browning. In "His Lady of the Lilac," when the hero Philip Allington arrives at Amberhill, his ancestral home, he finds a study "lined from top to bottom with dusty leather-covered volumes."[23] Books are also part of the "wonderful affinity" in "tastes and ideals" between Philip and the story's heroine, Esther Carfax.[24] When they picnic in the forest, Philip reads to Esther as she sews. He is also in the habit of "breaking now and then into quotation" when they walk together.[25] On one occasion, he quotes three lines from Christina Rossetti's "Amor Mundi" as they walk through the New Forest. Books and reading do not play a significant role in "The Nut Brown Maid" or "The Mistress of Boldre Farm," although the heroine of the latter story, Margaret Tyrell, attends a sewing party where she is asked to read to the other women from a book by Eden Phillpotts.[26] Thompson does not identify the novel, but she describes it as "the story of an injured wife."[27]

Struggling journalists are among Thompson's favorite characters in the short stories she published before and after World War I. In "The Toft Cup," as well as in six other short stories, at least one of the main characters is a struggling journalist.[28] Two of the stories Thompson published before the war feature a journalist. In "The Toft Cup," Edmund Varney is a freelance journalist for the *Christminster Herald.* When he meets Grace, he has just started publishing "little articles on 'Forest Lore'" in the *Simple Life Magazine.*[29] In "His Lady of the Lilac," the hero, Philip Allington, is a freelance journalist who has "supported himself meagerly by his pen," receiving a "weekly half guinea" for a "column of Nature Notes, and casual contributions to the magazines."[30]

Thompson's short stories are a source of character types, plot elements, and even complete passages that she would reuse in her later work. In "The Toft Cup," Thompson's description of a winter morning in the New Forest appears almost verbatim in her first nature essay for

Out of Doors, published in January 1921. In "The Toft Cup," Thompson writes: "During the night, the frost had cast its spell over the woods and glades of the New Forest. This morning, every branch and twig was hung with a pearly coating of hoar-frost. Over the narrow lane by which the two women had come, the morning star still glittered coldly. The silence of a winter dawn was only broken by the *crop, crop* of a forest pony as it picked its scanty breakfast on the heath by the roadside."[31] In her later nature essay, Thompson reused this passage, altering it to accommodate the switch from the third-person narrator in the short story to the first-person narration of "Flora."[32]

In "The Toft Cup" there are also early signs of the documentary impulse that would characterize Thompson's trilogy, *Lark Rise to Candleford.* In *Lark Rise*, Thompson carefully records many of the songs and ballads that the working people of rural Oxfordshire sang during the last two decades of the nineteenth century. In "The Toft Cup," Grace's grandmother sings a stanza from "an old song" that had been sung "by generations of foresters."[33] Thompson also uses Grace's grandmother to depict a country practice known as "telling the bees." "The Toft Cup" is the first-known, published work in which Thompson includes this tradition in one of her narratives. In this story, Grace's grandmother goes out to her hives to tell her bees:

> Bees, bees, there's joy in the house
> For a maid has promised to wed.

Thompson would later describe this country tradition, with modifications, in the nature essay that she published in *The Peverel Papers* in September 1922, in "Old Queenie," and in *Lark Rise.* Another incident in "The Toft Cup" would later appear in Thompson's posthumously published novel, *Heatherley.* In *Heatherley*, Laura and Richard Brownlow share a similar taste in literature, and "if one of the two began to quote poetry, the other capped the quotation."[34] In "The Toft Cup," Grace and Edmund share a similar taste in literature and spend evenings quoting and capping quotations as Grace's grandmother sits dozing by the fireside.

"The Mistress of Boldre Farm" and "The Education of a Genius" also include a number of plot and character elements that Thompson would later reuse in *Lark Rise, Candleford Green,* and *Heatherley.* In "The Mistress of Boldre Farm," Margaret Tyrell, like Laura's mother in *Lark Rise*, had once been a nursery governess and is consequently more refined than the other women of her village. Margaret attends a sewing party, a popular social activity that Thompson would later describe in great detail in *Candleford Green.* Thompson also recycled the basic plot of "The Mistress of Boldre Farm." After changing a few details,

Thompson republished this story in the *Catholic Fireside* in 1922 with a new title, "Where the Apple Reddens." In "The Education of a Genius," Mrs. Wellstead, the blacksmith's wife, remembers a brother who loved books but, for lack of money, could not continue his education. Her brother had joined the army and had been killed during the Boer War. In *Lark Rise,* Laura's brother Edmund also loves books. As a young boy of four, Edmund asks a visiting aunt, "Which college shall I go to when I am grown up, Oxford or Cambridge?"[35] His sympathetic aunt replies, "There won't be any college for you, my poor little man. . . . 'You'll have to go to work as soon as you leave school; but if I could have *my* way, you should go to the very best college in Oxford." In *Heatherley*, Laura's brother Edmund fights in the Boer War and survives, only to perish on the battlefield during World War I.

When Thompson wrote "His Lady of the Lilac," she reused several elements from "The Toft Cup." Like "The Toft Cup," "His Lady of the Lilac" is set in a derelict country home in the New Forest that features a picturesque room lined with books. The young lovers in both stories draw closer together due to a mutual love for books and a similar taste in literature. The heroes of both stories are freelance journalists who support themselves by writing weekly nature notes for a newspaper. Thompson also used the New Forest as both the inspiration and the setting for the first year of nature essays that she wrote for the *Catholic Fireside.* Thompson's narrative persona ("Flora") in *Out of Doors* and *The Peverel Papers*, like Philip Allington of "His Lady of the Lilac," comes to the New Forest to live the life of a hermit and eventually experiences the healing power of nature.

Short Fiction after World War I

The war years were particularly difficult for Thompson. In 1916 her beloved brother Edwin Timms, who had joined Canada's Eastern Ontario Regiment, was killed in action in Flanders.[36] Then in 1918, at the age of forty-one, Thompson was surprised to find herself pregnant.[37] Her third child, Peter Redmond, was born in 1918, just as the war ended. In 1919, soon after Peter's birth, Thompson enrolled in a writing course offered by the Practical Correspondence College of London.[38] Although Thompson stated that she wrote nothing during World War I and only resumed writing with the poems of *Bog Myrtle and Peat,* she actually revised a story that she had published in the *Lady's Companion* and submitted it to the *Catholic Fireside* in 1919.[39] It was a momentous step, for she would spend the next eight years writing for this publication.

"The Leper" was published in the *Catholic Fireside* on January 24, 1920. It was the first of six short stories that Thompson would publish in this magazine during 1920. Also published were "The Call," "The Uphill Way," "Sign and Countersign," "The Hermit's Yew," and "Ambrose." Three additional stories were published in 1921: "Bluebell's Luck," "The Mervyn Mystery," and "Our Contemporary." The year 1922 was the last year that Thompson published short fiction in the *Catholic Fireside.* The two stories that appeared that year were "The Hidden Power" and "Where the Apple Reddens." The short stories that Thompson published after World War I are all set in the English countryside or in provincial towns. Unlike the stories published before the war, these stories are not linked to a specific rural community. What does link most of the stories is the experience of life in postwar Britain.[40] Most of the stories that Thompson published in the *Catholic Fireside* in the 1920s are conventionally romantic, but they reflect a postwar sensibility. The central theme of two of the stories, "The Call" and "The Hermit's Yew," is the loss of traditional English values, a theme that would inform Thompson's descriptions of country life in "Old Queenie," "An Oxfordshire Hamlet in the 'Eighties," "May Day in the 'Eighties," and her trilogy, *Lark Rise to Candleford*. "The Uphill Way" and "Bluebell's Luck" are stories about selfless fathers who supplement their incomes by working as freelance writers. "The Profiteers," "Our Contemporary," "Ambrose," and "Sign and Countersign" are all traditional romances, but they reflect postwar social and economic conditions. In "The Profiteers" and in "Sign and Countersign" postwar attitudes about social class play an important role in the plots. Freelance journalism and changes in the newspaper industry are significant plot elements in "Our Contemporary" and in "Ambrose." "The Hermit's Yew," "The Uphill Way," "The Profiteers," and "Our Contemporary" are stories that provide an interesting glimpse of the themes and character types that Thompson favored in her postwar fiction.

"The Hermit's Yew"

The fate of an ancient yew tree, rumored to be a thousand years old, is the dramatic focus of Thompson's one-page short story, "The Hermit's Yew." The yew tree, standing at the top of a hill known locally as "the Hanger," is associated with the legend of a hermit "in Saxon times" who planted the "tiny slender, whispering slip" beside the door of his monastic cell.[41] Old Renshaw, hobbling about the village supported on two sticks, is the only villager who remembers the reverence that generations of local villagers felt for the ancient tree before "people had ceased to care for such things." However, all the villagers know the ancient curse associated with the tree: "Who strooks at me / Strooken shall be!" After the owner of the Hanger dies on the battlefield in Flanders, his land is sold to a "stranger," Mr. Pascoe. Mr. Pascoe, a "retired butcher who had made a fortune out of Government pork," is contemptuous of the villagers' affection for the wild cherry trees, the lilac hedge, and the yew tree on his newly acquired property. He dismisses the villagers' feelings as "a lot of sloppy sentiment," declaring, "I paid good money for this little show, and, as a business man, expect to see most of it back by the sale of the timber." The yew tree proves "so hard and sound" that it exhausts the four men Pascoe employs to cut it down. Pascoe then takes up the axe himself, determined to see his work of destruction to its end. The yew finally falls, but Pascoe's "exertion in the hot sun felling the Hermit's Yew" leads to his own fall as well. That same night Pascoe himself is "strook," and he dies several days later.

Mr. Pascoe represents a crass segment of the New Rich referred to contemptuously as *profiteers.* During the 1920s, many English men and women were disturbed by the crass materialism, self-indulgence, and iconoclasm of the era, and they viewed profiteers such as Mr. Pascoe with alarm.[42] In "The Hermit's Yew," Thompson does not punish Mr. Pascoe for being a profiteer, but for trampling on traditional English values by destroying an ancient landmark. The felling of the ancient yew provides a useful metaphor for the narrator's assessment of postwar Britain: "During the war, too many precious and sacred things *toppled and crashed* for us to have much feeling left" (emphasis added).

"The Hermit's Yew" expresses several ideas that Thompson would develop more fully in *The Peverel Papers* and in her later novels. Like the ancient trees that she describes in *The Peverel Papers*, the yew is a living witness to centuries of English history. It is both a precious historical artifact and a tangible link to the Anglo-Saxon monk who planted it, the Normans who noted it in the Domesday Book, and the fallen soldier who had once owned the land on which it stands. The curse associated with the tree is an example of the type of folklore and superstition that Thompson would document in *The Peverel Papers* and in *Lark Rise to Candleford.*

"The Uphill Way"

"The Uphill Way" opens with the first two lines of Christina Rossetti's poem "Up-Hill," which obviously inspired the title of the story as well. The hero of this story is Dr. Carstairs, an altruistic country physician with a large family and a poor country practice, whose life has been an "up-hill road."[43] Although resigned to the fact that "with so poor a practice and so many to keep out of it, every personal wish had to be stifled," Dr. Carstairs has still managed to spare some time for his work as an amateur astronomer. Despite working with an antiquated telescope that would be "disdained by an astronomically minded schoolboy," Carstairs has published articles in scientific papers and earned the respect and friendship of a distinguished astronomer. In his professional life, Dr. Carstairs must balance the demands of Lady Partington, a hypochondriac who pays her bills, against the more pressing needs of the impoverished cottagers who do not. In the homes of the cottagers, Carstairs is frequently overwhelmed by the "poverty and ignorance" that meets him "at every turn," and he often feels that he is "fighting his way through a jungle."[44] Two of Dr. Carstairs's children are taking their first steps out into the world. Derrick, who works in a laboratory, still depends on financial support from home. Rosalind, his beautiful and adoring daughter, needs additional funds to pay for the expenses associated with mixing in "good society."[45] Just when Carstairs is worrying how he will meet the medical needs of his impoverished patients and the financial demands of his family, he receives an offer from a weekly newspaper, the *People's Own,* to write an astronomy column for its weekly series, *The Sidereal Heavens*. This new source of income will not only allow Carstairs to ease the strain in family finances, but it will also enable him to purchase a telescope more suited to his research.

Most of the freelance writers and journalists in Thompson's stories are young and unmarried men and women, but in "The Uphill Way" and in another short story, "Bluebell's Luck," fathers use freelance journalism to supplement their modest incomes. In "The Uphill Way," purchasing a better telescope ensures Dr. Carstairs's future success as an amateur astronomer. In "Bluebell's Luck," winning £25 in a writing competition is "only the very beginning of all the good things that happened after" for a cabinetmaker and his family.[46] "The Uphill Way" and "Bluebell's Luck" are both sentimental and rather saccharine short stories, chiefly because the members of both families are so idealized. The husbands are clever, talented, and self-sacrificing. The mothers are attractive, cheerful, and supportive. Both mothers make the best of their straitened circumstances without complaint. The children in both stories are loving, obedient, and appreciative. Neither family is suffering from serious want.

What is most interesting in "The Uphill Way" and "Bluebell's Luck" is Thompson's portrayal of determined autodidacts whose talents triumph over education and social class. The middle-class Dr. Carstairs is a self-taught astronomer who achieves a level of expertise that enables him to publish his observations in professional journals. The cabinetmaker, known only as Bluebell's father, frequents the local reading room and spends his evenings at home reading and writing. His determined efforts to improve his education, combined with his writing talent, enable him to write a prize-winning play and short story. Thompson was herself a determined autodidact and freelance journalist who used her knowledge of nature and literature to supplement her own family's income. Yet Thompson chose fathers rather than mothers to be the writer-heroes in these two stories.

"Our Contemporary"

After World War I, publishing newspapers became an increasingly competitive business. Newspapers that failed to attract a mass audience did not survive. For this reason, many provincial papers went out of business in the years following the war.[47] This postwar reality is reflected in "Our Contemporary." The heroine, Gerda Kaye, is the editor of a failing provincial paper, the *Lynwood Courier.* Despite dire predictions of failure from her family and college friends, Gerda assumes the position of editor at the *Lynwood Courier* after her father's death. Gerda, a college-educated young woman with "bobbed, corn-coloured hair," is more accustomed to writing than editing.[48] She finds it "very difficult, in so small a town, to be sincere and yet please all and offend none." Circulation for the *Lynwood Courier* is already low when a rival newspaper, the *Herald*, appears in Lynwood. Even Gerda is forced to admit that the *Herald* "with its crisp news columns," and "its really first-rate stories and articles, was much as she imagined her ideal paper."[49] To make matters worse, free sample issues of the *Herald* are being distributed on the streets of Lynwood, further reducing the almost nonexistent circulation of the *Lynwood Courier.* A chance meeting between the rival editors, Gerda and Mr. Mostyn, brings predictable professional and romantic results. The morning following their meeting, Mostyn writes to Gerda, suggesting that they combine their two newspapers into "one really first-class paper."[50] In a matter of months, the *New Forest Times* replaces both the *Lynwood Courier* and the *Herald.* Thompson provides an abbreviated version of a conventional happy ending in the last sentence of this story: "But all this was only a prelude, the real romance came later!"

In "Our Contemporary" Thompson reveals the economic and social realities affecting provincial newspapers in the early twentieth century without engaging in controversy. Gerda has taken on the challenge of running a provincial newspaper out of loyalty to her father and his employees. A published author of short stories and articles on "legend and folklore," Gerda has put her own writing aside to fulfill her father's dying wish.[51] Mostyn is a wealthy Oxford graduate with an interest in philanthropy. Rather than standing for Parliament or joining a University Settlement, activities traditionally associated with his social class, Mostyn gives lectures about the starving Russians and founds a newspaper to educate the "rural population."[52] Unlike Gerda, who is a native of Lynwood, Mostyn is an outsider. He does not live in Lynwood or in the surrounding countryside. Instead, he comes to Lynwood "for a day or two each week" to see "his paper through the press," staying in the "expensive and exclusive 'Romney Arms.'" In the process of fulfilling his philanthropic dreams, Mostyn drives a provincial newspaper out of business. Unlike Gerda and the employees of the *Lynwood Courier*, Mostyn does not depend on the sales of the *Herald* to make his living. Thompson does not engage in a discussion of the ethics and economics inherent in this situation. Rather, the story's conflict is solved by a business and romantic merger.

"The Profiteers"

The redistribution of wealth brought about by the economic and social realities of World War I created a new class of people in postwar Britain known as the New Rich and the New Poor. The New Rich were those who had prospered and even amassed fortunes during the war. The New Poor were typically members of the middle classes whose incomes had decreased due to the death or disability of the family breadwinner. The New Rich and the New Poor were frequently discussed in magazines during the 1920s, including women's magazines.[53] In 1920 Thompson published an unsympathetic story about the New Rich ("The Hermit's Yew") in the *Catholic Fireside*. "The Profiteers," published in 1921, is a far more sympathetic portrayal of this new class.

"The Profiteers" is set at the Hotel Moorlands, an old-fashioned and exclusive country hotel "where families came year after year, and everyone was quite safe in making friends."[54] Sheila Morgan and her parents are newcomers to the hotel and have spent an uncomfortable two weeks being ignored by their fellow guests. It is obvious to the established guests that the Morgans are members of the New Rich, perhaps even members of the despised group of businessmen known as "profiteers." Each member of the Morgan family has a different understanding of his/her social position. Sheila, a modern young woman who spent the war working at a VAD hospital, feels that World War I was fought, at least in part, to create a caste-free society in Britain.[55] Sheila feels that her war service and her father's wealth entitle her to take her rightful place among the wealthy. Mr. Morgan, who made his fortune by running a condensed milk factory during the war, has no social ambitions. He is "well aware of the price he had to pay for the mere privilege" of sitting in the hotel dining room and does not worry about using the correct fork or chatting with his fellow diners. Mrs. Morgan, a lady's maid before her marriage, is miserably self- conscious and worries that someone will recognize her as a social imposter. The Morgans are made even more uncomfortable by the conversations they overhear at surrounding tables, conversations about aristocratic families financially ruined by the war and forced to sell their ancestral homes to "retired pork butchers."

Into this tense social scene walks the hero, Dr. Allan Neal, a young doctor who had spent many childhood summers staying at the Hotel Moorlands. Allan Neal is the type of hero Flora Thompson is fond of using in her short fiction. Neal is well educated and has "the eyes of a poet and dreamer."[56] More importantly, he is free of class prejudice and is devoted to improving the lives of the poor. Neal practices medicine at St. Chadwins, a clinic in the slums of Manchester. He quickly discovers that Sheila's father is the generous patron who supplied condensed milk to the children at St. Chadwins during a strike, probably the Railway Strike of 1919. When Sheila and Allan discover that they are both devout Catholics, the stage is set for a great romance. The only crisis in "The Profiteers" is the arrival of Lady Jollison, Mrs. Morgan's former employer. After Lady Jollison snubs the Morgans in the hotel dining room, the family and Dr. Neal move to the Wheatsheaf, a less exclusive hotel nearby.

"The Profiteers" explores the shifting social landscape in postwar Britain, especially the resistance the New Rich faced in their social interactions with the New Poor and members of the upper classes. Each of the significant characters in the story has a different social standing. Dr. Neal has abandoned the upper classes by becoming a physician and practicing medicine in the slums. Unlike the other guests at the Hotel Moorlands, he is more liberal in his social outlook. Mr. Morgan, a grocer and the owner of Morgan's Stores, is a hard-working member of the working classes. After his condensed milk factory became unexpectedly profitable during the war, he found, to his surprise, that he was a very wealthy man. His wife, a former lady's maid, feels totally "inadequate," despite being more tastefully dressed than the other women at the hotel.[57] Sheila, who had urged her parents "to launch out a little" and abandon "their usual seaside apartments" for the Hotel Moorlands, is not prepared for the chilly reception her family receives. At first, her youthful disdain of social class makes it difficult for her to sympathize with her parents. The arrogant Lady Jollison is also placed in an uncomfortable position when she encounters Mrs. Morgan at the Hotel Moorlands. Mrs. Morgan knows that her old employer is the wife of a wealthy brewer who was only knighted because "he happened to be mayor the year the king came" to Belminster.[58] Encountering her former lady's maid as a fellow guest in the same hotel she frequents can only remind Lady Jollison of her own humble origins.

Although Thompson's short stories are predictable and sentimental, it is a mistake to dismiss them as artistic failures. Thompson was not attempting to write great literature during this period of her life; she was working to provide her children with a better education. Since periodicals for women of the upper classes published less fiction than those for the middle and lower middle classes, Thompson wrote the type of story that magazines for middle- and lower middle-class women were more likely to buy. The conventional elements in her stories (the beautiful heroines and handsome heroes, the noble and self-sacrificing mothers, and the invariably happy endings) are all informed by Thompson's sensibilities and provide interesting links to her essays and novels.

The Poetry of *Bog Myrtle and Peat*

Thompson expressed her deep love for English poetry in many of the short stories and essays that she published during the 1910s and 1920s. There are only scattered lines of poetry in her short fiction, but the nature essays and literary essays that Thompson wrote for the *Catholic Fireside* are filled with poetry excerpts.[59] Thompson's poetic ambitions were encouraged by her friend and mentor Dr. Ronald Campbell Macfie. At his suggestion, Thompson submitted a collection of her poems to the publisher Philip Allan and Company.[60] The resulting book was entitled *Bog Myrtle and Peat.*

Bog Myrtle and Peat, a slim paperbound book, sold for 3 shillings 6 pence when it was published in 1921. In a brief introductory note, Thompson thanked the editors of the "various periodicals" in which her poems had appeared for permission to reprint them. She also dedicated the first poem in the collection, "To Ronald Campbell Macfie," to her poetic mentor. Reviews for Thompson's book began to appear in March 1921.[61] The review in the *Daily Chronicle*, entitled "Woman of Letters: Village Postmistress Poetess," described *Bog Myrtle and Peat* as a "slim volume of considerable merit" that is "being looked for with a good deal of interest locally." [62] The review further noted that Thompson's poems were "well written" but bore "traces of [the author's] having laboriously built up her technique upon the models of the greater poets." The *Daily Chronicle* review also contains some of the few recorded statements that Thompson made about being a writer, her love for literature, and her childhood. On being a working writer and mother, Thompson noted practically, "I am generally too busy in the mornings to write [. . .] but I make use of my ideas later." She added, "I work at my writing when my other housework is done." Thompson also revealed the loneliness she experienced while following her literary pursuits, telling her interviewer, "I sometimes think I must be the most isolated of women who write poetry." Thompson projected a similar sense of loneliness and isolation in the nature essays that she was publishing in *The Peverel Papers* at this time.

Subsequent reviews of *Bog Myrtle and Peat* expressed a similarly qualified praise for Thompson's poetry. *Bog Myrtle and Peat* received a brief (one-sentence) mention in the prestigious *Times Literary Supplement.* The mention was kind but tepid: "A passion for the open English country—a keen receptiveness to its sights and scents and sounds are the notes of the pieces collected in this slim volume, and they are given adequate and tasteful expression."[63] In *Ideas* the reviewer offered this opinion: "I should not call Mrs. Thompson a great poet, but there is considerable beauty in her efforts and she may go a long way."[64] The *Evening Standard* praised Thompson's "charming lyrical faculty" and "serene spirit" but also offered the following blunt criticism: "When Miss Thompson disciplines her rather too facile Muse and rejects the easy adjective and the time-worn poetic attitude, she will probably advance considerably on the present volume."[65] *The Bookman* credited Thompson's verse for having a "singing note" and a "very pleasant lilting quality" but found "no great freshness of vision" in her "simple songs of April and wild-thyme and heather."[66] Perhaps "the author may have work of more considerable style and quality to give us," this reviewer concluded sympathetically. Reviews in *Tit-Bits* and the *Lady* were less exacting. The review in *Tit-Bits* stated (rather inaccurately) that *Bog Myrtle and Peat* had been "highly praised by critics."[67] The *Lady* simply praised Thompson for her "imaginative sense" and "splendid ideas."[68]

Bog Myrtle and Peat was also noted in the *Civilian*, a publication for Civil Service employees to which Flora and John Thompson subscribed. The *Civilian* published a one-page article on Thompson, entitled "Flora Thompson: Poet and Nature Lover." This article included excerpts from three of Thompson's poems ("Shallows," "Paper Boats," and "Flood Time") and praised Thompson's poetry for its "sincerity" and "melodic sweetness."[69] However, the review also faulted Thompson for "falling victim to the present tyrant of the poetic world, verse libre" in her poem "The Earthly Paradise" and further commented that readers "enamoured" of "complex and transcendant truths" expressed in "felicitous language" would not find Thompson "numbered with their favourites."

In 2001 John Ferns of Mc Master University published a more generous assessment of Thompson's poetry in his entry for the author in the *Dictionary of Literary Biography.* Based on his close study of individual poems in *Bog Myrtle and Peat*, Ferns portrayed Thompson as an Edwardian-Georgian poet who "wrote from a perspective of being in immediate and intimate contact with the natural world as well as the world that literature opens."[70] As Ferns observes, Thompson worked "outside the literary circles in which Eliot and other modernists were moving."[71] Consequently, her poetry did not reflect a modernist sensibility but expressed instead a vein of "Edwardian-Georgian nostalgia."[72]

The Poems

Thompson did not explain why she chose the title *Bog Myrtle and Peat* for her book of poetry, but her title was probably inspired by the bog myrtle and peat that she observed growing on the heath near her home in Liphook, Hampshire. Curiously, there is no poem about bog myrtle or peat in this collection, although one line in "Home Thoughts from the Desert" contains a reference to the "good smoke of burning peat."[73] The poems of *Bog Myrtle and Peat* reveal that Thompson had carefully studied poetic form and was eager to attempt exacting verse forms when writing her own poetry. Among the poems of *Bog Myrtle and Peat* are a Petrarchan sonnet, a triolet, and a villanelle. Most of the poems found in this volume are nature or love poems, but Thompson also included a handful of poems on less traditional subjects. "The Airman" and "Flight at Sunset" are poems about pilots. "Ocean Malignant" and "You Have Forgotten Our Cave" are poems about prehistoric men and women. "Shallows" is a poetic critique of the superficiality of polite conversation.

Despite her careful attention to poetic form and her willingness to experiment with nontraditional poetic subjects, Thompson's poetic skill falls short of her gift for writing descriptive prose. In lesson 3 of the *The Peverel Literary Society Verse Writing Course* that Thompson later wrote for members of the Peverel Society, she was to describe the importance of selecting "fresh and distinctive words" to express poetic thought.[74] Her guidelines for selecting the "perfect word in poetry" were that each word "must express the exact shade of meaning required," "be musical in itself," and "not be hackneyed."[75] In her poetry, Thompson seemed to have great difficulty in selecting her own "perfect" words. Judging by the nature essays that Thompson was writing during this same period, her vocabulary was rich and varied. Perhaps the precision and economy of language required for the poetic genre ran counter to her gift for writing richly detailed prose.

Six poems from *Bog Myrtle and Peat* provide a useful illustration of the uneven quality of Thompson's poetic expression and her preference for traditional verse forms. Three of these poems are written in fixed forms: the triolet ("April"), the Petrarchan sonnet ("Ocean Malignant"), and the villanelle ("A Villanelle of Spring"). The three remaining poems represent the verse forms that Thompson used most frequently in her other poems. Thompson's adaptation of the ballad stanza is seen in "August Again." "Home Thoughts from the Desert" is a poem that reflects her use of refrains and repeated lines. "To One in Prison" is a passionate love poem written in another of Thompson's favorite verse forms: the octosyllabic couplet.[76]

"April"

In "April," Thompson closely follows the formal constraints of the eight-line French verse form, the triolet. The opening line ("Now that April is here") is repeated in lines four and seven, and the second line ("With her blackthorn ablow") is repeated in the last line of the poem.[77] Like the traditional triolet, the rhyme scheme of "April" is ABaA abAB. The first two lines of this poem, which form the repeating lines of the poem's structure, are adequate, if unremarkable, lines of poetry. Unfortunately, the remaining lines of the poem ("I will say to my dear:-" "With her smile and her tear," and "To the greenwood we'll go!") are so hackneyed that the resulting poem seems as if it were written by a child. Thompson also uses the triolet's pattern of repeated lines in her nine-line poem "If We Were Young Together." Unfortunately, "If We Were Young Together" suffers from the same flaws found in "April."

Thompson published "April" at least two more times after its publication in *Bog Myrtle and Peat.* This poem opens the nature essay that Thompson published in *Out of Doors* in April 1921. Thompson also used this poem as an example of the triolet in *The Peverel Literary Society Verse Writing Course.* Thompson included a triolet by Frances Cornford in the text of a nature essay that she published in *The Peverel Papers* in June 1923. "To a Fat Lady Seen from a Train" succeeds in the very manner that "April" fails. The repeated lines in Cornford's poem address a "fat white woman whom nobody loves," a surprising form of poetic address. In addition, the lines that describe grass, "soft as the breast of doves / And shivering sweet to the touch," conjure images of the fat woman's quivering flesh as she walks "through the fields in gloves." The novelty of these poetic lines diverts the reader's attention from the simplicity and potential monotony of this verse form.

"Ocean Malignant"

Thompson chose the Petrarchan sonnet to write about a caveman's love for the ocean in "Ocean Malignant." In most respects, Thompson follows the Petrarchan model in this poem. The rhyme scheme of the initial octet conforms with the classic rhyme scheme abbaabba, although the concluding sestet (cddede) deviates from the more usual cdecde or cdccde. Like the Petrarchan sonnet, each line of "Ocean Malignant" is composed of five metrical feet, but in three lines Thompson deviates from the more standard iambic pentameter. Lines 1 and 2 begin with a dactyl, and in line 14 the initial unstressed syllable is followed by a spondee.

"Ocean Malignant" is one of Thompson's more successful poems because her personification of the ocean as a seductive mistress allows a more erotic reading of its poetic lines. In addition, the lover in this sonnet is a caveman, not a courtier, and the object of his desire is the ocean rather than a beautiful woman. The dangerous love affair described in this sonnet begins with "the first caveman" who "flung himself down" on the ocean's "gold-fretted shore."[78] The caveman, "enamoured" of the ocean's "sinuous azure grace," is disarmed by "her soft, sweet breath" and "gentle waves." He mistakes the treacherous mistress for the "Mother of our Race" and is lured to his death in her "caverns dim." The ocean is a wily mistress who holds "high sport" with the caveman's body and then flings "his carrion back to Earth again" after "entwining" his hair with seaweed. The final line of this sonnet echoes a lover's complaint: "So cruel false! But fair–Ah, God, how fair!"

"Villanelle of Spring"

The title of this poem boldly announces the complex verse form in which it is written. Thompson's poem obeys all the rules of this challenging verse form. "A Villanelle of Spring" is composed of five tercets and a concluding quatrain. Line 1 ("I sing a villanelle of Spring") and line 3 ("And primrose dells where throstles sing") in the first tercet are systematically repeated in the remaining stanzas of the poem.[79] Unfortunately, like "April," Thompson's "Villanelle of Spring" is a meticulous example of a verse form, but it is not satisfying as poetry. A few individual lines create pleasant images of "long, lush hedgerows, white with may" and "bluebell, and pink crab-apple spray," but these individual lines are not complemented by the repeated lines of the poem. This problem is especially obvious in the clumsy and hackneyed language of the poem's concluding quatrain:

> Hark to the swallows twittering!
> *They're* mending their old nests with clay;
> I sing a villanelle of Spring
> Of primrose dells where throstles sing!

"Home Thoughts from the Desert"

"Home Thoughts from the Desert" is a twenty-line poem composed of four five-line stanzas. The rhyme in each stanza is found in alternating lines of iambic tetrameter. The iambic dimeter of the fifth-line refrain, "In Hampshire now!" remains unchanged, even in the last stanza of the poem, where the refrain changes to "Ah, Hampshire dear!"[80] Thompson used repeated lines or refrains in several of the poems in *Bog Myrtle and Peat.* There is a fifth-line refrain in the two-stanza poem "Cuckoo."

There is also considerable repetition in another poem, "You Have Forgotten Our Cave." The title of this thirty-five-line poem is used as a poetic line three times in the poem. The opening phrase ("You have forgotten") is used twice, and another phrase ("Forgotten the . . .") begins six different lines.[81]

In "Home Thoughts from the Desert," the speaker dreams of the Hampshire landscape, remembering the "heath-sands" of "tawney-gold," the wind that "comes screaming from the sea," and the "good smoke of burning peat."[82] Thompson's gift for describing the sights, sounds, and scents of the Hampshire countryside, which figure so prominently in *The Peverel Papers*, is used to good effect in this poem.

"August Again"

"August Again" is a balladlike poem, composed of two eight-line stanzas. Although the poem is not written in four-line ballad stanzas, it uses the distinctive metrical pattern of the ballad: alternating lines of iambic tetrameter and iambic trimeter. In the first stanza, the speaker of the poem laments the death of "My Love" who "lies cold and still" on "that far Flemish plain."[83] Since this poem was published only three years after the end of World War I, it probably alludes to a soldier, like Thompson's brother Edwin Timms, who died in Flanders during the war. The pathos of the poem is intensified by the speaker's knowledge that her love "does not know that the heath-bells blow / On the Hampshire hills again!" In the second stanza, the speaker imagines that, sensing the depth of her faithful love and profound grief, her lover stirs sympathetically in his grave. The poetic lines of "August Again" could easily be mistaken for the lyrics of a traditional ballad. The image of the lover stirring in his grave and the language in individual lines such as "My Love lies cold and still" is quite similar to the imagery and language found in English and Scottish ballads. In addition, Thompson's use of the ballad stanza meter gives this poem such a musical quality that it could easily be sung to the tune of a traditional ballad.

"To One in Prison"

"To One in Prison" is the last poem in *Bog Myrtle and Peat*. This nine-line poem is composed chiefly of octosyllabic couplets, a verse form that Thompson used frequently in her poetry. In the second line of the poem, an allusion to Beatrice provides a framework of meaning for the erotic and spiritual intensity of the following lines. The allusion to Beatrice suggests that the speaker's love for the unidentified "poet-hero, poet-king" is akin to the love Dante expressed for Beatrice in *La Vita Nuova* and *La Divina Comedia.*[84] The speaker, whose soul is in "a white-heat of desire" and whose lips are "aflame with holy fire," expresses a passionate and idealistic love for the beloved that, through the allusion to Beatrice, translates into spiritual love. The meaning of the first line of this poem ("Had I the power to match my love") is explained in line 4 when the speaker says, "were mine but a poet's fate." Just as Dante immortalized Beatrice Portinari in his work, the speaker desires the "power" of a poet to "hymn" the excellence of the unidentified "poet-hero, poet-king" to "endless time." Although the gender of the speaker is not identified, the gender of the beloved is male. The title is mysterious. There is no clue in the poem that identifies the prisoner to whom the poem is addressed, and there is no indication whether the prison is real or metaphorical.

Thompson's love of English poetry was expressed in most of her published work. In her short stories, in the nature essays that she wrote for *The Peverel Papers*, and in the novels of *Lark Rise to Candleford* and *Heatherley*, Thompson invariably included some reference to poetry or incorporated poetic excerpts into her texts. However, despite the encouragement of Dr. Ronald Campbell Macfie and her own concerted efforts to write poetry, Thompson did not write memorable verse. In reality, Thompson's greatest poetic gift was for writing lyrical descriptions of nature in prose. Her poetic descriptions of nature, found most frequently in *The Peverel Papers,* are also found scattered throughout her short stories, literary essays, and novels. And, as the literary essays of *The Fireside Reading Circle* and *The Peverel Literary Society Verse Writing Course* reveal, Thompson was a knowledgeable teacher and a sympathetic critic for other aspiring poets.

Literary Essays

On June 5, 1920, Thompson published her first literary essay in the *Catholic Fireside.* This essay, entitled "Skerryvore: The Bournemouth Home of Robert Louis Stevenson," was the precursor of a series of literary essays that Thompson published two years later in the *Catholic Fireside* for a series entitled *The Fireside Reading Circle.*[85] Although this first essay is only one and a half columns long, Thompson accomplishes in miniature what she would later accomplish in the expanded three-page format of *The Fireside Reading Circle.* In "Skerryvore," Thompson reviews Stevenson's life and works, emphasizing the famous works that he composed while living in Bournemouth: *Dr. Jekyll and Mr. Hyde*, *Kidnapped*, and *A Child's Garden of Verse.* Stevenson's family life, health problems, and friendships with literary figures such as George Meredith and Thomas Hardy are all mentioned. Thompson would return to Robert Louis Stevenson in

January 1924, when she published a three-page essay on this writer in *The Fireside Reading Circle.*

In January 1923, Thompson published the first of thirty-five literary essays that she was to write for *The Fireside Reading Circle.*[86] From January 1923 to November 1925, she published a monthly literary essay in *The Fireside Reading Circle* as well as a monthly nature essay in *The Peverel Papers*, an impressive output for a woman who was still raising three children and keeping house in an era with few modern conveniences. Thompson had already been including many references to English literature in *The Peverel Papers*; however, *The Fireside Reading Circle* allowed her to fully express her literary interests. *The Fireside Reading Circle* also gave Thompson an opportunity to run a writing competition similar to the competitions sponsored by the *Lady's Companion* in *Our Book Club* during the 1910s. Thompson achieved her first success as a writer in these competitions and wished to help other aspiring writers in a similar way.

The literary essays that Thompson wrote for *The Fireside Reading Circle* fall into different categories.[87] Eleven of the thirty-five essays are devoted to specific nineteenth-century novelists: Sir Walter Scott, Charles Dickens, George Eliot, the Brontës, Robert Louis Stevenson, William Makepeace Thackeray, George Meredith, Joseph Conrad, Arnold Bennett, Rudyard Kipling, and J. M. Barrie. There are two different essays on the Romantic poets. One of these essays is devoted to William Wordsworth, and the other is devoted to Percy Bysshe Shelley and John Keats. The Victorian poets Robert Browning, Alfred Lord Tennyson, and Dante Gabriel Rossetti are each discussed in an essay. There is also one essay on English women poets. Victorian essayists are represented by Thompson's separate essays on Thomas Carlyle and John Ruskin. She also wrote four essays on Catholic writers: the Catholic poets Coventry Patmore, Francis Thompson, and Alice Meynell, as well as the novelist and Catholic apologist G. K. Chesterton. There are six essays on literary genres: the English novel, the English short story, the lyric, the English sonnet, and the English essay (discussed in two separate essays). Thompson wrote two essays on nature poetry and one essay entitled "Christmas with the Poets." The essays entitled "Atmosphere in Literature," "Seaside Reading," and "The Sea in Literature" are primarily essays about poetry. The essay entitled "Atmosphere in Literature" mentions George Eliot, Thomas Hardy, and Joseph Conrad but is essentially a discussion of poetry. In "Seaside Reading," Thompson identifies the best poetry to read while vacationing at the seaside. It is interesting to note that Thompson did not write an essay on Shakespeare or on English drama for this series, although she refers to Shakespeare and quotes from his sonnets and plays in several of her essays.

The Fireside Reading Circle is an impressive accomplishment for one whose formal education ended at the age of fourteen. Considerable research must have gone into each of the essays, since Thompson typically includes historical and biographical detail, information about the critical reception of specific works, and direct quotations from the novels, poems, and essays under discussion. Four of Thompson's literary essays are representative examples of her treatment of novelists, poets, and essayists in *The Fireside Reading Circle.* The subjects of these four essays are Sir Walter Scott (untitled, January 1923); Charlotte, Emily, and Anne Brontë ("The Three Brontës," June 1923); English women poets ("The Women Poets," October 1923); and essayist John Ruskin (August 1924).

Untitled (January 1923)

The first essay that Thompson published in *The Fireside Reading Circle* is untitled and consists of two sections. In the first half of this essay, Thompson introduces her new series and states her authorial intent. The second half of the essay is devoted to a discussion of the life and works of Sir Walter Scott. It appears that Thompson may have intended to publish her literary essays in book form. Thompson edited a printed copy of this essay by, crossing out the first section and then writing "Chapter I Sir Walter Scott" at the beginning of the second section.[88] In 1943 Geoffrey Cumberlege expressed an interest in publishing a selection of her essays for *The Peverel Papers.* Perhaps Thompson decided to edit *The Fireside Reading Circle* essays as well, hoping to include them in the proposed book. Thompson edited most of *The Fireside Reading Circle* essays by crossing out the sections that pertained to the monthly writing competition and reader correspondence. Unfortunately, Thompson never published a collection of the essays that she wrote for *The Peverel Papers* or *The Fireside Reading Circle.*

Thompson begins her first essay for *The Fireside Reading Circle* by criticizing the majority of English men, women, and children for their indiscriminate reading of newspapers, popular fiction magazines, and "vulgar and highly-coloured comics."[89] Opposed to this cultural majority, Thompson says, are those few individuals whose "inborn taste revolts against the lurid atmosphere, the strained pathos, the extravagant luxury," and "the exaggerated virtue and vice, which have delighted so many millions of readers and cinema-goers." Thompson honors autodidacts (like herself) who, without the advantage of "lessons in literature" and "lectures upon art," have still managed to discover the works of great writers on their own. Thompson expresses her hope that her new series will enable her readers to get "into touch with those who love the things they love, think the same thoughts, and speak the same language."[90] Thompson addresses her readers directly, sharing her plans for upcoming essays and expressing her desire to create a circle of literature enthusiasts:

> Let us, then, consider ourselves a circle of invisible friends reading the same book at the same time, and each in turn expressing our opinion upon it. In this way we will take the novelists, Dickens and Scott and George Eliot and the Brontës, with many others down to our own day. Some months we will turn aside and study the poets, try to think their thoughts and breathe their atmosphere, until the petty slights and stings of daily life are forgotten, and we gain fresh strength and are inspired to greater effort by their wisdom.

The second half of Thompson's essay is devoted to the life and works of Sir Walter Scott. She opens with an anecdote taken from Scott's childhood. One afternoon, the young boy was caught in a thunderstorm while playing in his grandfather's pasture. When he was found, his family was amazed to see the "little kilted child of four" clapping his hands "with delight" and crying "Bonny! Bonny!" after each clap of thunder.[91] Thompson would often use such endearing personal stories to make famous writers come to life in the pages of her essays. In addition, Thompson's essays on individual poets, authors, and essayists always include a biographical sketch that describes the writer's family background, significant childhood experiences, early works, and artistic development, as well as the critical reception of his or her most famous works. Thompson also describes any personal challenges that the literary figure had to overcome. In this essay, Thompson points to Scott's lameness as having given him periods of rest when he was able to immerse himself in the history, poetry, and legend that would inform his later novels. Thompson credits Scott for rescuing the novel from its "retrograde condition" after the deaths of Fielding, Sterne, Smollett, and Goldsmith, when the novel "relapsed into dull artificial accounts of fashionable life on the one hand and blood curdling tales of murder and mystery on the other." Despite Scott's genius, Thompson says, his novels "bear traces of haste." She comments, "Had he laboured to polish and perfect, his place would be beside Shakespeare and Dante." Thompson describes in detail Scott's rise to fame, his enjoyment of his success, his generosity, and the economic circumstances that led to his financial ruin. She reports that, on his death bed, Scott murmured the lyrics of "Stabat Mater Dolorosa," a detail that would have favorably impressed her Catholic readers.[92] Thompson concludes this essay with a brief description of plot and characterization in *The Heart of Midlothian.* She advises her readers to purchase or borrow a copy of this novel if they wish to become familiar with Scott's novels.

"The Three Brontës"

Thompson opens her essay on "The Three Brontës" (June 1923) with a discourse on solitude. Solitude, she declares, "appears to have formed an almost essential element in the education of nineteenth-century genius."[93] For writers like Charles Dickens, George Eliot, and Mrs. Gaskell, Thompson says, solitude had been a temporary state "forced upon them in the first place by outward circumstances." However, Charlotte, Emily, and Anne Brontë had a "brooding solitude of soul" that would have kept them "solitary at heart" even if they had not lived a secluded life at Haworth Parsonage. Thompson structures her essay around the intertwining lives of Charlotte, Emily, and Anne, beginning with the arrival of Reverend Patrick Brontë and his young family at Haworth Parsonage in 1820 and ending with Charlotte's death in 1855. She provides detailed information about the series of tragic deaths in the Brontë family, the three sisters' attempts to earn their livings, their literary careers, and the critical and popular reception of their work. Thompson says little about Anne Brontë but calls Emily "the first potentially great woman poet of our nation," whose promise "was to be cut short by death."[94] She describes Emily's *Wuthering Heights* as "a tale of wild, almost incredible barbarity" and "tremendous creative power."[95] Thompson also comments on the controversy surrounding the publication of Charlotte's *Jane Eyre.* The sensationalism in *Jane Eyre,* Thompson says, was only "put on like a garment, to please her prospective publisher and prospective public." Charlotte's true achievement in *Jane Eyre,* Thompson says, was making her heroine a "pale, plain-faced little governess" whose "intellect and inner being" glows "with a fire often denied to the fair and fashionable." *Villette* is Charlotte's "most perfect" work of art, Thompson states, because she "kept entirely within the field of her own experiences and from those slender materials constructed a masterpiece."[96] It is interesting that, after attributing the sensationalism in *Jane Eyre* to the demands of her reading public, Thompson feels no need to defend the sensational elements in *Villette.* There is no mention of Lucy Snowe's mental breakdown, the apparition of the ghostly nun, or the episode in which a hallucinating Lucy Snowe wanders through the streets of Brussels in the dead of night after being drugged with an opiate.

Thompson was eager to minimize any scandalous behavior on the part of the writers that she loved, always casting the best light on their misdeeds or sliding over them without comment. In her essay on George Eliot, published in April 1923, Thompson referred to the author's unconventional relationship with G. H. Lewes as "that one false step in her life with which we will not concern ourselves."[97] In her untitled essay on John Keats and Percy Bysshe Shelley, published in May 1923, Thompson passed quickly over Shelley's abandonment of his first wife and his subsequent elopement with sixteen-year-old Mary Godwin, stating, "The full story of that marriage and its consequences most of my readers know already; it is sufficient here to say that he suffered the extreme penalty for his mistaken action."[98]

Thompson also seeks to minimize the rumors of Charlotte Brontë's infatuation with M. Heger, her married literature instructor at the Pensionnat Heger in Brussels. A bundle of old letters written by Charlotte to Heger had surfaced in 1911, Thompson explains to her readers, and these letters had rekindled an old controversy. Thompson declares that the "passion and pleading" found in Charlotte's letters to M. Heger were not evidence of an "unworthy passion" but of the "rarer bond of affinity of soul."[99] More recent scholarship suggests that, although M. Heger and Charlotte may not have had an adulterous affair, Charlotte, in the words of Juliet Barker, "gradually slipped from normal feelings of respect and esteem for her teacher into an unhealthy and obsessive dependency."[100] Perhaps Thompson based her estimation of Charlotte's relationship with M. Heger on her own relationship with Dr. Ronald Campbell Macfie. Thompson dedicated her first book of poetry to Macfie and deeply grieved the loss of her friend when he died unexpectedly in 1931. Ten years after his death, Thompson wrote to a nephew, "the chief friend of my life was a Scotsman Dr. Ronald Macfie and I lost him by death ten years ago, a loss never to be replaced." [101]

"The Women Poets"

In 1922 Thompson discussed the dearth of female artists and poets in two nature essays that she published in *The Peverel Papers.* In these essays, Thompson attributed this fact to the overwhelming demands placed on women as wives, mothers, and household drudges. She returned to this topic in her literary essay entitled "The Women Poets," published in October 1923. The purely literary focus of *The Fireside Reading Circle* allowed Thompson to expand more fully on a topic that resonated with her own experience as a wife, mother, and writer.

Thompson begins "The Women Poets" by enlarging on the conditions that had prevented women from becoming poets in their own right. For the inadequately educated women of the middle classes, leisure time for reading and writing was made virtually impossible by the unending tasks of cooking, soap and candle making, spinning, and sewing. The economic and social circumstances of working-class women reduced them to "illiterate drudges in house and field."[102] "For a poet to have sprung from their ranks would have been a miracle," Thompson declares. Thompson passes quickly over the "'blue stockings' of Doctor Johnson's time" and "the small group of Scotswomen who stole into the lists as song writers" to discuss the life and works of Joanna Baillie. While acknowledging Baillie's prolific output, her immense popularity, and the esteem in which she was held by literary figures such as Sir Walter Scott, Thompson states, "No reader of the present day would dream of placing her beside Goldsmith, much less Shakespeare." She identifies Bailie as the precursor of other women poets, like Letitia Landon and Mrs. Hemans, whose work was published in popular anthologies of sentimental verse known as "keepsakes." Commenting unfavorably on the sentimentality of the "sugar and water" verse found in the "Keepsake," Thompson concludes that Felicia Hemans "might now occupy a higher place in our literature" if she had "been born in a sterner time."

The poet whom Thompson discusses in the greatest detail in this essay is Elizabeth Barrett Browning. Thompson says little about Barrett Browning's life, concentrating instead on her poetry. Thompson praises the poet for flinging "a mantle of feminine grace" around the ageless poetic themes of "life, death, the immortality of the soul," and "the fall and redemption of man" in her poetry.[103] She also praises Barrett Browning for being the first Englishwoman to tell "the story of a woman's love from a woman's own point of view" in *Sonnets from the Portuguese.* [104] To illustrate her point, Thompson includes the first five lines of Sonnet 38 ("The first time that he kissed me") and the first six lines of Sonnet 43 ("How do I love thee?") in her text. Thompson also praises Barrett Browning's "The Cry of the Children" and includes an eight-line excerpt from this poem in her text. Thompson is quick to point out that she does not admire the poem for "being versified blue-book" but for being "a natural expression of outraged love and pity."

After briefly mentioning the poets Dora Greenwell, Adelaide Procter, and Jean Ingelow, Thompson shifts her focus to the poetry of Emily Brontë and Christina Rossetti. In this essay, Thompson repeats much of what she had already written about Emily Brontë in "The Three Brontës," but she also includes eight lines from Brontë's poem "Last Lines." Thompson singles out Christina Rossetti as a poet who proved that a woman could be "as excellent an artist as man."[105] She describes *Goblin Market* and *The Prince's Progress* as "word pictures" with "all the richness of colour her brother and his followers put into their pictures." Thompson also praises Rossetti for the spiritual themes found in *Monna Innominata* and describes her devotional verse as glowing with "the white heat of intense adoration." During Christina Rossetti's lifetime, Thompson notes with satisfaction, the number of women poets increased so steadily that the quaint term "poetess" finally became obsolete. [106] In her closing comments, Thompson expresses regret that the poetry of Augusta Webster, Mary F. Robinson, and Emily Hickey have suffered "an eclipse." Thompson declares, "If but the best work of each of such writers . . . could be gathered together in one volume, that volume would be a priceless national possession." The essay concludes with five lines from Alice Meynell's "Builders of Ruins," a poem that Thompson describes as "the work of one peerless woman poet who has recently gone from us."[107]

"John Ruskin"

Although Thompson did not write any essays on English drama, she did write two essays on the history of the English essay. "English Essayists" was published in November 1924, and it was followed in December 1924 by "English Essayists II." Thompson also published separate essays on the two great Victorian essayists, Thomas Carlyle and John Ruskin. Thompson's three-page essay on John Ruskin, which was published in August 1924, is more simple and straightforward than many of her other literary essays.

The Ruskin essay is primarily structured around the events in John Ruskin's early life, particularly the years leading up to the publication of *Modern Painters* (1843). Thompson continually emphasizes Ruskin's close relationship with his parents and the unique privilege of his early life. She passes quickly over his marriage to Euphemia Chalmers Gray, noting only that Ruskin had "married unsuitably" and that the five-year marriage was "dissolved by a degree of nullity."[108] She sums up Ruskin's later life as a time of service to humanity followed by a period of quiet retirement.

Rather than identifying the unique characteristics of Ruskin's prose style or engaging in a close examination of his works, Thompson uses her essay to discuss Ruskin's importance as a Victorian thinker. She identifies Ruskin as "the very incarnation" of the Victorian age in his "intensity of purpose," his "passion for social betterment," and his "love of the solid and genuine in art as in life."[109] She credits Ruskin for inspiring "a revolution in the art of painting," for raising "architecture from the state of tame commonplace," and for sowing "seeds of social reform which are still germinating." His ideas, so advanced and daring in his day, have now become "matters of course," she observes. Ruskin grew up, Thompson says, "surrounded with all the advantages of wealth, without its usual distractions." The family home was filled with "the glowing colours of good oil-paintings" by "genuine artists." Thompson further observes: "Costly foreign travel, access to libraries and picture galleries, together with a thorough grounding in the technique of art, were all essential features in the education his particular genius required."[110] Thompson summarizes the importance of Ruskin's greatest works, *Modern Painters*, *The Seven Lamps of Architecture*, *The Stones of Venice*, and *Sesame and Lilies*, without quoting any passages from these works, saying only that they offer the "truest impression of what is essential and enduring in Ruskin's teaching."

Theme- and Genre-Based Essays on Literary History

Thompson wrote a total of nine essays on literary history. Three of these essays are based on a literary theme: "The Sea in Literature," "The Poetry of Nature," and "Modern Nature Poetry." The remaining six essays are based on specific literary genres. The titles of these essays are "The English Short Story," "The Sonnet in English Poetry," "The Lyric," "The English Essayists," "English Essayists 2," and "The Evolution of the Novel." Thompson's essays on literary history are written to appeal to a general audience, and they vary in literary scope and content. However, most of these essays combine interesting incidents in English history, short portraits of individual authors, and illustrative excerpts from the literary works under discussion. Thompson does not deal with individual works in detail but concentrates on providing enticing glimpses of a variety of works, no doubt with the intention of tempting her readers to sample these works for themselves.

Thompson's theme-based essays on literary history are far ranging and include the works of writers from Saxon times to the early twentieth century. "The Sea in Literature," published in August 1923, is a short history of English poetry. It begins with a discussion of *Beowulf* and concludes with John Masefield's "Sea Fever." In this essay, Thompson also discusses representations of the sea found in the works of Cynewulf, Chaucer, Spenser, Milton, Dryden, Cowper, Wordsworth, Coleridge, Shelley, Keats, Tennyson, Robert Browning, Arnold, Kipling, Alfred Noyes, and Sir Henry Newbolt. In addition, Thompson refers to the plays of William Shakespeare, Dibdin's seafaring ballads, *Hakluyt's Voyages*, Defoe's *Robinson Crusoe*, and the novels of Sir Walter Scott and Joseph Conrad in her discussion. Twenty-one separate quotations from the works of the writers Thompson discusses are sprinkled throughout the text. In the essay entitled "The Poetry of Nature," published in April 1924, Thompson traces the development of nature poetry from the medieval "Sumer is icomen in" to the poetry of Wordsworth, Byron, Shelley, and Keats. Included in this discussion are specific works by Chaucer, Shakespeare, Spenser, Milton, Vaughan, Crashaw, Herrick, Goldsmith, Thomson, Cowper, and Burns. Once again, Thompson uses quotations (thirteen in this essay) to illustrate the specific works that she discusses. The sequel to "The Poetry of Nature" was published in June 1924. This essay, entitled "Modern Nature Poetry," touches briefly on the Romantic poets and then moves on to the nature poetry of seventeen different poets, ranging from Tennyson and

Robert Browning to A. E. Housman and Francis Thompson.[111] There are twenty-one different quotations from the poetry Thompson mentions in this three-page essay.

Thompson's essays on specific genres are uneven in scope. For example, in "Evolution of the Novel," published in January 1925, she limits her discussion to the works of specific nineteenth-century novelists in what is otherwise a loose discussion of romanticism and realism. The novelists to whom she refers are Dickens, Thackeray, Meredith, Stevenson, Bennett, Conrad, and Hardy, although Thompson focuses most closely on Dickens, Thackeray, and Bennett. Without naming particular novelists or novels, she expresses her disgust with the "sickly, poisonous mist of sex obsession" found in European fiction that has influenced "present-day writers."[112] Her essay entitled "The Sonnet in English Poetry" is more inclusive and traces the history of the sonnet in England from the introduction of the Petrarchan sonnet in the sixteenth century to its use by twentieth-century poets such as Rupert Brooke in *War Sonnets*.[113]

After World War I, women's magazines, particularly those for the middle classes, placed a new emphasis on "rendering service" to their readers.[114] The essays that Thompson published in *The Fireside Reading Circle* reflect her desire to not only share her love of literature but also to educate her readers and help them cultivate literary taste. In her monthly essays, she introduced the readers of the *Catholic Fireside* to the masterpieces of English literature and provided them with information about literary history and literary genres. Using monthly writing competitions, Thompson also fostered a sense of community among her faithful readers that would lead to the foundation of the Peverel Society, a postal writing society that would thrive for fourteen years.

The Peverel Society

Thompson's first modest attempts at encouraging aspiring writers can be found at the end of each of the literary essays that she published in *The Fireside Reading Circle* between 1923 and 1925. In the beginning, Thompson announced the subject for the new competition, as well as the winners of the previous competition, at the end of her monthly literary essays. She gradually expanded this format, using the end of her essay to reply to correspondence from her readers and to give advice to those who had submitted their work to her for comment. By 1925 Thompson's replies to her readers sometimes occupied an entire page. The last writing competition in *The Fireside Reading Circle* was announced in October 1925. Thompson announced the winners of the October competition in December 1925 without commenting on the end of her series.

Thompson had decided to end *The Fireside Reading Circle* with the essay published in November 1925 in order to devote more time to mentoring aspiring writers. With the assistance of Mildred Humble-Smith, she founded a postal writing society for literature lovers that she named the Peverel Society of Poets and Prose Writers.[115] Mildred Humble-Smith (1886-?), who had studied English language and literature at Oxford University, came from a prosperous family of ship chandlers and nautical instrument makers in Newcastle on Tyne.[116] A fellow writer for the *Catholic Fireside*, Humble-Smith met Thompson around 1923.[117] The two women became close friends.

For an annual membership fee, members of the Peverel Society could submit one original work per month (a poem, short story, or article) for comment. Thompson grouped members into different circles, and work submitted by circle members was mailed from member to member until everyone had a chance to offer helpful criticism to the writer. For an additional fee, members could also receive lessons in a writing course that Thompson created for society members. Thompson wrote the curricula for her writing courses on topics such as short story writing, poetry writing, literature techniques, and general culture.[118] In 1926 Thompson compiled an anthology of verse written by members of the Peverel Society that the society published as *The Peverel Society Book of Verse.* Two of Thompson's poems that had been previously published in *Bog Myrtle and Peat* were included in this collection: "May Moonlight" and "Garden Fires." The Peverel Society remained an active organization until 1941. Mildred Humble-Smith and Flora Thompson decided to disband the Peverel Society after each lost a son in combat that year.

Only one of the writing courses that Thompson developed for the Peverel Society can be found in the Flora Thompson archive. *The Peverel Literary Society Verse Writing Course* consists of six separate lessons. These are Lesson 1: "Subject and Form"; Lesson 2: "Rhythm and Metre"; Lesson 3: "Choice of Words"; Lesson 4: "Rhyme"; Lesson 5: "Poetic Form"; and Lesson 6: "The Sonnet and Marketing Verse." Thompson offers basic instruction and practical advice to aspiring poets in these lessons. Each is clearly written and includes helpful examples of the topic she discusses. The literary advice contained in the essays that Thompson wrote for *The Fireside Reading Circle,* as well as the activities of the Peverel Society, would provide an interesting new area of research into Thompson's life and works. The documents associated with the society, such as the various writing courses, Thompson's critiques of members' work, the manuscripts that circulated among circle members, and "The Chats Book," in which members shared their thoughts with each other, would cast an important light on the seventeen years that Thompson spent instructing and mentoring other writers. According to Thompson's biographer,

Gillian Lindsay, Thompson's daughter, Winifred, wrote a letter to the Oxford University Press in which she stated that many of the writers who had belonged to the Peverel Society "got into print and are going strong now."[119] It would be interesting to discover the identity of these writers and to assess the role that the Peverel Society played in their success.

Conclusion

Flora Thompson's success as a novelist was built upon a long series of small successes: her prize-winning essays, the short fiction that she published before and after World War I, the poetry of *Bog Myrtle and Peat*, and the essays written for *The Peverel Papers* and *The Fireside Reading Circle*. In the Flora Thompson archive, there are a handful of unpublished poems and short stories that have yet to be studied, as well as a number of poetry and story fragments. Undoubtedly, there are still short stories, essays, and poems that Thompson published in women's magazines that have yet to be discovered. Although individual stories, poems, and essays may fail to impress literary scholars, these minor works provide fascinating glimpses of Thompson's artistic development and of her determined efforts to become a successful writer. Further research into the seventeen-year period that Thompson spent instructing and mentoring other aspiring writers through *The Fireside Reading Circle* and the Peverel Society may reveal the role she played in helping other talented writers into print.

5

Thompson and the Intellectual Life of the Working Classes

FIFTEEN YEARS BEFORE RICHARD ALTICK PUBLISHED *The English Common Reader* (1957), his groundbreaking study of the rise of the nineteenth-century mass reading public, Flora Thompson began writing her own account of the same historical phenomenon in *Lark Rise.* Laura's story, as told in *Lark Rise* and in the subsequent novels, *Over to Candleford, Candleford Green,* and *Heatherley,* is set in the English countryside during the last two decades of the nineteenth century, a time when the English book and periodical trade was finally bringing a wide variety of cheap books and periodicals to the mass reading public.[1] In the subtext of these four novels, Thompson not only traces the development of Laura's intellectual and artistic sensibilities, but she also traces the gradual expansion of intellectual and cultural opportunities for the rural working classes, as reflected in their reading habits and access to printed material. Woven into Laura's story are specific details about the children's books, schoolbooks, novels, poetry collections, and periodicals that were available to members of the working classes living in Juniper Hill, Cottisford, Twyford, Fringford, and Grayshott, rural communities that became the fictional Lark Rise, Fordlow, Candleford, Candleford Green, and Heatherley. With the same loving attention to detail, Thompson also describes the oral tradition of these agricultural communities: the storytelling, ballads, rhymes, sayings and proverbs, witticisms, and wordplay that served as an alternative literary culture before books and periodicals became widely available.

THE WRITTEN WORD: BOOKS AND PERIODICALS

Laura's story begins in the 1880s, in the pages of *Lark Rise* and *Over to Candleford.* In these books, Thompson reveals the material and intellectual poverty of agricultural workers, poignantly symbolized by the meager contents of the cottage bookshelf and the woefully inadequate country school. In *Candleford Green,* which is set in the 1890s, Thompson depicts the growing access to books and periodicals made possible by the appearance of mechanics' institutes and penny readings in rural working-class communities. In *Heatherley*, Thompson describes reading habits and cultural activities in a rural village in Surrey that was frequented by famous writers during the late 1890s. The mutual improvement societies, penny readings, and public lectures depicted in *Heatherley* are evidence of what Jonathan Rose has called the "shared literary culture" created by the British working classes before the advent of public libraries.[2] Half a century before Rose published *The Intellectual Life of the British Working Classes,* Thompson traced the development of this "shared literary culture" on her own terms, in the pages of her novels about Laura, the stonemason's daughter.

In *The English Common Reader,* Altick systematically analyzed the changing social, historical, and political conditions that eventually led to what he termed "the democratizing of reading."[3] Alticks's findings illuminatc the cultural and educational circumstances that Thompson describes so thoroughly in her novels. Like the residents of the fictional hamlet of Lark Rise, the working classes, particularly those who lived and worked in the English countryside, lived in conditions that made reading nearly impossible for most of the nineteenth century. Members of the working classes were poorly paid and often worked twelve- to fourteen-hour days. Consequently, they did not have leisure time for reading or the income needed to buy books and periodicals.[4] In addition, country dwellers had little access to the inexpensive publications that were becoming increasingly available to the urban working classes, starting at midcentury. Country people had to wait until the end of the century, when the cheap presses began to distribute their publications via the railways and through local distributors, before they could buy cheap books and periodicals.[5] For all these reasons, as both Altick and Rose have pointed out, members of the rural working classes were forced to rely on the family bookshelf for reading matter. Thompson describes a variety of family bookshelves in the novels of *Lark Rise to Candleford* and *Heatherley.* These range from the humble cottage bookshelves found in *Lark Rise* and the family bookshelf of Laura's employer in *Candleford Green* to the private library of the big-game hunter, Mr. Foreshaw, in *Heatherley.*

The Family Bookshelf

The typical cottage bookshelf was an extremely limited resource; generally it only contained a few volumes that had either been passed down from previous generations, acquired as school prizes, borrowed from neighbors, or scavenged.[6] As Richard Altick notes, the Bible, *Pilgrim's Progress,* and *Robinson Crusoe* were the three books typically found on a cottage bookshelf in this era.[7] In *Lark Rise,* Thompson writes that "every well-kept cottage" had "its little row of books."[8] In Laura's home, "Mother's Bible and *Pilgrim's Progress*" were on the family bookshelf, along with "a few children's books" that a local family "had turned out from their nursery when they left the neighborhood."[9] These extra books included Jonathan Swift's *Gulliver's Travels*, *Grimm's Fairy Tales*, Charlotte M. Yonge's *The Daisy Chain* (1856), and two books by the children's author Mrs. Molesworth (1839–1921): *The Cuckoo Clock* (1877) and *Carrots* (1876).

Although most family bookshelves in the hamlet of Lark Rise held only a "family Bible and a prayer-book or two," other families had "a few extra volumes which had either belonged to parents or been bought with other oddments for a few pence at a sale."[10] These extra volumes were mostly "old books of travel and sermons," a class of books that was relatively affordable during the nineteenth century.[11] Two of the "extra volumes" mentioned in *Lark Rise* fall into this general category: *Drelincourt on Death* and Belzoni's *Travels*.[12] Laura finds a "battered old copy" of Belzoni's *Travels* propping open a neighbor's pantry window. Samuel Richardson's *Pamela* (1740) and *Anna Lee: The Maiden Wife and Mother* (1875) by the American temperance author T. S. Arthur (1809–85) are also mentioned in *Lark Rise*. These particular books reflect an interesting aspect of the English book trade during the nineteenth century. Because classic works by Shakespeare or by eighteenth-century authors and poets were often available as cheap reprints or could be scavenged from estate sales, it would not have been unusual to find *Pamela* on a poor cottager's bookshelf.[13] However, for most of the nineteenth century, works by contemporary British authors were too expensive for working-class readers. Cheap reprints of Sir Walter Scott's works were available only after the 1860s, and cheap editions of standard classics were not widely available until the early 1870s.[14] During the same period, works by American authors were relatively inexpensive because they were not covered by British copyright law until 1891.[15] This explains why T. S. Arthur's *Anna Lee: The Maiden Wife and Mother*, published in 1875, could find its way to a cottage bookshelf in the 1880s. It also explains why so many women and girls in *Over to Candleford* were reading *The Wide Wide World* (1851) and *Queechy* (1852), two popular religious novels by the American author Susan Bogert Warner (1819–85).

When Laura leaves her home in the hamlet of Lark Rise, she meets other booklovers and discovers new sources of reading material in their homes. In *Over to Candleford*, Laura spends a summer with her Uncle Tom and his family and discovers a treasure trove of books that her uncle had scavenged from the unsold volumes at an estate sale. Most were volumes of "old sermons" and natural history, grammars, lexicons, "keepsakes," old poetry, and novels.[16] Being a book lover, Uncle Tom allows Laura to read all the books in his attic, even the rather scandalous *Pamela*. In *Candleford Green*, when Laura moves from her birthplace to take her first post office position, she finds a new family bookshelf to explore—the bookshelf of the postmistress, Dorcas Lane. In Miss Lane's cottage, copies of *Cooking and Household Management*, *The Complete Farrier,* and Dr. Johnson's *Dictionary* lie casually on a kitchen window seat. The postmistress's most cherished books are stored "behind glass doors above the bureau in the parlour."[17] Miss Lane's book collection, which had originally belonged to her father, was "an unusual one to be found in a tradesman's parlour at that time." Miss Lane's father had been an "unusual man" because he was "a lover of poetry, especially of Shakespeare, and a student of history and astronomy." Among the volumes on Miss Lane's bookshelf Laura finds "*The Works of William Shakespeare* in two large, flat volumes, and Hume's *History of England* in at least a dozen small fat ones, Scott's *Poetical Works* and a number of the Waverley Novels, Cowper's poems and Campbell's and Gray's, Thomson's *Seasons* and many other such books."[18]

Miss Lane is "very particular about her books" and requires that each "be fitted with a brown-paper jacket" before it is loaned to Laura.[19] Miss Lane's personal reading taste is decidedly more modern than the contents of her family bookshelf would indicate. Miss Lane is interested in the latest discoveries in science and psychology and studies Charles Darwin's *On the Origin of Species* during her free time. In *Heatherley,* Laura meets another book lover when she moves from Candleford Green to take a new post office position. In the village of Heatherley, she meets a retired big-game hunter, Mr. Foreshaw. Laura becomes thoroughly acquainted with Mr. Foreshaw's reading tastes, soon discovering that his favorite authors are Dickens and Thackeray. In the course of her visits to his home, Laura observes that Mr. Foreshaw, who normally refused to read anything written by modern novelists, did read "every new book which appeared about Africa," as well as travel books and biographies.[20]

Schoolbooks, Gift Books, Prize Books, and Borrowed Books

For poor country children, school was another source of reading material. In addition to reading the Bible and studying the Church catechism, students in the one- room schoolhouse in *Lark Rise* read excerpts from the works of Sir Walter Scott, James Fenimore Cooper, and Washington Irving in the *Royal Reader.*[21] English schoolbook publishers often incorporated works by nineteenth-century American authors into their anthologies because these works were not protected by copyright law. James Fenimore Cooper, Washington Irving, and the poets Longfellow, Poe, Bryant, and Whittier were frequently anthologized for this reason.[22] In *Lark Rise*, the schoolchildren also read the poetry of British poets such as Scott, Byron, Tennyson, Hogg, and Henry Glassford Bell in the *Royal Reader.*[23]

Once the family bookshelf and schoolbooks were exhausted, even the most determined reader had difficulty finding new books to read. In the hamlet of Lark Rise during the 1880s, Laura and her brother Edmund, though "voracious readers," only read books that came into their hands "by chance," and these books were "few and not selected."[24] In *Lark Rise*, several books are given to the children as prizes or gifts. For her winning essay on "The Life of Moses," Laura receives a "large, calf-bound, gilt-edged 'Book of Common Prayer.'"[25] The saintly Anglo-Catholic curate, Mr. Marley, gives Edmund a copy of Sir Walter Scott's *Complete Poetical Works* when he discovers the boy has only read the poet in extracts. Mr. Marley also gives Laura a copy of *The Imitation of Christ,* "daintily bound in blue and silver" so she "might not feel neglected."[26] In 1887, as Queen Victoria's Golden Jubilee draws near, Laura is given a bound copy of *Good Words*, in which she reads a serialized version of *Leaves from Her Majesty's Life in the Highlands*.[27] In *Over to Candleford*, the kindly schoolmistress Miss Shepherd gives eleven-year-old Laura a copy of *Ministering Children* (1857), a religious novel by Maria Louise Charlesworth (1819–80).

Occasionally, Laura read books borrowed from neighbors, the school library, or the local Sunday School library. In *Over to Candleford*, Laura's family borrows a copy of Ainsworth's *Old St. Paul's* and several of Scott's Waverley novels from their neighbors.[28] Laura and Edmund, who love the romantic novels of Sir Walter Scott, are not interested in the "goody-goody, Sunday-school prize type" of books found in the school library.[29] Such books, "though better than nothing to read," made "little impression" on Laura and her brother. Books available at the Sunday School library were no better. Approximately one in every five English Sunday Schools had its own library by 1834, but most were stocked exclusively with pious works.[30] In *Over to Candleford*, the "Sunday School Lending Library" is stocked with books about London slum life. [31] The London slums, the narrator of *Over to Candleford* comments, were "then a favorite subject with writers of that class of fiction." The urban slums not only served as "a striking background for some ministering lady or child," but they also gave the country reader "a cheering sense of superiority." In *Over to Candleford,* the women and children who read *Christie's Old Organ* (1874) by Mrs. F. O. Walton and *Froggy's Little Brother* (1875) by Brenda New congratulate themselves on having "a whole house" and not having "to 'pig it' in one room" or sleep on "bundles of rags in corners" like urban slum dwellers. As Jonathan Rose observes, books about the London slums conveyed "profoundly conservative values to working-class readers.[32] Such books reassured the rural working classes that they were "at the midpoint of the economic pyramid rather than at the bottom."[33]

Mechanics' Institutes

In his *History of Public Libraries in Great Britain, 1845–1975* (1977), Thomas Kelly traces "the series of reforming measures" that eventually led to the creation of a public library system in Great Britain.[34] As Kelly notes, during the first half of the nineteenth century, most libraries in Britain were either associated with institutions (such as mechanics' institutes and private societies) or were subscription libraries run by private or commercial concerns. Despite passage of the Public Libraries Act in 1850, national enthusiasm for building public libraries did not truly gain momentum until the Queen's Jubilee in 1887.[35] Even then, by 1914, a full two-fifths of the population of Great Britain (mostly living in agricultural areas) still did not have access to a public library.[36] For this reason, the residents of agricultural communities, such as the fictional Candleford Green, continued to rely on the local mechanics' institute for access to books and periodicals.

In *Candleford Green*, when Laura moves from her birthplace, Lark Rise, to take her first job in Candleford Green, she enters a new phase in her life. She is no longer dependent on the family bookshelf, her neighbors, the school library, or the Sunday School library for reading matter. After she reads most of Miss Lane's "parlour books," Laura follows Miss Lane's suggestion and takes out a ticket at the local mechanics' institute .[37] Thanks to the "Mechanics' Institute in Candleford town," Laura finally reads "such of the Waverley Novels as had not before come her way," the novels of Dickens, Trollope, and Austen, and the works of "many other writers hitherto unknown to her." Laura's experience at the mechanics' institute offers the narrator of *Candleford Green* an opportunity to challenge prevailing assumptions about the "booklessness of the poor": "But there was no dearth of books. After she left home, Laura never suffered in that way. Modern writers who speak of the booklessness of the poor at that time must mean books as possessions; there were always books to borrow."

Living in a Literary Community

For the working classes, living in the countryside meant not having easy access to inexpensive books and periodicals for most of the nineteenth century. In *Heatherley*, Laura moves from Candleford Green to take a new post office position in a country village that serves a distinctly literary clientele. So many famous writers and poets live in the area that a local hill is renamed "the Lesser Parnassus."[38] Thompson took such a job in Grayshott, a village in Hampshire that became the inspiration for the fictional Heatherley. Working behind the post office counter in Grayshott, Thompson (like her fictional counterpart, Laura) overheard conversations between the famous literary figures who came to buy stamps and send telegrams—men such as George Bernard Shaw, Sir Arthur Conan Doyle, Grant Allen, and Richard Le Gallienne. For an avid reader like Thompson, and her fictional counterpart, Laura, there was another advantage to living and working in a literary community. The local shops were well stocked with current books and periodicals. In *Heatherley,* "Madame Lillywhite's," a shop that caters to the sophisticated tastes of local writers, is located across the street from the post office where Laura works.[39] Madame Lillywhite, the proprietor, receives "frequent boxes from Mudie's" and stocks her library shelves with "modern books." Thanks to Madam Lillywhite, Laura finally gets "in touch with current literature."[40] She reads modern novels, poetry, and plays, as well as back numbers of sophisticated periodicals such as the *Nineteenth Century*, the *Athaneum,* and the *Quarterly Review.*

Periodicals

Periodicals played an increasingly important role in rural working-class communities during the last half of the nineteenth century. Since Laura's story begins in rural Oxfordshire in the 1880s, Thompson depicts communities that have already benefited from the rise of the periodical press. Because most working-class individuals did not read daily newspapers until the 1890s, weekly newspapers were an important part of working-class life.[41] In the hamlet of Lark Rise, the weekly newspapers that "came into every house, either by purchase or borrowing," became a vehicle for social change.[42] Even though some of these papers "were still written by educated men for the educated," the new ideas they contained "were slowly percolating" through this tiny hamlet. Previous generations had relied on the Bible as an unfailing guide and source of truth. Gradually, this reliance was being transferred to newspapers. In *Over to Candleford,* the narrator observes that, although many people no longer believed "every word in the Bible to be literally true," everyone believed in the newspapers. Any argument could be settled with "I seed it in the paper, so it must be true." With few exceptions, the periodicals that appear in the novels of *Lark Rise to Candleford* and in *Heatherley* are periodicals that were in actual circulation during the period in which each novel is set. In addition, these periodicals reflect the varied interests of the mass reading public of that time, from leftist politics and serialized fiction to news and family entertainment.

Political Weeklies

In the period between 1851 and 1900, apart from the *Illustrated London News*, the most popular weeklies "were all to the left of center politically."[43]

Like many of the working-class men of their time, the working men in *Lark Rise* prefer papers with a leftist political slant. In the hamlet of Lark Rise, the men read three of the most popular weeklies: the "*Weekly Despatch*" (*Weekly Dispatch*), "*Reynolds News*" (*Reynolds' Weekly News*), and "*Lloyd's News*" (*Lloyd's Weekly Newspaper*). Conservatives were deeply concerned about the political radicalism found in these weekly papers. In 1880 an unnamed critic in the *Quarterly Review* criticized these particular weeklies for "the violence and even brutality of their tone."[44] The *Weekly Dispatch*, this critic stated, had "very strong writing" and "somewhat gross personalities." In *Lloyd's Weekly*, "the staple of the leading article" was "discontent . . . with everything . . . which is not of the lowest workingman level." *Reynolds' Weekly Newspaper*, this critic asserted, was "even worse than *Lloyd's*."

Serialized Fiction and Novelettes

Serialized fiction weeklies or "novelettes" are the reading matter of choice for hamlet women in *Lark Rise*. The "comfortable, pink-cheeked" Mrs. Braby subscribes to two periodicals that were particularly popular among the working classes for their fiction: the *Family Herald* and *Bow Bells*.[45] Altick described the *Family Herald* as a sensational fiction weekly meant for the "indifferently educated."[46] It featured escapist fiction (mostly short fiction and serialized novels) about members of the British aristocracy. *Bow Bells* appealed to its female audience by combining serial fiction with needlework and dress patterns.[47] Even in a poor hamlet like Lark Rise, "there was always quite a library of them in circulation," and they "were handed round until the pages were thin and frayed with use."[48] Since these fiction weeklies only cost a penny, several hamlet women had their own subscriptions. Additional copies also "found their way" to Lark Rise from "neighbouring villages, or from daughters in service." As the narrator of *Lark Rise* notes, "novelettes" followed a specific formula: "The novelette of the 'eighties was a romantic love story, in which the poor governess always married the duke, or the lady of title the gamekeeper, who always turned out to be a duke or an earl in disguise. Midway through the story there had to be a description of a ball, at which the heroine in her simple white gown attracted all the men in the room; or the gamekeeper, commandeered to help serve, made love to the daughter of the house in the conservatory." When Laura meets Mrs. Braby on her way home from school, the talkative matron entertains her with a synopsis of *His Ice Queen*, a novelette that she is currently reading. In *Over to Candleford*, Laura's employer, Dorcas Lane, is one of the few women who does not read these fiction weeklies. A woman "in advance of her own day," Miss Lane takes the

Times to keep herself "well-informed of what was going on in the world, especially in the way of invention and scientific discovery."[49]

Weekly Miscellanies: Tit-Bits *and* Answers

Although a few of the tradesmen's daughters who become Laura's friends in *Candleford Green* have fathers who read the *Daily Telegraph,* the majority of Candleford Green residents were reading the popular miscellanies *Tit-Bits* and *Answers*. *Tit-Bits*, first published in 1880, was a penny paper composed of short excerpts from books, periodicals, and newspapers.[50] In the town of Candleford Green, *Tit-Bits* "was taken by almost every family, and the snippets of information culled from its pages were taken very seriously indeed."[51] The "Candleford Greenites" also took the "all-conquering weekly periodical called *Answers,*" a paper based on the *Tit-Bits* formula. According to Altick, *Tit-Bits* and *Answers* filled their pages with jokes, riddles, and excerpts—"nothing which required sustained attention on the part of their readers."[52] "The majority of younger people" in Candleford Green, Thompson writes, took great delight in reading these papers and finding out "how many months of his life a man spent shaving and a woman doing her hair."[53] They also loved to repeat the jokes found in the pages of these weeklies. The narrator notes that the title of *Tit-Bits* became a "catchword" for the unfamiliar. If someone expressed an unfamiliar taste or opinion he or she was likely to be told, "Don't try to be funny. We've read about you in Tit-Bits!" In *Serializing Fiction in the Victorian Press,* Graham Law notes that *Tit-Bits* also offered "a guinea a column" for contributions from its readers, "including letters to the 'Correspondence' page."[54] Although few readers responded to this general call for reader contributions, specific "prize fiction competitions" in *Tit-Bits* and other papers were very popular to the end of the nineteenth century. Thompson began her own writing career by entering such competitions in the *Lady's Companion.*

Local Papers, Trade Publications, and Religious Periodicals

In addition to the political weeklies favored by the men, the fiction weeklies favored by the women, and the weekly miscellanies favored by young and old alike, the residents of Lark Rise, Candleford town, and Candleford Green read a variety of trade publications, local papers, and religious periodicals. Laura's father, a stonemason, subscribes to the *Carpenter and Builder* (a trade publication) in addition to the "*Weekly Despatch.*"[55] In the hamlet of Lark Rise during the 1880s, "a few remained faithful to that fine old local newspaper, the *Bicester Herald.*" In *Candleford Green,* a local vicar is so famous for giving excellent sermons that a local paper, the fictional *Candleford News,* sends a reporter to record Mr. Delafield's sermon verbatim. Once the sermon is printed in the *Candleford News*, copies are "posted to sons and daughters in London, in the North of England, or out in the Colonies" to prove that Candleford Green was no longer a "poor little stick-in-the-mud spot."[56]

Many tradesmen's families in *Candleford Green* owned bound copies of periodicals that were particularly useful for Sunday afternoon reading: the *Quiver* and the *Sunday at Home*. The *Quiver*, a family magazine, was one of "eight monthly magazines and nearly fifty other serials" that the publishing firm of Cassells ran during the 1890s.[57] The *Sunday at Home,* published by the Religious Tract Society, was what Altick calls "typical village reading."[58] The local girls read another Religious Tract Society publication, the *Girls' Own Paper.* As the narrator of *Candleford Green* wryly comments, local girls used the *Girls' Own Paper* for their "public reading."[59] In secret, "the more daring and up to date" girls who "liked a thrill in their reading" hid the romantic novels of Ouida under their mattresses and read them in secret.

Reading as a Social Activity: Sewing Parties, Penny Readings, and Book Teas

A distinctive feature of hamlet, town, and village life in the novels of *Lark Rise to Candleford* and *Heatherley* is the presence of informal groups of working-class women who meet to discuss what they are reading, from novelettes to poetry. In a time before cheap books and periodicals or even public libraries appeared in the English countryside, these groups provided entertainment, conversation, and a bit of culture. Even in the poor hamlet of Lark Rise, there was a "genteel section of the community" that met while husbands were at work and children were at school.[60] These women, mostly under the age of forty, met in each other's homes to drink tea and discuss the latest fashion or the novelettes they were reading.

In *Candleford Green,* various social activities involve some form of literary entertainment, from sewing parties to penny readings. For sewing parties, village women met in each other's homes to sew while one woman read aloud. In sewing parties for the "better-to-do," the women drank tea and "sewed garments for the heathen or for the poor in cities."[61] Poor women also had sewing parties, but they sewed for their own families, using fabric "provided at under cost" by a ladies' committee.[62] The poor women did not drink tea. Penny readings were a favorite family activity in Candleford Green. Although "already out of date in most places," in Candleford Green the penny reading was "still going strong in the 'nineties." Entire families attended these public readings for an evening of entertainment and for "the excitement of going out after dark." The "star" of the penny readings in Candleford Green was old Mr. Greenwood. In his youth, Mr. Greenwood had heard Dickens "read his own works in public and aimed at reproducing in his own rendering the expression and mannerisms of the master."[63] Another favorite reader was Mrs. Cox, who "was said to be an American by birth." Mrs. Cox always read from *Uncle Remus* in a "plantation dialect."[64] Although the audience loved to hear Mr. Greenwood and Mrs. Cox read passages from Dickens and from *Uncle Remus*, they had no interest in reading these books for themselves, even when copies were available in the parish library. This audience wanted to be entertained. As the narrator comments, they were "a public ready-made for the wireless and the cinema."[65]

In *Heatherley*, when Laura takes a post office position in a village popular with famous writers, she encounters a seemingly more sophisticated set of girls who invite her to a "book tea."[66] Those invited to the book tea were instructed "to wear or to bear something signifying a book title." Although "nobody guessed the meaning of half the symbols," a few were easier to guess at: "One girl carried a small globe and that was plainly *The Wide Wide World*; another kissed and fondled a flaxen-haired doll, and those who had recently read the book exclaimed '*My Little Sweetheart*'. *Great Expectations* was represented by the facial expression of a guest who, on entering the room, pointed to the already laid tea-table and mimed pleasurable anticipation, then turned a little sulky when someone suggested *A Lunatic at Large*." The idea of a book tea had been suggested by an article in a "women's paper" that also suggested several "bookish games." One of the games played at this book tea began with the questions, "Do you prefer Dickens or Thackeray? Tennyson or Browning?"[67] However, the questions soon degenerated into "White meat or brown? Apples or pears?" In reality, these girls were not sophisticated readers. They lived in homes "where cookery books were the favourite reading," and they preferred reading sentimental fiction, such as *My Little Sweetheart* and *The Wide Wide World,* or crime fiction, such as *A Lunatic at Large* (1893) by J. Storer Clouston.[68] As the narrator comments, "The creature comforts were maybe superior in quality to the intellectual entertainment" at this particular book tea.[69]

Public Readings, Performances, and Public Lectures

In *Heatherley,* Thompson describes the variety of readings, performances, and lectures held in a local parish hall before the advent of the cinema, the wireless, and the television. Such activities are examples of what Jonathan Rose terms the working-class passion for "mutual education."[70] One advantage of living in a rural village frequented by literary figures was that public readings were sometimes given by authors reading from their own works. Laura attends one of these readings to hear the Scottish author Ian McLauren read from *Beside the Bonny Briar Bush* (1894). Another advantage of living in Heatherley was that popular entertainers were sometimes persuaded to leave London to perform in the local parish hall. One evening the parish hall hosted a magic act that was "all the rage in London at that time."[71] "The famous Cappers" entertained the audience by reading "everyone's most secret thoughts" and finding lost articles.[72] Some of the programs at the parish hall were more high culture than popular culture. Laura's favorite program was a performance of handbell ringing, Elizabethan part songs, and songs from the plays of Shakespeare performed by actors in Elizabethan dress.

The parish hall also hosted public lectures on a wide variety of topics, from spiritualism and vegetarianism to "unrest in the Balkans" and the role of women.[73] Laura hears George Bernard Shaw lecture on socialism several times, and she is surprised to find that Shaw was "freely interrupted and questioned by his audience, to which at that time the initials G. B. S. had no special significance."[74] In contrast to the wide variety of programs presented at the parish hall are the private Sunday afternoon classes given in Mrs. Camden's home. Laura does not attend these classes, but her friend and co-worker, Alma Stedman, is one of a select group of young women invited to attend. Mrs. Camden, intent on forming "the taste" of the girls, dictates which books and poems are worthy of their attention. [75] Unlike Laura, who enjoys the thrill of discovering that a book or poem she loves is an "acknowledged masterpiece," Alma relies on the opinions of Mrs. Camden, rather than on "her own taste and judgment." Unfortunately for Alma, the narrator comments, Mrs. Camden's method "had worked very well."

The Oral Tradition in Hamlet and Village

What the residents of the fictional Lark Rise, Candleford, Candleford Green, and Heatherley may have lacked in books, periodicals, and other reading material was supplied by a rich and diverse oral tradition. The older residents told stories about bygone days, and younger adults told stories about themselves and their families. Gossip was another unfailing source of exciting stories. Laura's imagination was fed by all of these community stories as well as by the stories her father and mother told her. In an era before the radio, the movies, and television were staples of daily life, ghost stories, ballads, "men's stories," conversion stories, and sermons often provided entertainment and excitement. In addition to stories, there was a wealth of rhymes, sayings, and proverbs, as well as witticisms and wordplay.

Stories about the Past

In *Lark Rise*, "older people" are a particularly valuable source of stories about the past.[76] For Laura, "the old people were the most interesting of all, for they told her about the old times and could sing old songs and remember old customs."[77] In all four novels, Laura gravitates towards this older generation, not only to hear their stories but also because old people like and trust her. This is a particularly gratifying experience for Laura, who often feels unaccepted and unliked. The narrator of *Lark Rise* defends the old men and women of the hamlet, who were often dismissed as illiterate and ignorant: "Statistics of illiteracy of that period are often misleading, for many who could read and write sufficiently for their own humble needs would modestly disclaim any pretensions to being what they called 'scholards.'" [78] Despite their lack of formal education, the narrator informs us, many of these older people "could yet read a little," certainly enough to read one-syllable words in the Bible or in the newspapers. For Laura, the special wisdom of this older generation really lay in its life experience and in its link with a disappearing way of life.

In *Lark Rise*, Thompson provides her most extensive treatment of the elderly, devoting an entire chapter to the older residents of the hamlet. In "Survivals," two couples are the primary representatives of this older generation. Sally and Dick, the first couple, live in a "long, low, thatched cottage with diamond-paned windows."[79] They are described as "survivals from the earliest hamlet days" who, due to "their hard work and self-denial," were living a more comfortable life than other old people in the hamlet.[80] Sally and Dick had married and lived together in Lark Rise for over sixty years. Sally "had many tales to tell of the fun they had had carting their bit of hay or hunting for eggs in the loft."[81] At the age of twelve, Laura becomes "their little woman of business" by "writing letters to seedsmen" and performing other tasks on their behalf.[82] This close relationship allows Laura to learn "a great deal about the past life in the hamlet."

The second couple, Queenie and Twister Macey, represent "another phase" of hamlet history that "had also ended and been forgotten by most people."[83] Queenie, "a little, wrinkled, yellow-faced old woman in a sunbonnet," was the hamlet lacemaker and beekeeper. Her husband, Twister, was known as "a slack-twisted sort o' chap" who was not above posing as the local half-wit "for the sake of a pint of beer."[84] A tale about Queenie and her husband that circulated in the hamlet attested to Queenie's ability to manage her husband. It was said that Queenie had cured her husband of wife-beating by baking his belt in a pie and serving it to him for dinner. When Twister died, Queenie took the story of his death to her bees. She "tapped on the roof of each hive," telling the bees: "*Bees, bees, your master's dead an' now you must work for your missis.*"[85]

Queenie's lacemaking was a rich source of stories for the hamlet children, for "every bobbin weighted with its bunch of bright beads" had "its own story."[86] One blue bunch of beads had been part of a necklace belonging to Queenie's sister who had died at the age of five. A black bunch had been found "in a work-box belonging to a woman who was reputed to have been a witch." The cottage industry of lacemaking provided another source of stories. Queenie was a survival from the days when many girls were "brought up to the pillow" and, as Queenie explained, gathered with the older women of the hamlet for a day of lacemaking, "gossiping, singing old songs, and telling old tales."[87] Queenie's stories often harkened back to a more prosperous time in the hamlet. On the theme of "Them wer' the days!" Queenie would tell the children about "the bargains she had bought with her earnings." These bargains ranged from "Good brown calico" to "rag dolls and ginger-bread for the 'little 'uns'" and "snuff for the old grannies." The children of Lark Rise came to know these stories "by heart."[88]

In "Survivals," there is also a rather unflattering portrait of another old woman: Laura's maternal grandmother, Hannah. Hannah's stories about the past are strictly romantic stories about herself. She often tells Laura of the time in her youth when her hair "had reached down to her knees, like a great yellow cape."[89] Once known as the "Belle of Hornton," she particularly likes to tell her tale of dancing with a young lord at his coming-of-age party. According to old Hannah, he "had passed over his own friends and the daughters of his tenants in favour of one who was but a gamekeeper's daughter." The young lord had "whispered in her ear that she was the prettiest girl in the county," a compliment she still cherished as a "thin, frail old woman."

The old also figure briefly in *Over to Candleford* and *Candleford Green,* although none attain the prominence of Sally and Dick or Queenie and Twister as sources of stories about the past. However, in *Heatherley* Laura meets Mr. Foreshaw, an elderly gentleman with a reputation for being a "woman-hater," who tells her of his adventures as a big-game hunter in British and Portuguese East Africa.[90] Laura, now a postal clerk and still "exceptionally fond of aged people," becomes Mr. Foreshaw's friend after delivering a telegram to his bungalow after hours. They spend many hours together, surrounded by Mr. Foreshaw's books and exotic trophies. Since "almost every article in his large collection had a story," Mr. Foreshaw regales Laura with tales of adventure such as escaping from a rampaging elephant, being attacked by a pack of wild dogs, and stumbling across an elephant cemetery.[91] His stories are also flavored with the mystery and menace of colonial cultures, such as the time when he saw "the Hindoo kill, pluck and roast a chicken and burn the feathers, then bring it back to life again."[92] As in the previous novels, Laura appreciates the attention she receives from this old man, feeling more comfortable with him than with her peers. Mr. Foreshaw treats her with courtesy and attention, a delightful experience for Laura, "unused as she was to such consideration."[93] Laura also likes Mr. Foreshaw for his "originality, his raciness, his immense store of experience and his biting wit."

Laura realizes later that, although Mr. Foreshaw "would talk freely about his thirty years of big-game hunting in Africa," he never told her anything about his personal life before or after his African adventures.[94] Mr. Foreshaw also had nothing to say about the history of Heatherley and its environs. Unlike the hamlet of Lark Rise or the villages of Candleford and Candleford Green, Heatherley was not a village in the traditional sense. Rather, it was "a settlement of recent growth" that attracted visitors with its health-giving "moorland air."[95] Moreover, Mr. Foreshaw had only moved to Heatherley in "extreme old age" and preferred living alone rather than mingling with the locals.[96]

Personal Stories

Just as the old people told stories about the past, younger adults in hamlet, town, and village told stories about themselves and their families. For country people, whose lives were defined by poverty and hard work, these stories, with their hints of drama and romance, were a pleasant diversion. The stories also served as an outlet for individuals who wished to distinguish themselves from the common herd. In a chapter of *Lark Rise* entitled "A Bit of a Tell," Patty, Gertie, and Mrs. Merton are three women whose personal stories not only distinguish them from the other women of the hamlet but also create a bit of drama. Patty Wardup comes to the hamlet to be a housekeeper after living in a workhouse. Although in her forties and "evidently belonging to a slightly higher stratum of society," she says nothing about her past or the period she spent living in the workhouse.[97] After she marries a younger man and moves her personal possessions into her new home, her feather bed, leather-covered couch with matching chairs, and stuffed owl tell their own story. These items prove that Patty *is* a superior sort of person, one who had once lived a more prosperous life. Patty's silence about her past is finally explained when local residents observe that Patty is "fond of her glass of stout." It is only when Patty invites the local children in to see her "her stuffed owl and other treasures" that she talks about her "better times" as the wife of a publican, always ending these talks with, "Yes, I've seen better times, but I've never seen a better husband than Amos."[98]

Unlike Patty, Gertie is a young married woman who delights in regaling the women of Lark Rise with stories about her past. She had been a housemaid in a country house before marrying "her kind, honest great cart-horse of a husband."[99] Gertie has "romantic ideas," and her stories are full of past romantic conquests, such as the time "Mr. Pratt, the butler, had danced with her four times at the servant's ball." However, Patty's stories are told at the expense of her husband. Patty characterizes her husband as a "great gowk" who was perpetually jealous of his future wife's many admirers during their courtship. Over time, Gertie forgets "her past triumphs" and transfers her romantic ideas to her children.[100] When Laura meets Gertie years later, she is a "red and lumpy" older woman who speaks of her daughter's marriage to a stable boy as "a regular romance in real life."

Mrs. Merton is another local woman who affects a romantic air. The stories Mrs. Merton tells about her life are all tinged with suffering and melancholy. Mrs. Merton's personal afflictions are no different from those of her neighbors. She had lost a child in infancy, her father had died of old age, and the family pig had died of swine fever. However, unlike the other women in Lark Rise, Mrs. Merton cultivates a tragic persona based on these events, often ending her ruminations with, "I've supped sorrow with a spoon and sorrow will always be my lot."[101] Perpetually dressed in black, Mrs. Merton "might have sat for a picture as the Tragic Muse"—at least in the eyes of a young girl like Laura. Ironically, in old age Mrs. Merton does become "the tragic figure she had looked when young." She is already a widow when she loses her only son and two grandsons during Word War I.

In *Over to Candleford*, in a chapter entitled "Uncle Tom's Queer Fish," Laura encounters a commercial traveler who constructs a dramatic tale out of his marital discontent. Sitting in her Uncle Tom's workshop, Laura observes Uncle Tom listening patiently as the young man "launched on a long story of how he had that very morning taken up his wife's breakfast to her in bed."[102] But when the young man begins to complain, "Of all the spiteful, contrary cats . . . ," Uncle Tom interrupts his story to chide him for speaking so disrespectfully of his wife.[103] Uncle Tom supplies the missing side of the young man's story. His new wife was lonely, and she was finding marriage to a commercial traveler more difficult than she had expected. Uncle Tom tells the young man to "bite on it" when he is tempted to complain about his marriage. For Uncle Tom, "most married folks have their little upsets" and a husband should not construct a dramatic tale from them.

In *Heatherley*, the wife of Laura's employer, the tragic Mrs. Hertford, tells Laura the story of her engagement and marriage to George Hertford. The only romance in this story concerns George's previous relationship with a girl named Letty. As Laura listens to Mrs. Hertford tell the story of Letty and George's love affair, she recognizes it as the type of story "beloved of minor Victorian novelists."[104] It contained all the conventional ingredients of "a father's pride, an obedient daughter's broken heart, and the faithfulness of a lover." Sadly, Mrs. Hertford's account of George's proposal and their subsequent marriage lacks all the romance and drama of George and Letty's love story. As Mrs. Hertford tells Laura, George had proposed to her by saying, "I'll marry you if you will have me, but my heart is buried in poor Letty's grave."[105] In time, Mrs. Hertford's life story ends even more tragically than Letty's. She is eventually murdered by her criminally insane husband as she leans over a tub, bathing her new baby.

Family History

In an effort to rise above the poverty and tedium of their daily lives, people told stories about their family history that proved their families had once held a higher position in society. In *Over to Candleford,* a favorite story in Laura's family centers on "Granny's Golden Footstool."[106] In this story Laura's paternal grandmother had been a "lady by birth" who had run away to marry her sweetheart.[107] This story about Laura's paternal grandparents featured the grandfather handing his wife into a carriage, placing "a box containing a thousand pounds in gold at her feet, saying: 'It's not every lady who can ride in her own carriage with a golden footstool.'"[108] The thousand pounds had been the purchase money for a public house and livery stables the grandparents had once owned in Oxford. Since this business had failed and the money was long gone, family members could only "try to imagine what so much gold together must have looked like and to plan what they would do with such a sum if they had it now."[109] Another of Laura's family stories involved one of her mother's uncles who "shut his father in a box" and ran away to look for gold in Australia. This story set the family to wondering if the long-dead uncle had ever found gold and if there might be an unclaimed fortune waiting for them all. As the narrator comments, "Almost every family in the hamlet prided itself upon some family tradition which . . . raised it above the common mass of the wholly uninteresting." Such family stories would inflate the cottage a great uncle had owned to "a whole row of cottages" or support a claim to noble blood, "even if it came illegitimately." Family stories could also support a family's dreams for its children. When Laura's mother imagines Edmund and Laura's future, she pictures Edmund as a carpenter's apprentice and Laura as the head nursemaid in an imaginary "good family" that would love her and take care of her for life.[110] The scenario that Edmund and Laura imagine is far simpler. They would have houses of their own "in which they could do as they liked."[111]

Gossip

Gossip is a perennial feature of community life and plays a featured role in the novels of *Lark Rise to Candleford.* In *Lark Rise*, gossip is seen as both a source of stories and an outlet for lonely characters like Mrs. Mullins and Mrs. Andrews. Mrs. Mullins was the most dreaded of gossips because she was a "melancholy bore."[112] She "talked no scandal" but "just babbled on, about the weather, or her sons' last letters, or her pig, or something she had read in the Sunday newspaper." She was known as a "standing gossip," after the hamlet saying: "Standing gossipers stay longest." Mrs. Mullins's social calls were dreaded because she "visited every cottage in turn" on the pretense of asking the time or borrowing some small item. Once over the cottage threshold, she would stand "just inside the door, twisting her door-key and talking." Another hamlet gossip, and an even greater talker, was Mrs. Andrews. Like Mrs. Mullins, she had no family at home and too much time on her hands. However, Mrs. Andrews was a more entertaining gossip than Mrs. Mullins. If there was no interesting news or story to tell, Mrs. Andrews was "quite capable of inventing something." She would "take up some stray, unimportant fact, blow it up like a balloon, tie it neatly with circumstantial detail and present it to her listener, ready to be launched on the air of the hamlet."[113] Even though local women knew that most of Mrs. Andrews's gossip was based on lies, they still enjoyed talking with her because "it made a bit of a change" in a hamlet "without cinemas or wireless and with very little reading matter."[114]

In the opening chapter of *Over to Candleford,* gossip is presented as a relief from the tedium of daily life in a hamlet where "nothing of outside importance ever happened."[115] In a community with few books and before the advent of film, "many a satisfying little drama" was constructed out of complications in the lives of local residents. The chapter entitled "A Bit of a Tell" is devoted to the social life of the hamlet women, including their sharing of news and gossip. For the sake of a "tell" (the local term for gossip), women would burst into each other's homes "to relate some breathless item of news" or "spend the afternoon shouting it across gardens or from doorsteps."[116] Unlike Mrs. Andrews of *Lark Rise*, Rachel is a gossip worth hearing. She has the reputation for knowing everything that is happening in the hamlet, and she is even willing to approach the subject of the gossip to make sure she has her facts straight. When women gathered for "a bit of a tell" they were careful to drop their voices or send children from the room if the stories became too racy. The lives of the local gentry sometimes provided an exciting source of such racy stories, particularly stories about the behavior of the "wild young devils" in these families.[117] One story claimed that one of these young men had been responsible for "lurid orgies" in his ancestral home. It was also reported that a saintly old curate was kicked down a flight of stairs when he went "to admonish the young spark."

When Laura and Edmund go to Candleford and visit their Aunt Ann, they are sometimes drawn into the kitchen by Bertha, the kitchenmaid. Bertha, normally silent around adults, is quite talkative around children. She is eager to gossip about everything, including "children's squabbles, children's tea parties and children's holidays."[118] Bertha is simple and impulsive, and despite her "spreading figure and greying hair" she is more child than adult.[119] She often begs her audience to never repeat a bit of gossip she has impulsively told them. Swearing her to secrecy, Bertha one day tells Laura that Elsie, Bertha's pretty young sister, is actually her own child. Bertha tells Laura the story of how she had "made a fool of herself with a soldier when she was thirty" and how she had given birth to her child in a workhouse.[120] Laura finds this story a burden until she discovers that Bertha was in the habit of sharing this particular secret on a regular basis. Bertha was "so proud of 'our young Elsie' she must tell somebody or burst."

In *Candleford Green*, gossip is once again presented as a source of entertainment at a time when the cinema "had yet to be invented" and countrywomen "read little."[121] As seen in *Lark Rise* and *Over to Candleford*, there were gossips who "could take some trifling event and so expand, distort, and embroider it" that it would bear no "resemblance to the facts." The narrator comments that these stories usually did no great harm. However, in one case, gossip caused needless suffering for a young girl in service who had come home to recuperate after an illness. After her arrival, a story circulated that the girl had really come home because she was pregnant; the story even named her seducer. As the girl was "modest" and "sensitive" and in a "weak condition" she suffered greatly when she heard this gossip.[122] This type of malicious story, the narrator assures the reader, was the product of "a few of the evil minded people such as may always be found in any place."

Bedtime Stories

Another source of stories in Laura's childhood were her mother's bedtime stories. Although her father would occasionally contribute a story about his family or stories about Roman warriors, Laura's mother was a born storyteller. Included in her repertoire were fairy stories, animal stories, and "stories of good and bad children" with conventional endings.[123]

Most of her mother's stories came from her own imagination; these were the stories that Laura, her brothers, and her sisters liked best. One of Laura's favorites was about a young girl who found a passage to an underground palace "in which all the furniture and hangings were pale blue and silver."[124] This room "shone with a kind of moonlight radiance" in Laura's imagination, long after she had forgotten the details of the story. Some of her mother's stories were "serial stories" that lasted for weeks or months, especially when her children did not want the story to end. Sometimes Laura's mother sang popular ballads that contained stories of "fair maidens who pined and faded for love."[125] When Laura grows older, she loves to see how her younger brothers and sisters react to stories her mother had told *her* as a child, and she sometimes corrects her mother "when her memory went astray."[126]

Ballads, Ghost Stories, Men's Tales, and Conversion Stories

Ballads, ghost stories, "men's stories," and even conversion stories told in Methodist chapels provided another source of entertainment for the rural communities Thompson describes in her novels. Ballads were a source of musical entertainment as well as a source of stories. In *Lark Rise*, men gathered to drink, discuss politics, and sing ballads in the taproom of the local inn, the Wagon and Horses. A variety of ballads were sung, depending on the age and taste of the singer. The middle-aged men were "inclined more to long and usually mournful stories in verse, of thwarted lovers, children buried in snowdrifts, dead maidens, and motherless homes."[127] In the chapter entitled "At the Wagon and Horses," Thompson documents some of these ballads with verse excerpts. Two of the ballads that tell stories about knights and young maidens are quoted at length; there are seven verses of "Lord Lovell Stood" and eleven full verses of "Outlandish Knight" in this chapter.

Stories about the supernatural were a thrilling source of entertainment in country villages. In *Lark Rise*, the men who drank at the Wagon and Horses also enjoyed telling ghost stories. "With curdling blood and creeping spine," children crouched outside the door to hear tales about the "turnpike ghost" or "the lady dressed in white." [128] The lady in white was reported to ride a white horse over the bridge at midnight, "minus her head." The men also told tales about dead relatives who came back "to warn, counsel, or accuse."[129] In another local tale, the people of the hamlet had once seen "a regiment of soldiers marching in the sky, all complete with drum and fife band." This unusual occurrence was believed to be the "freak reflection" of a regiment that had been marching on a nearby road at the same time. [130] A real-life horror story, the exploits of Jack the Ripper, "furnished other tales of dread."[131]

In *Over to Candleford*, the people of Lark Rise told "ghost stories and stories of witchcraft" that "lingered and were half believed."[132] There were tales of Dickie Bracknell, who was buried at the crossroads "with a stake through his entrails." There was also a local pool known as "the beast's pond." It "was said to be bottomless and haunted by a monster." An elder tree beside a brook was rumored to "bleed human blood when cut." In the popular imagination, this tree was a witch who had transformed herself while being chased by local men brandishing pitchforks. Laura tells a ghost story of her own after she imagines seeing something move in her bedroom closet. When closely questioned, she fabricates a description of the "ghost" until her mother reprimands her for "fibbing."[133]

In *Candleford Green*, the narrator comments that some of the "more simple people" may have believed ghost stories were true, but most people enjoyed them "for the sake of a thrill, as we now enjoy reading mystery stories."[134] Laura's mother is the only person Laura knows who had "an open mind on the subject of the supernatural." Some of the stories her mother had heard had "almost convinced her that there *was* something outside the range of ordinary earthly life."[135] One of her mother's family stories seemed to suggest a supernatural event. A dying relative saw a vision of unexpected visitors stopping to pick blackberries. When the visitors arrived with the blackberries, her vision was confirmed. As the narrator notes, by the beginning of the twentieth century, previously well-known ghost stories started to disappear. In *Heatherley*, the local story of a "dead horseman" had survived for eighty to ninety years "only in man's memory."[136] After World War I, many of these old ghost stories were forgotten.

Some of the stories told in the hamlet of Lark Rise were intended only for a small and select audience. In *Lark Rise*, agricultural workers sometimes told "men's tales" as they stopped their work in the fields to eat lunch under the shadow of a hedge or hayrick.[137] These stories about the men's sexual exploits were "kept strictly to the fields and never repeated elsewhere."Taken together, the narrator says, they formed a "rustic Decameron" that was rumored to be "extremely indecent." Ironically, Methodist services sometimes provided thrilling or scandalous stories. When a church member would "stand up to testify," it was always possible that he/she would reveal the "exciting transgressions" that were the "conventional prelude" to a conversion story.[138]

Rhymes, Sayings, and Wordplay

Hamlet and village life was also enriched by various rhymes, popular verse, local sayings, and proverbs. One chapter of *Lark Rise* is devoted to documenting the various games children played in the 1880s, including the game rhymes and songs. In "Country Playtime," Thompson describes how girls gathered in open areas and "went through the game movements" and sang or chanted the rhymes "as their mothers and grandmothers had done before them."[139] These rhymes "had been handed down for a time long before living memory," yet "no one inquired the meaning of the words of the game rhymes."[140] Some of these game rhymes, such as "Poor Mary Is A-Weeping" and "Waly Waly Wallflower," told melancholy tales of weeping or dying maidens. Other game rhymes alluded to historical figures, such as "Queen Ann" and "Queen Caroline."[141] An inquisitive and thoughtful girl like Laura would puzzle out the meanings of the rhymes or speculate about the historical origins of the enigmatic stories they told. Many of the game movements, rhymes, and songs that Thompson describes in "Country Playtime" were also collected and published by Alice Bertha Gomme in her two-volume *Traditional Games of England, Scotland and Ireland* (1894, 1898). Iona and Peter Opie's *The Singing Game* (1985) also contains variants of the games Thompson describes.

Particular rhymes and songs were associated with holidays or special events, such as May Day, Guy Fawkes Day, and Harvest Home. Thompson devotes a chapter in *Lark Rise* to documenting May Day customs and May Day songs. Particular songs were sung as the children took the May garland from door to door. The words of songs such as "All hail gentle spring" were poetic, containing images of flowers, bees, and fairies.[142] In *Lark Rise,* the boys of the hamlet go door to door to collect fagots for the Guy Fawkes Day bonfire, chanting the verse beginning, "Remember, remember, the fifth of November."[143] For the celebration of Harvest Home, men and boys returning from the fields would shout, "Harvest home! Harvest home!/ Merry, merry, merry harvest home!"[144] In *Candleford Green,* agricultural workers are entertained by an elderly haymaker named Mr. Beer who recites a poem about the "adventures of an Oxfordshire man on a trip to London."[145] This performance, "half-song, half-recitation," was a yearly feature of the supper held after haymaking. In *Over to Candleford,* the ritual that girls perform to find a sweetheart is associated with its own verse. An "ash leaf with nine leaflets" was placed "in the seeker's bosom" while she recited a verse that began, "Here's an ash leaf with nine leaves on / Take it and press it to your heart / And the first chap you meet'll be your sweetheart."[146] There were even verses recited about more mundane subjects, such as lightning. During a thunderstorm, someone might quote a verse that began, "Under oak there comes a stroke."[147] In *Candleford Green*, local boys had composed a rhyme about the collapse of a merry-go-round. This rhyme was still being recited fifty years later, although few villagers actually remembered the incident.

Some rhymes or verses were used to make fun of an unpopular person or group. In *Lark Rise,* a children's bedtime prayer that begins "Matthew, Mark, Luke and John / Bless the bed where I lie on" is a sweet religious verse, especially when juxtaposed with the rhyme shouted at local Catholics on their way to Mass:

O dear Father, I've come to confess.
Well, my child, and what have you done?
O dear Father, I've killed the cat.
Well, my child, and what about that?
O dear Father, what shall I do?
You kiss me and I'll kiss you.[148]

Children from rival towns sometimes shouted versified insults at each other. One of these began:

Old Hardwick skags!
Come to Fordlow to pick up rags
To mend their mothers' pudding-bags,
Yah! Yah! [149]

In *Candleford Green*, small boys also shouted insults at the local policemen:

There goes the bobby with his black shiny hat
And his belly full of fat
And a pancake tied to his nose. [150]

Some popular verse provided mild social commentary. There is a verse in *Candleford Green* about women riding bicycles:

Mother's out upon her bike, enjoying of the fun
Sister and her beau have gone to take a little run.
The housemaid and the cook are both a-riding on their wheels;
And Daddy's in the kitchen a-cooking of the meals.[151]

Sayings and proverbs also played a special role in the lives of country people, serving as homespun expressions of local wisdom. In *Lark Rise*, nonchurchgoers rely on sayings and proverbs for moral guidance. Such "homely precepts" as "Pay your way and fear nobody" and "Tell the truth and shame the devil" are considered words to live by.[152] The desire to have a bit of fun resulted in a popular form of wordplay: *capping* sayings and proverbs. In *Over to Candleford*, popular sayings such as "Two heads be better n'r one" came with humorous rejoinders such as "That's why fools get married."[153] In *Heatherley,* another form of wordplay is fashionable at the turn of the century: *punning*. "All who could articulate punned away merrily," from servant girls and music hall stars to "learned doctors and university dons."[154] Among the young women Laura knew, "puns dropped as profusely as gold, diamonds, and pearls dripped from the lips of the girl in the fairy tale." "But," as the narrator comments, "fashions in wit, like fashions in dress, can never survive extreme popularity, and at the turn of the century the pun had become too cheap to last much longer in favour." Perhaps the punster's use of words was too facile and superficial for a serious reader and autodidact like Thompson and Laura.

Conclusion

Like many working-class novelists of the 1930s and 1940s whom Gustav Klaus describes in *The Literature of Labour*, Thompson created the narrative of *Lark Rise, Over to Candleford, Candleford Green*, and *Heatherley* by drawing deeply from her own life experience. Incorporating the details of daily life in the working-class communities she described allowed Thompson to both document a particular way of life and to represent her own social class. Like the working-class autobiographers whom John Burnett, David Vincent, and David Mayall describe in their introduction to *The Autobiography of the Working Class*, Thompson also used her novels to "describe often in passionate detail" her "pursuit of knowledge" and the books that "had transformed [her] mental world."[155] However, in the novels of *Lark Rise to Candleford* and *Heatherley,* Thompson moved beyond the conventions of the working-class novel and the working-class autobiography. Her careful documentation of the reading habits of *other* working-class people and her detailed descriptions of the oral traditions that sustained their communities argue that, despite popular stereotypes, people living in poor agricultural communities did indeed have an intellectual and cultural life. Although social class, poverty, and geography had severely limited their educational opportunities and access to reading material, poor country people enjoyed a lively and creative literary culture of their own. Thompson's use of detail in describing the books and periodicals that country people read, the stories they told, and the rhymes, sayings, and proverbs they repeated form a part of Thompson's larger argument that there is dignity and significance in the lives of the poor.

6
Flora Thompson Revalued

For over sixty years, Flora Thompson's literary reputation has been based on *Lark Rise to Candleford*, a trilogy that is still perceived as the author's autobiography and only significant work. Thompson is deservedly praised for *Lark Rise to Candleford*. Despite the fact that the trilogy has been enshrined as the author's autobiography, critics, biographers, and scholars have recognized that it resists simple classification. A true estimation of the trilogy will be possible only if *Lark Rise*, *Over to Candleford*, *Candleford Green*, and the posthumously published *Heatherley*, are treated equally in future studies. Publishing all four books in one volume would also correct the perception that *Heatherley* is an inferior sequel to *Candleford Green*. To fully appreciate Thompson's achievement, one must also view the trilogy within a larger context, acknowledging that it combines elements of various fiction and nonfiction genres and subgenres. Studying these books as novels provides one new way to discuss the trilogy. Exploring the connections between *Lark Rise to Candleford* and the genres of working-class writing and literary autobiography provides another.

Between 1918 and 1938, many novels, autobiographies, documentaries, and short stories by working-class writers were published in the mainstream press as well as in liberal, left-wing journals.[1] In *Rewriting English: Cultural Politics of Gender and Class*, authors Janet Batsleer, Tony Davies, Rebecca O'Rourke, and Chris Weedon explore the "cultural-political context of working-class writing" in the 1930s, the very period in which Flora Thompson wrote and published *Lark Rise*. As the authors note, during the interwar period, "working-class writing" commonly referred to texts written by men "from an industrial working-class background."[2] Working-class women, constrained by "the dual role of wage-earner and housewife-mother," typically published short pieces in journals.[3] Working-class fiction published between the wars was predominantly realistic. "It was assumed," the authors note, that "the realistic representation" of working people's poverty and suffering was "in itself a political statement."[4] "Most working-class writing" of this period also had a "marked regional character, drawing on the history and social conditions" of a work's setting.[5] Another common feature of this genre was an omniscient narrator that "silently" imposed a point of view and offered evaluative comments based on a particular set of values or a political perspective.

Although *Lark Rise*, *Over to Candleford*, *Candleford Green*, and *Heatherley* portray the working classes in a rural rather than an industrial or urban setting, these novels do share some of the characteristics of working-class fiction identified in *Rewriting English*. All four books focus on the lives of working-class people in specific rural communities, portraying their everyday life through the use of realistic detail. The overt narrator in these novels also functions like the omniscient narrator found in working-class fiction, although Thompson's narrator does not impose an overtly political set of values in her texts.

Since Thompson was born into the working classes and her trilogy has always been classified as an autobiography, it would seem reasonable to classify *Lark Rise to Candleford* as a working-class autobiography. However, the trilogy differs in significant respects from working-class autobiographies of the 1920s and 1930s. This subgenre was dominated by male writers who wrote "militant self-portraits" of their political development or rise from humble working-class origins.[6] *Lark Rise*, *Over to Candleford*, *Candleford Green*, and *Heatherley* actually have more in common with the working-class autobiographies written by Victorian women that Julia Swindells describes in *Victorian Writing and Working Women*. Although Thompson uses a third-person narrator to write about Laura in these novels, she describes Laura's experience in much the same way that Victorian working-class women described their own lives. For example, Laura reflects on her father's occupation and on her family's social class. She also remarks on the social and educational limitations imposed on her by her social status.[7] Like the working-class autobiographers that Swindells describes, Laura's "interest in reading is part of a lifelong commitment, initiated in childhood," that she must sometimes pursue in secret to avoid criticism.[8] Despite the poor quality of her formal education, Laura thirsts for knowledge and perceives the pursuit of knowledge as a form of "spiritual and intellectual self-advancement." Her aspirations differentiate her from her peers, leading her to experience a "class otherness." And, like the working-class women in Swindells's study, Laura expresses a desire to become a writer, despite knowing that her social class and inadequate education would make it impossible for her to achieve professional literary status.[9]

During the 1930s, the new technologies of photography, film, and radio gave rise to a new cultural form: the documentary.[10] "At the heart of documentarism," notes H. Gustav Klaus, stood "the poor, the damaged, the inconspicuous and the ordinary."[11] This genre became so "active" during the 1930s that it "spread and became rooted" in "diverse cultural forms," from film, photography, and Mass Observation to works such as George Orwell's *Road to Wigan Pier* (1937).[12] The documentary of the 1930s focused primarily on contemporary social problems such as unemployment, housing, and slum life, in "hope that public exposure of these issues [would] pave the way for processes of improvement."[13] Documentarism was also seen in novels, such as John Sommerfield's *May Day* (1936). In this novel, Sommerfield described two days in London across all ranks of society as people prepare for May Day celebrations.[14] *May Day* was not focused on "the inner lives and destinies of a handful of characters," Klaus comments, but on a "cross-section of the London population," particularly on those in the working classes. In *Lark Rise*, Thompson also documents the life of the working classes and exposes various social problems that plagued late Victorian rural society. However, because it represented late nineteenth-century society rather than twentieth-century urban or industrial society, *Lark Rise* did not have the same political value as contemporary accounts of working-class life published during the 1930s.

Since Thompson's four novels about Laura have continued to be classified by her publishers as works of autobiography, it is not difficult to find an autobiographical approach to *Lark Rise to Candleford* and *Heatherley*. In essence, much of what has been written about Thompson by Margaret Lane, Gillian Lindsay, John Owen Smith, and Christine Bloxham has advanced the identification of autobiographical content in these books. However, the literary autobiography described by Linda H. Peterson in *Traditions of Victorian Women's Autobiography* (1999) might offer an additional autobiographical approach. In *Lark Rise to Candleford* and *Heatherley*, Thompson portrays Laura (and, arguably, herself) as a young girl whose identification with the "life of the mind" and "passion for books" are early signs of her eventual literary career.[15] Such elements are found, as Peterson notes, in the autobiographical writings of Victorian writers such as Felicia Hemans, Harriet Martineau, and George Eliot. The possibility of approaching *Lark Rise to Candleford* and *Heatherley* as works of literary autobiography also suggests that these works, if approached as works of fiction, could also be studied as *künstlerromane*.

In "The Regional Novel: Themes for Interdisciplinary Research," K. D. M. Snell offers a solution to the problems encountered in studying writing about the English countryside, arguing persuasively for what he calls "academic open-mindedness."[16] The extent to which "fiction and non-fiction have now interpenetrated" in works of rural fiction, historical fiction, and even rural autobiography, Snell astutely observes, has led to "a breakdown of conventional artistic and disciplinary boundaries." Snell argues for a new approach to writing about the English countryside, one that would employ the critical standards and methodology of a variety of academic disciplines, such as "literary criticism, cultural, regional, and social history, culture and media studies, geography, and literary sociology." Such an approach would greatly benefit critical scholarship on Thompson's novels, as it would break down the barriers imposed by the standard autobiographical approach to her work.

To truly reassess Thompson's literary legacy, one must move beyond her famous trilogy and fully consider her neglected rural novel, *Still Glides the Stream,* as well as the nature essays, literary essays, and short stories that she published in women's magazines during the 1910s and 1920s. It must be acknowledged that in her early writing career Thompson was a freelance journalist who wrote with an awareness of the women's periodical market rather than an unsophisticated hack. The nature essays that she wrote for *The Peverel Papers*, for example, were not trivial entertainment. Instead, they were serious essays aimed at improving her readers' knowledge and appreciation of nature and literature. Thompson's gift for writing richly descriptive prose is displayed to its best advantage in *The Peverel Papers*, where she evokes the sights, sounds, and fragrances of the English countryside. The nature essays not only reveal Thompson's knowledge of plants, animals, insects, and birds, but they also reveal her impressive knowledge of English literature, particularly English poetry. The nature essays prove that Thompson was an accomplished writer nearly twenty years before the publication of *Lark Rise*. Furthermore, *The Peverel Papers* is more than a long series of individual nature essays; it is an extended narrative that is (arguably) equal in importance to *Lark Rise to Candleford*.

The Peverel Papers is also a significant work in Thompson's *oeuvre* because it sheds light on her narrative technique in *Lark Rise to Candleford*. Thompson's narrative persona in *The Peverel Papers* ("Flora") was not a direct representation of herself, but a literary creation, consciously crafted to suit Thompson's narrative purpose and Catholic audience. This suggests that, although *Lark Rise to Candleford* and *Heatherley* are based on Thompson's life experience, readers should not assume that the narrator of these novels is a simplistic third-person disguise for the adult Flora Thompson. Like "Flora," the narrator of *Lark Rise to Candleford and Heatherley* is a literary creation. *The Peverel Papers* also provides interesting insight into the ways in which Thompson reused or refashioned themes, characters, and events for use in later works. In her nature essays, Thompson's portrayal of gypsies, "Flora's" brother Edmund, and the country practice of "telling the bees" differs in important ways from her portrayal of these same elements in *Lark Rise to Candleford*.

The literary essays that Flora Thompson published in *The Fireside Reading Circle* should not be neglected in any serious study of the author's literary legacy. Although these essays are uneven in scope and content, they are impressive examples of the post–World War I emphasis on "rendering service to readers" found in many periodicals for middle-class women.[17] Thompson's literary essays are designed to both inform her readers and to tempt them to explore the masterpieces of English literature for themselves. Like the essays of *The Peverel Papers*, *The Fireside Reading Circle* essays reveal Thompson's impressive knowledge of English literature and her gift for writing intelligent but accessible prose for a general audience. Even Thompson's much-maligned short stories deserve a modicum of respect, if only as sources of interesting links to Thompson's later work. Sadly, despite her passion for English poetry, Thompson's writing in this genre is mediocre.

The evidence of her work proves that Thompson's writing career did not begin in 1939, when *Lark Rise* was first published, but in 1911, when her first prize-winning essay was published in the *Lady's Companion*. For the next thirty-five years, Thompson continued to defy the limitations imposed upon her by the inadequacies of her formal education and her social class. She was a tireless reader and researcher, as well as an author of short fiction, poetry, nature essays, literary essays, and novels. Thompson's literary interests were not confined to furthering her own writing career. Through the writing competitions that she initiated in *The Fireside Reading Circle* and through the activities of the Peverel Society, Thompson devoted herself to mentoring other aspiring writers for seventeen years.

Although scholars and critics have appreciated Thompson for the light she has shone upon the lives of the rural working classes in late Victorian England, her reputation has suffered from the assumption that her earlier writing for women's periodicals was both trivial and forced upon her by financial circumstances. The perception of Thompson as a working-class writer has also led to assumptions about her education, her writing career, and her literary sophistication that have proven to be inaccurate. Perhaps the time has finally come when a new generation can appreciate the full complexity of Flora Thompson's work and recognize her accomplishments as a twentieth-century woman writer.

Appendix A: Sources of Literary Quotations in *The Peverel Papers*

FLORA THOMPSON FREQUENTLY USED LITERARY QUOTATIONS IN *The Peverel Papers,* the nature series that she published in the *Catholic Fireside* from January 1921 to December 1927. The works listed in this appendix provide a basis for assessing the extent of Thompson's own reading and literary interests. The following is a selected, alphabetical list of the poet/author and work from which individual literary quotations are taken. This list is based on the essays discussed in chapter 2.

AUTHOR/TITLE OF SOURCE	MONTH/YEAR OF ESSAY
Arnold, Matthew	
"Philomela"	June 1922
The Bible	
Proverbs 6.6	November 1922
Luke 12:24	September 1926
Bridges, Robert	
"Nightingales"	June 1922
"Last Week of February 1890"	February 1924
Brontë, Emily	
"No Coward Soul is Mine"	April 1922
Browning, Elizabeth Barrett	
"Cheerfulness Taught by Reason"	March 1922
Browning Robert	
"The Last Ride Together"	July 1922
Chaucer, Geoffrey	
Canterbury Tales: General Prologue	April 1924
Coleridge, Samuel Taylor	
"Dejection: An Ode"	April 1924
Cornford, Frances	
"To a Fat Lady Seen from a Train"	June 1923

Gerard, John	
Herball of General Historie of Plantes (1633)	January 1925
	May 1923
Herrick	
"A Christmas Carol Sung to the King in the Presence in White Hall"	December 1927
Hood, Thomas	
"Ruth"	May 1923
Keats, John	
"Ode to a Nightingale"	June 1921
"To Autumn"	November 1921
"Ode to a Nightingale"	June 1922
"To Autumn"	November 1924
"La Belle Dame Sans Merci"	January 1926
Koran	March 1922
Lowell, James Russell	
"The Vision of Sir Launfal"	June 1922
Marvell, Andrew	
"The Garden"	July 1923
	May 1924
	July 1927
Meredith George	
"Ode to the Spirit of Earth in Autumn"	September 1921
	November 1922
	March 1924
"Modern Love"	October 1925
Monk of Reading	
"Sumer is icomen in"	February 1922
Morris, William	
"August"	August 1926
Patmore, Coventry	
"Winter"	January 1926
Ruskin, John	
Proserpina	August 1924
Russell, George (*AE*)	
"3. Prayer"	January 1922
"Carrowmore"	June 1922

"Sacrifice"	November 1922
"The Twilight of Earth"	February 1925
Shakespeare, William	
Richard III (1.1.1–2)	April 1922
Love's Labour's Lost (5.2.885)	July 1922
First Part of Henry IV (2.4.237)	September 1924
Sonnet 98 (line 2)	April 1925
Love's Labour's Lost (5.2.908)	September 1926
Third Part of Henry VI (5.6.44)	September 1926
The Winter's Tale (4.4.121–24)	July 1927
Shelley, Percy Bysshe	
"To a Skylark"	June 1921
Prometheus Unbound	March 1922
"To Mary"	July 1922
"Cloud"	December 1922
"To a Skylark"	October 1923
Prometheus Unbound	December 1923
Julian and Madallo	August 1924
Tennyson, Alfred	
"Afterthought"	August 1922
"Early Spring"	April 1924
"Flower in the Crannied Wall"	July 1925
Tennyson, Frederick	
"Skylark"	June 1921 February 1924
Thompson, Flora	
"To a Poet"	February 1921
"April"	April 1921
"Emancipation"	March 1922
Thompson, Francis	
"The Hound of Heaven"	July 1922
"The Mistress of Vision"	April 1922
"Ode after Easter"	March 1925
Paganism Old and New	December 1925
de Vere, Sir Aubrey	
"Spring"	April 1925
Watson, Sir William	
"Song"	April 1925

White, Gilbert	
Natural History of Selborne	February 1923
Wordsworth, William	
"Intimations of Immortality"	May 1923
	May 1925

Appendix B: Selected Poems from *Bog Myrtle and Peat*

In chapter 5 ("Minor Works") I discuss the following six poems from *Bog Myrtle and Peat,* a collection of Flora Thompson's poetry that was published by Philip Allan and Company in 1921. The poems are listed in alphabetical order.

April

Now that April is here,
With her blackthorn ablow,
I will say to my dear: -
'Now that April is here,
'With her smile and her tear,
'To the greenwood we'll go!'
Now that April is here,
With her blackthorn ablow! (14)

August Again

The heather flings her purple robe
Once more upon the hill;
Beneath a shivering aspen-tree
My Love lies cold and still;-
Ah, very deep my Love must sleep,
On that far Flemish plain,
If he does not know that the heath-bells blow
On the Hampshire hills again!

O, other maids take other men,
And just a passing sigh
Will not disturb the lightest dream;
But my poor heart would die
If so very deep my Love should sleep
Beneath his foreign tree,
That he did not stir at the thought of her
Who could love so faithfully! (23)

Home Thoughts from the Desert

In Hampshire now, the woods are brown,
The heath-sands tawny-gold with rain;
The mist lies blue on Bratley Down,
The firelight flecks the window pane-
In Hampshire now!

The wind comes screaming from the sea,
The wild sea-horses champ and roar,
And every oak on Dudman's Lea
Echoes the tumult of the shore-
In Hampshire now!

The 'Wight lies wrapt in cloud and mist,
Scarce once a week they'll see it clear,
And then it glows like amethyst-
And Oh, I would that I were there,
In Hampshire now!

Amidst the desert sand and heat,
I hear the wheeling seabirds scream,
Scent the good smoke of burning peat,
Then wake and find it but a dream-
Ah, Hampshire dear! (10)

Ocean Malignant

When the first cave-man, wearied from the chase,
Flung himself down on her gold-fretted shore,
And heard her gentle waves lap o'er and o'er,
And felt her soft, sweet breath upon his face;
Enamoured of her sinuous azure grace–
And dreaming not of tempests' crash and roar,
When storm-winds rage and yeasty billows pour-
He fondly named her 'Mother of our Race.'

No Mother, but a Mistress; crafty, vain,
She loves to lure man down to caverns dim,
And there for nine days hold high sport with him,
Entwining with dank weeds his sodden hair,
Then fling his carrion back to Earth again,
So cruel false! But fair- Ah, God, how fair! (15)

To One in Prison

Had I the power to match my love,
Not Beatrice herself should be
Hymned higher unto heaven than thee!
And were mine but a poet's fate,
The body lorn and desolate,
The soul a white-heat of desire,
The lips aflame with holy fire;
To endless time, thy praise should ring,
My poet-hero, poet-king. (28)

A Villanelle of Spring

I Sing a villanelle of Spring,
Of long, lush hedgerows, white with may,
And primrose dells where throstles sing.

Of woods, where tawny squirrels swing
From bough to bough the livelong day;
I sing a villanelle of Spring.

Of brooding bird, with downy wing;
(O, tread you gently here I pray!)
In primrose dells where throstles sing.

Lo, from the wood our spoils we bring;
Bluebell, and pink crab-apple spray;
I sing a villanelle of Spring.

The orchard trees their petals fling,
To greet us on our homeward way,
From primrose dells, where throstles sing.

Hark to the swallows twittering!
They're mending their old nests with clay;
I sing a villanelle of Spring,
Of primrose dells where throstles sing! (26)

Appendix C:
Literary Essays in *The Fireside Reading Circle*

THOMPSON PUBLISHED THIRTY-FIVE LITERARY ESSAYS IN *The Fireside Reading Circle* between January 1923 and November 1925. The following lists the title and month/year of publication for each essay.

DATE	SUBJECT/TITLE
January 1923	Untitled (Sir Walter Scott)
February 1923	Untitled (Charles Dickens)
March 1923	Untitled (William Wordsworth)
April 1923	Untitled (George Eliot)
May 1923	Untitled (John Keats and P. B. Shelley)
June 1923	"The Three Brontës"
July 1923	"Robert Browning"
August 1923	"The Sea in English Literature"
September 1923	"Alfred Lord Tennyson"
October 1923	"The Women Poets"
November 1923	"The English Short Story"
December 1923	"Christmas with the Poets"
January 1924	"Robert Louis Stevenson"
February 1924	"The Sonnet in English Poetry"
March 1924	"Thomas Carlyle"
April 1924	"The Poetry of Nature"
May 1924	"William Makepeace Thackeray"
June 1924	"Modern Nature Poetry"
July 1924	"Dante Gabriel Rossetti"
August 1924	"John Ruskin"
September 1924	"The Lyric"
October 1924	"George Meredith"
November 1924	"The English Essayists"
December 1924	"English Essayists: 2"
January 1925	"The Evolution of the Novel"
February 1925	"Joseph Conrad"
March 1925	"Catholic Poets of the Nineteenth Century: 1, Coventry Patmore"

April 1925	"Arnold Bennett"
May 1925	"Catholic Poets of the Nineteenth Century: 2. Francis Thompson"
June 1925	"G. K. Chesterton"
July 1925	"Atmosphere in Literature"
August 1925	"Seaside Reading"
September 1925	"Some Catholic Poets of the Nineteenth Century: 3. Alice Meynell"
October 1925	"Rudyard Kipling"
November 1925	"Sir James M. Barrie"

Appendix D:
Gates of Eden

THOMPSON PUBLISHED INSTALLMENTS OF HER NOVEL, *GATES OF EDEN*, IN the Peverel Society's *Peverel Monthly* during 1928. The original 352-page typewritten manuscript is located in the Flora Thomson archive. The title of the novel refers to the biblical Garden of Eden, guarded by angels with flaming swords. For the novel's protagonist, Berengaria (Berry) Verlander, who feels abandoned and unloved, the Garden of Eden represents her personal dream of human love. The novel opens immediately after the death of Berry's father, an alcoholic stonemason named Edmund Verlander. Verlander's death results in a life of increasing poverty and isolation for his wife, young son, and sixteen-year-old Berry. One year after her father's death, Berry runs away from home, and, after a series of adventures, she comes to live in a boardinghouse in the seaside town of Avonmouth, working as the companion of a blind woman. At the boardinghouse Berry meets and falls in love with Heath Francis, a refined poet and freelance journalist who is trapped in a loveless marriage. Francis reveals that, although he has not lived with his wife for ten years, his Catholic faith prevents him from divorcing her. The lovers briefly contemplate living together, but Berry's conscience leads her to renounce Francis. The novel ends as Berry finds a new home with a grandfatherly old friend, Edward Morgan.

Thompson probably began writing *Gates of Eden* during the 1920s when she was also writing short fiction for women's magazines. The romance between Heath Francis and Berry Verlander is stereotypical romantic fare, but there are many interesting connections between this novel and *Lark Rise to Candleford* (such as the stonemason father) that would make *Gates of Eden* an interesting addition to studies of the trilogy. *Gates of Eden* is also interesting because, in addition to depicting life in a country village, it also depicts boardinghouse life in a modest seaside resort community in the years following WWI. Characters include a landlady, an auto mechanic, the children of an actress in a traveling theater company, a freelance journalist, a Catholic priest, and a warm and loving Jewish family. Berry's best friend, the daughter of a Jewish pawnbroker, is a talented vocalist who leaves England to study on the Continent. Thompson also portrays a darker side of humanity in *Gates of Eden*. Berry is viciously bullied by two girls in her native village, and she is assaulted by a sailor after she runs away from home. Berry also spends one night sleeping in an abandoned barn, only to discover, the next day, that she had been sharing this space with the corpse of a drowning victim.

Notes

Chapter 1. Flora Thompson: An Introduction

1. In 2005 the music performed for these productions (originally recorded by the Albion Band in 1980) was rereleased by Talking Elephant Records as a musical CD entitled *Lark Rise to Candleford.*

2. After it was vandalized, the bust was moved to its present location inside the Liphook Public Library.

3. Lane, *Flora Thompson*, 4.

4. "In a Victorian Village," *New York Herald Tribune Weekly Book Review*, June 20, 1943, 22.

5. Ronald Bythe, "Natural Involvements," *Times* [London] *Literary Supplement.* Nov. 23, 1979, 9.

6. O'Rourke, "Were There No Women?" 60.

7. The following information about Thompson's literary career is a composite account based on Lindsay's *Flora Thompson: The Story of the Lark Rise Writer.*

8. Thompson, "A Country Child Taking Notes," 7. This statement appears to conflict with a statement Thompson made to the *Civilian* (in 1921) that she was a functionally illiterate country girl who could "barely read and write and nothing more!" when she left school at the age of fourteen. Thompson's account of her life in the *Civilian* interview, although similar to her depiction of Laura in *Lark Rise to Candleford*, differs from the novels in important ways. In *Lark Rise to Candleford*, Laura is depicted as a voracious reader from early childhood, who read the novels of Sir Walter Scott as a young girl. It is possible that either Thompson or the interviewer from the *Civilian* exaggerated some of these personal details for dramatic effect.

9. "C.," "Flora Thompson: Poet and Nature Lover," *Civilian* May 14, 1921, 171.

10. Ibid.

11. *Woman of Letters. Village Postmistress Poetess*, Mar. 2, 1921. From press clippings in the Flora Thompson archive.

12. Although I refer to *Lark Rise, Over to Candleford, Candleford Green,* and *Heatherley* as novels, they are generally classified as the author's memoirs or as lightly fictionalized autobiography. I present my rationale for reclassifying these works in chapter 3.

13. Thompson's first published book, *Bog Myrtle and Peat*, was not received with the same degree of enthusiasm. For reviews of *Bog Myrtle and Peat*, see chapter 4.

14. "*Lark Rise* by Flora Thompson," *Literature and Life*, May 1939, 16. Thompson's books were widely reviewed in Great Britain. Additional British book reviews can be found in the Flora Thompson archive.

15. E. A. Wolfe, "Village and Grandmother," *Time and Tide*, Apr. 14, 1939, 479.

16. "The English Village: Passing of an Era," *Times* [London] *Literary Supplement*, May 13, 1939, 278.

17. "Yesterday in England," *New York Times*, Aug. 6, 1939, 9.

18. George Dangerfield, "English Village Life," *Saturday Review*, July 8, 1939, 12.

19. Lindsay, *Flora Thompson*, 150–51.

20. Unsigned review of *Over to Candleford* by Flora Thompson, *Spectator*, Aug. 22, 1941, 189–90.

21. "Village Childhood: A Vanished Life," *Times* [London] *Literary Supplement*, July 12, 1941, 338.

22. "Candleford Again," *Times* [London*] Literary Supplement*, Mar. 13, 1943, 128.

23. Hampson, review of *Candleford Green* by Flora Thompson, *Spectator*, Feb. 12, 1943, 156.

24. Jane Spence Southron, "A Village Chronicle," *New York Times Book Review*, May 2, 1943, 24.

25. "In a Victorian Village," *New York Herald Tribune Weekly Book Review*, June 20, 1943, 22.

26. Lindsay, *Flora Thompson*, 163.

27. V. C. Clinton-Baddeley, review of *Lark Rise to Candleford*, *Spectator*, June 22, 1945, 582.

28. Harold Hobson, "True Serenity Lingers in the Close of Salisbury Cathedral," *Christian Science Monitor*, June 16, 1945, 12.

29. John T. Frederick, "A Candid Account of 'The Good Old Days,'" *Chicago Sun Book Week*, Aug. 19, 1945, 2.

30. Struthers Burt, "Panorama of English Rural Life," *New York Times Book Review*, Sept. 23, 1945, 4.

31. "Village Annals," *Times* [London] *Literary Supplement*, May 22, 1948, 284.

32. Thompson, *Still Glides the Stream*, 232–33.

33. Ernestine Evans, "Fresh from an Ancient Spring," *New York Herald Tribune Weekly Book Review* Aug. 1, 1948, 2.

34. Eric Forbes-Boyd, "The Texture of a Victorian Village," *Christian Science Monitor*, July 15, 1948, 11.

35. Pamela Taylor, "Golden Time," *Saturday Review*, July 24, 1948, 9.

36. Lindsay, *Flora Thompson*, 160.

37. Chase, "Massingham," 235–36.

38. Quoted in Lindsay, *Flora Thompson*, 161.

39. Massingham, introduction, *Lark Rise to Candleford*, ix.

40. Ibid., xiii.

41. Ibid., x.

42. Ibid., xii.

43. Hastings, "Lane," 432.

44. Lindsay, *Flora Thompson*, 175.

45. Lane, introduction, *A Country Calendar*, 4.

46. Ibid., foreword.

47. Ibid., introduction, 17.

48. Lindsay, *Flora Thompson*, 162.

49. Lane, introduction, *A Country Calendar*, 8. Lane does not identify the date or recipient of this letter.

50. Ibid., 4.

51. Ibid., 3–4.

52. Ronald Blythe, "Natural Involvements," *Times* [London] *Literary Supplement*, Nov. 23, 1979, 9.

53. Neither Margaret Lane nor Ronald Blythe identified the source of information for their statements about Flora Thompson's marriage.

54. Of these photographs, only three are of Thompson and her family members: one of Flora, one of her brother Edwin Timms, and one of her mother, Emma Timms. There is also a photograph of Eliza Massey, a Juniper Hill resident who found her way

into the pages of *Lark Rise* and *Over to Candleford* as the old lacemaker and beekeeper, Queenie. There are two photographs of the Fox Inn, an establishment in Juniper Hill that became the Wagon and Horses in *Lark Rise*. There is also a photograph of the school that Thompson attended in Cottisford, which later became Fordlow National School in *Lark Rise* and *Over to Candleford*, as well as a photograph of the forge and post office in Fringford that inspired Thompson's depiction of the post office and forge in the fictional village of Candleford Green. The remaining photographs are of general country subjects such as "Ploughing," "Driving Bees," and "A Two Man Band."

55. Casson, introduction, *Lark Rise*, 13.

56. Ibid., 15–16.

57. Ibid., 16.

58. Shuckburgh, introduction, *The Peverel Papers*, 15.

59. Ibid., 7.

60. Ibid., 9.

61. Ibid., 7.

62. Ibid., 13.

63. Ibid., 8, 14.

64. Ibid., 13. The suffering of a sensitive protagonist, paired with a brutish spouse, is a familiar theme in the British novel. Since Thompson admired Thomas Hardy, this plot idea could have as easily been inspired by the doomed marriages of Tess Durbeyfield and Alec D'Urberville in *Tess of the D'Urbervilles* or Jude Fawley and Arabella Donn in *Jude the Obscure*.

65. Ibid., 8.

66. Thompson, *Lark Rise to Candleford*, 553–54.

67. Shuckburgh, introduction, *The Peverel Papers*, 9.

68. Trodd, *Women's Writing in English*, 109.

69. Because the subject of Thompson's novels is the life of the agricultural working classes, she does not appear in significant works about the industrial working classes, such as Martha Vicinus's *The Industrial Muse* and Phyllis Ashraf's *Introduction to Working Class Literature in Great Britain* (1979)

70. Cavaliero, *The Rural Tradition in the English Novel*, 28.

71. Keith, *The Rural Tradition*, 255.

72. Wade, *In My Own Shire*, 110.

73. I found an additional seven references in the first forty-five pages alone.

74. Kodish, "Moving Towards the Everyday," 94.

75. Ibid., 95.

76. Ibid., 94.

77. Ibid., 95.

78. Ibid., 103.

79. Pickering, "Popular Song at Juniper Hill," 482. In her study of church choir music, *Fact and Fiction: Flora Thompson and the Fewcott Part Book* (2003), Gillian R. Warson discusses a different musical connection to *Lark Rise*. However, this connection is tenuous and, at best, biographical. Thompson's grandfather, John Dibber, had been a member of the choirband at Ardley Church. According to Warson, the Ardley choirband may have used the *Fewcott Part Book*, a handwritten manuscript of psalms and hymn music. In *Lark Rise*, Emma tells Laura that her grandfather once played the violin in a church choir, but the *Fewcott Part Book* is never mentioned.

80. Ibid., 485.

81. Judge, "Fact and Fancy," 174.

82. Ibid., 182.

83. In a 1979 review of *A Country Calendar* in *Lore and Language*, D. Hey sounded a similar note of caution regarding Thompson's reliability as a primary source of information about country life and folkways. While noting that *Lark Rise* is "a marvelous evocation of a vanished way of life in the countryside" and "a work of social history as well as compelling literature," Hey asked the question, "But how true is *Lark Rise* of the realities of rural life in late-Victorian England?" He concluded, "The skill of the writing must not lure us into an uncritical acceptance of the book as a piece of true social history" (130).

84. Williams, *The Country and the City*, 261. In *Akenfield: Portrait of an English Village*, Ronald Blythe creates a nonfiction portrait of a small agricultural village in East Anglia. The book is based on the information that Blythe collected during his study, as well as on the first-person testimony of specific village residents.

85. Rose, *The Intellectual Life of the British Working Classes*, 2.

86. Ibid., 84.

87. Ibid., 387. In his *Notes*, Rose misidentifies this passage as coming from *Lark Rise.*

88. English, "Lark Rise and Juniper Hill," 11.

89. Ibid., 14.

90. Ibid., 17.

91. Ibid. The introductory note to *Lark Rise* states: "This book tells of the life in an Oxfordshire hamlet in the 'eighties. The drawings were made by Mr. Lynton Lamb in the village around which the story is written. The setting has remained unchanged since the period described by the author." English, perhaps, places too much significance on Thompson's use of the word story in this note. Thompson's note *does* emphasize the realistic setting of Lark Rise, but her use of the word story does not constitute an explicit statement that *Lark Rise* is a work of fiction.

92. Ibid. The essays to which English refers are "Old Queenie," "An Oxfordshire Hamlet in the 'Eighties," and "May Day in the 'Eighties."

93. Ibid., 18.

94. Ibid., 18, 19. English notes that Thompson made this statement in a letter to Edmund A. Greening Lamborn. This letter was found pasted into one of the Bodleian Library's copies of *Lark Rise.*

95. Ibid., 34, 33–34.

96. Burnett, Vincent, and Mayall, *The Autobiography of the Working Class*, vol. 1, 314.

97. O'Rourke, "Were There No Women?" 54.

98. Ibid., 55.

99. Ibid., 58.

100. Ibid., 59.

101. Ibid.

102. Ibid., 60. O'Rourke does not identify specific works that Thompson published in the *Daily News.* However, in 1919, Thompson did respond to an advertisement for the Practical Correspondence College of London that was published in this periodical.

103. Thompson, *A Country Calendar*, 306.

104. O'Rourke, "Were There No Women?" 61.

105. Sara Mills's article is published in the proceedings of the 1989 conference on *Working -Class and Feminist Literature in Britain and Ireland in the 20th Century.* Among the conference papers is Monika Ruthe's "20th Century Working-Class Autobiography—Changing Features and Functions," which serves as a brief introduction to the article by Mills.

106. Mills, "Problems in the Analysis of British Working Class Women's Writing in the Thirties," 51.

107. Ibid., 50.

108. Ibid., 53, 54.
109. Ibid., 54, 51.
110. Ibid., 54.
111. Lindsay, *Flora Thompson*, 13–14.
112. Mills, "Problems in the Analysis of British Working Class Women's Writing in the Thirties," 56.
113. Ibid.
114. Ibid., 58.
115. Dusinberre, "The Child's Eye and the Adult's Voice," 61.
116. Ibid., 62, 62–63.
117. Ibid., 69.
118. Ibid., 67.
119. Ibid., 68.
120. Zagarell, "Narratives of Community," 499.
121. Ibid., 514.
122. Ibid., 519.
123. Ibid., 524.

CHAPTER 2. *THE PEVEREL PAPERS*

1. Margaret Lane was introduced to Thompson's work through her friend Joan Hassall. After Thompson's death, Lane and Hassall traveled to Oxfordshire to discover the real "Lark Rise" and to gather information about Thompson's life. Lane eventually interviewed Thompson's daughter, Winifred, who allowed Lane to read her mother's papers (Lindsay, *Flora Thompson*, 175).

2. Lane, *Flora Thompson*, 4. The biographical sketch that Lane originally published in the *Cornhill* was republished in 1976 as the memorial pamphlet *Flora Thompson*.

3. Thompson's knowledge of the area surrounding Liphook was so extensive that she was asked to write the text for the 1925 *Guide to Liphook Bramshott and Neighbourhood*.

4. First published on January 31, 1879, *The Catholic Fireside* ceased publication on September 29, 1978.

5. Lindsay, *Flora Thompson*, 99.

6. At the end of the nature essay published in September 1922, Thompson acknowledged the "Yorkshire reader" who had made this request (*Peverel Papers*, *Catholic Fireside*, Sept. 2, 1922, 242).

7. I viewed this letter from Geoffrey Cumberlege while working with the Flora Thompson archive.

8. The essays with Thompson's editorial markings are found in the Flora Thompson archive.

9. The first, full text edition of *Out of Doors* and *The Peverel Papers,* published by John Owen Smith in May 2008, was the result of a collaborative effort. Using scanned copies of the original essays that I obtained from Gillian Lindsay and the British Library, John transcribed the essays using a voice recognition system. Proofreading the resulting 450 pages of text was a task we both shared. This edition is illustrated with two pages of photographs and with pen and ink sketches of nature subjects by John Reaney.

10. In "January," for example, the first excerpt is taken from the essay published in 1926. This is followed by excerpts from 1924, 1921, and 1925, respectively.

11. Thompson, *A Country Calendar*, 40.

12. Ibid., 117.

13. Two excerpts for "March" are misidentified; one is from "April" 1922 and another from "April" 1924. One excerpt for "April" is from "March" 1924. One "June" excerpt is from "March" 1924, and one of the "July" excerpts is actually from "November" 1923. Of the three excerpts Lane selected for "August," two are misidentified. One is actually from "November" 1922, and the other is from "September" 1922. One "October" excerpt is from "November" 1924. Finally, two of the excerpts Lane selected for "November" were taken from one essay published in "December" 1922.

14. To avoid confusion, in this chapter, I refer to Flora Thompson's fictional persona as "Flora."

15. *Out of Doors*, *Catholic Fireside*, Mar. 5, 1921, 254.

16. "April" was originally published in *Bog Myrtle and Peat.*

17. *Out of Doors*, *Catholic Fireside* Apr. 2, 1921, 2.

18. *Out of Doors*, *Catholic Fireside,* June 4, 1921, 238.

19. Ibid.

20. *Out of Doors, Catholic Fireside,* July 2, 1921, 2.

21. Ibid., Aug. 6, 1921, 130.

22. Ibid., Oct.1, 1921, 2.

23. Ibid., Nov. 5, 1921, 134.

24. *Peverel Papers*, *Catholic Fireside,* Jan. 7, 1922, 7.

25. Ibid.

26. "Lines Written a Few Miles above Tintern Abbey" by William Wordsworth; *Peverel Papers*, *Catholic Fireside,* Jan. 7, 1922, 7.

27. In "April" 1921, "Flora" says that she has lived on Peverel Downs for three years.

28. *Peverel Papers*, *Catholic Fireside,* Jan. 2, 1922, 7.

29. Lindsay, *Flora Thompson*, 92.

30. *Out of Doors*, *Catholic Fireside,* June 4, 1921, 238.

31. Ibid., July 2, 1921, 2.

32. Ibid., Apr. 2, 1921, 2.

33. *Peverel Papers*, *Catholic Fireside*, Apr. 21, 1923, 64.

34. *Out of Doors*, *Catholic Fireside*, Apr. 2, 1921, 2.

35. *Peverel Papers*, *Catholic Fireside*, Apr. 21, 1923, 64.

36. *Out of Doors*, *Catholic Fireside*, May 7, 1921, 134.

37. Ibid., 150.

38. Ibid., June 4, 1921, 238.

39. Ibid., Nov. 5, 1921, 134.

40. Lindsay, *Flora Thompson*, 133.

41. *Peverel Papers*, *Catholic Fireside,* Jan. 7, 1922, 8. Thompson also criticized the Protestant Reformation in several essays that she wrote for *The Fireside Reading Circle.*

42. Ibid., July 1, 1922, 8.

43. *The Noble Army* was published in 1921 by J. Bale. (London).

44. For a list of the source of specific quotations, including the months in which they appear, see appendix A.

45. *Peverel Papers*, *Catholic Fireside*, Mar. 4, 1922, 224.

46. *Out of Doors*, *Catholic Fireside*, Oct. 1, 1921, 2.

47. *Peverel Papers*, *Catholic Fireside*, May 13, 1922, 172.

48. Ibid., Jan. 7, 1922, 8.

49. Ibid., June 3, 1922, 249. Thompson misquotes this line. The original reads "What is so rare as a day in June?"

50. Ibid., Aug. 13, 1926, 205. In Morris's *The Earthly Paradise*, "August" is one of twelve lyrical poems dedicated to the months of the year.

51. *Out of Doors*, *Catholic Fireside*, Nov. 5, 1921, 134.
52. *Peverel Papers*, *Catholic Fireside*, Nov. 15, 1924, 548.
53. This phrase appears in *The Peverel Papers* in "July" 1923, "May" 1924, and "July" 1927.
54. *Peverel Papers*, *Catholic Fireside*, Sept. 2,1922, 242.
55. Ibid., Dec.15, 1923, 653.
56. Ibid., Aug. 16, 1924, 185.
57. Thompson paraphrases line 545 from P. B. Shelley's *Julian and Madallo.*
58. *Peverel Papers*, *Catholic Fireside*, July 1, 1922, 8.
59. Ibid., Aug. 5, 1922, 136.
60. Ibid., Apr.1, 1922,16.
61. Another of Thompson's poems, "A Villanelle of Spring," was published in *The Catholic Fireside* on April 16, 1921.
62. *The Fireside Reading Circle* essays are discussed in chapter 4.
63. Lindsay, *Flora Thompson*, 122.
64. *Out of Doors*, *Catholic Fireside*, Jan. 1, 1921, 2.
65. Bloxham, *The World of Flora Thompson*, 212–13.
66. Lindsay, *Flora Thompson*, 103.
67. *Out of Doors*, *Catholic Fireside*, Jan. 1, 1921, 2.
68. *Peverel Papers*, *Catholic Fireside*, Dec. 19, 1925, 653.
69. Thompson illustrated five essays published in 1922 with black-and-white photographs that she had taken with a box camera (Lindsay 113). These photographs are entitled "The Hermit's Bridge" (February), "A Corner of the Cottage" (March), "Home of the Water Rat" (April), "Left in Charge" (May), and "The Valley Stream" (June). In the introduction to his edition of *The Peverel Papers*, Julian Shuckburgh notes that, even when viewing photographs like "A Corner of the Cottage," the reader "must reckon with Flora's powers to deceive, for although the cottage in the photograph is indeed identifiable, it does not correspond in every other respect with her descriptions—which are themselves mutually contradictory!" (Shuckburgh 11).
70. *Out of Doors*, *Catholic Fireside*, Apr. 2, 1921, 2.
71. *Peverel Papers*, *Catholic Fireside*, Mar.4, 1922, 223.
72. Ibid., Oct.18, 1924, 438.
73. Ibid., Jan. 17, 1924, 63.
74. Ibid., Sept. 15, 1923, 300.
75. Ibid., Feb. 21, 1925, 213.
76. Ibid., July 21, 1923, 77.
77. Hughes, *Selected Poems*, 41–42.
78. *Out of Doors*, *Catholic Fireside*, Jan. 1, 1921, 2.
79. *Peverel Papers*, *Catholic Fireside*, Sept. 2, 1922, 242.
80. Ibid., June 16, 1923, 288.
81. Ibid., Apr. 19, 1924, 436.
82. Ibid., July 18, 1925, 35.
83. Ibid., Aug. 5, 1922, 134.
84. Ibid., Sept. 20, 1924, 315.
85. Ibid., Sept. 15, 1923, 299.
86. *Out of Doors*, *Catholic Fireside*, Mar. 5, 1921, 254.
87. *Peverel Papers*, *Catholic Fireside*, Apr. 21, 1923, 65.
88. Ibid., Apr. 19, 1924, 435.
89. Ibid., June 16, 1923, 289.
90. *Out of Doors*, *Catholic Fireside*, Sept. 3, 1921, 234.
91. *Peverel Papers*, *Catholic Fireside*, Sept. 15, 1923, 299.

92. Ibid., Nov. 4, 1922,120.
93. Ibid., Nov. 15, 1924, 547.
94. Ibid., Apr. 19, 1924, 435 and 436.
95. Ibid., Mar. 17, 1923, 289.
96. Ibid., Aug. 18, 1923, 189.
97. Ibid., Mar. 15, 1924, 316.
98. Ibid., Sept. 17, 1926, 366.
99. Ibid., 365, 366.
100. Ibid., Nov. 4, 1922, 121.
101. Ibid., Sept. 1922, 241.
102. Ibid., 242.
103. Ibid., Mar. 17, 1923, 289.
104. Ibid., Dec 20, 1924, 682.
105. Ibid., Apr. 21, 1923, 64.
106. *Out of Doors*, *Catholic Fireside*, May 7, 1921, 134.
107. *Peverel Papers*, *Catholic Fireside*, June 3, 1922, 250.
108. Ibid., July 19, 1924, 64.
109. *Out of Doors*, *Catholic Fireside*, Aug. 6, 1921:130; *Peverel Papers*, *Catholic Fireside*, Apr. 19, 1924, 436.
110. Ibid., Feb. 5, 1921, 142.
111. *Peverel Papers*, *Catholic Fireside*, Mar. 17, 1923, 288.
112. Ibid., Aug. 18, 1926, 205.
113. Ibid., Jan. 20, 1923, 66.
114. Ibid., Aug. 16, 1924, 184.
115. Ibid., Feb. 17, 1923, 176.
116. Ibid., Aug. 16, 1924, 185.
117. Ibid., Jan. 15, 1926, 74.
118. Ibid., Jan. 17, 1925, 65.
119. Ibid.
120. Ibid., 66.
121. Ibid., Oct. 20, 1923, 429.
122. Ibid., Nov. 17, 1923, 541.
123. Ibid., May 19, 1923, 184.
124. Ibid., Oct. 20, 1923, 428.
125. Ibid., Mar. 15, 1924, 316.
126. Ibid.
127. Ibid., Dec. 16, 1927, 778.
128. Ibid., Aug. 5, 1922, 134.
129. Ibid., Dec. 2, 1922, 240.
130. Ibid., Dec. 15, 1923, 651.
131. Ibid., 651, 652.
132. Ibid., 652.
133. Ibid., July 21,1923, 78.
134. Ibid., Dec. 15, 1923, 651.
135. Ibid., Oct. 7, 1922, 26.
136. Ibid., Aug. 13, 1926, 206.
137. *Out of Doors, Catholic Fireside*, Feb. 5, 1921, 142.
138. *Peverel Papers*, *Catholic Fireside*, Mar. 4, 1922, 223.
139. Ibid., Aug. 5, 1922, 135.
140. Ibid., June 3, 1922, 250. Horatio Herbert Kitchener (1850–1916), Secretary of State for War from 1914 to 1916, expanded the regular force at the beginning of World War I

through mass recruitment of volunteers. This new force was known as Kitchener's Army (Neilson, "Kitchener," 834).

141. *Out of Doors*, *Catholic Fireside*, Mar. 5, 1921, 254.
142. *Peverel Papers*, *Catholic Fireside*, Oct. 20, 1923, 428.
143. Ibid., Sept. 20, 1924, 317.
144. Sampson, *The Scholar Gypsy*, 143.
145. Ibid., 145.
146. *Out of Doors*, *Catholic Fireside*, Jan, 1, 1921, 2.
147. Ibid., Nov. 5, 1921,134. This appears to be the same gypsy who tells Laura's fortune in *Candleford Green*; she is also dressed in a brightly colored men's dressing gown (Thompson, *Lark Rise to Candleford*, 473).
148. *Peverel Papers*, *Catholic Fireside*, Feb. 4, 1922, 119.
149. Ibid., Dec. 16, 1927, 778.
150. Ibid., 779.
151. *Out of Doors*, *Catholic Fireside*, July 2, 1921, 2.
152. *Peverel Papers*, *Catholic Fireside*, May 13, 1922, 172.
153. Ibid., Dec. 16, 1927, 778.
154. Ibid., May 13, 1922, 172.
155. Ibid., July 18, 1925, 36.
156. Ibid., 37.
157. Ibid., May 13, 1922, 172.
158. Ibid., July 18, 1925, 36.
159. Ibid., Mar. 4, 1922, 224.
160. Ibid., June 3, 1922, 249.
161. Ibid., Oct. 17, 1925, 401.
162. Ibid., Sept. 17, 1926, 367.
163. Ibid., Mar. 15, 1924, 316.
164. Ibid., Oct. 7, 1922, 26.
165. Ibid., Aug. 16, 1924, 184.
166. *Out of Doors*, *Catholic Fireside*, May 7, 1921, 150.
167. *Peverel Papers*, *Catholic Fireside*, Nov. 17, 1923, 541.
168. *Out of Doors*, *Catholic Fireside*, Mar.5, 1921, 254.
169. Ibid., July 2, 1921, 2.
170. *Peverel Papers*, *Catholic Fireside*, Feb. 4, 1922, 120.
171. Ibid., Oct. 7, 1922, 26.
172. Ibid., Apr. 1, 1922, 16.
173. Ibid., Aug. 13, 1926, 206.
174. Ibid., Aug. 5, 1922, 134.
175. Ibid., Dec. 20, 1924, 683.
176. Ibid., 684.
177. Lane, *Flora Thompson*, 4.
178. O'Rourke, "Were There No Women?" 58.

Chapter 3. The Major Works

1. Although *Lark Rise to Candleford* and *Heatherley* are still perceived to be essentially autobiographical, I have classified them as novels, for reasons that are explained later in this chapter.
2. Thompson, "A Country Child Taking Notes," *Readers News*, 6–7.

3. Thompson's paraphrase of lines 5 and 6 from Robert Burns's poem "On the Late Captain Grose's Peregrinations."

4. Lindsay, *Flora Thompson*, 133, 135. For a summary of *Gates of Eden*, see appendix D.

5. Ibid., 151–52.

6. Ibid., 167.

7. Thompson, "A Country Child Taking Notes," 7. Thompson refers to *The Peverel Papers,* which she published in the *Catholic Fireside* from 1921–27.

8. Lindsay, *Flora Thompson*, 140.

9. Upon Thompson's death, Geoffrey Cumberlege wrote an obituary for the London *Times* in which he referred to *Lark Rise*, *Over to Candleford*, and *Candleford Green* as "autobiographical novels." This reflects, perhaps, his true estimation of Thompson's famous trilogy. I viewed the original typescript of this obituary while working with the Flora Thompson archive in August 2005.

10. Ironically, had the books of *Lark Rise to Candleford* been published as works of fiction, they might have faded from view, like many other rural novels published during the 1930s.

11. Lindsay, *Flora Thompson*, 145.

12. *Lark Rise to Candleford*, 3.

13. Thompson uses the first name of her own mother (Emma Dibber Timms) for the name of Laura's mother in *Lark Rise*, a departure from her usual practice of using pseudonyms when describing characters based on people she had known during her childhood. Laura's father is not given a name in *Lark Rise*, but he is named Robert in *Over to Candleford*. Thompson's father was named Albert Timms.

14. *Lark Rise to Candleford*, 6.

15. Ibid.

16. Ibid., 34.

17. Ibid., 38.

18. Ibid., 64, 217.

19. Ibid., 28.

20. Ibid., 243.

21. Ibid., 244.

22. Lindsay, *Flora Thompson*, 148.

23. Ibid., 150.

24. *Lark Rise to Candleford,* 247.

25. Ibid., 254.

26. Ibid., 391.

27. Ibid., 317.

28. Ibid., 261.

29. Ibid., 317.

30. Ibid., 259.

31. Ibid., 326.

32. Ibid., 267.

33. Ibid., 337.

34. Ibid., 339.

35. Ibid., 305.

36. Ibid., 394.

37. Ibid., 392.

38. Ibid., 393.

39. Ibid., 254.

40. The Morrison shelter, named for Herbert Morrison, the minister of Home Security during World War II, was a rectangular steel bomb shelter with wire mesh sides that could be used as a table or enclosed bed (http://www.richmond.edu/~wgreen/ECDmorrisonsh.html).

41. Lindsay, *Flora Thompson*, 152–53.

42. *Lark Rise to Candleford*, 402.

43. Ibid., 408.

44. Ibid., 403.

45. Ibid., 405.

46. Ibid., 429.

47. Ibid., 406.

48. Ibid., 458.

49. Ibid., 436.

50. Ibid., 495.

51. Ibid., 503.

52. Ibid., 404, 405, 405.

53. Ibid., 405.

54. Ibid., 435, 461.

55. Ibid., 461.

56. Ibid., 481.

57. Ibid., 541.

58. Ibid. 520.

59. Ibid., 532.

60. Ibid., 528.

61. Ibid., 466.

62. Ibid., 428.

63. Ibid., 427.

64. Ibid., 509.

65. Ibid., 528.

66. Ibid., 542.

67. Ibid., 553–54.

68. Ibid., 554.

69. Ibid., 553.

70. Ibid., 555.

71. These "gossamer threads" are the webs produced by gossamer spiders. Thompson describes this phenomenon in *The Peverel Papers* in August 1926.

72. *Lark Rise to Candleford*, 556.

73. Lindsay, *Flora Thompson*, 162.

74. *Heatherley*, 154.

75. Ibid., 211.

76. Ibid., 216.

77. Ibid., 269, 258.

78. Ibid., 210.

79. Ibid., 211.

80. Ibid., 155.

81. Ibid., 166, 167, 167.

82. Additional information about the famous literary figures who lived in the region surrounding Hindhead, Surrey, can be found in W. R. Trotter's *The Hilltop Writers: A Victorian Colony Among the Surrey Hills*.

83. *Heatherley*, 175, 174.

84. Ibid., 174.
85. Ibid., 237.
86. Ibid., 258. Margaret Lane and Julian Shuckburgh have both speculated that this passage refers to Flora's marriage to John Thompson. This assumption demonstrates the ease with which events in Thompson's novels are uncritically linked to events in the author's life. Based on existing records, it appears that Thompson did not meet her future husband until she left Grayshott (the fictional Heatherley) in 1901. See chapter 1, n. 64.
87. Ibid., 306.
88. Ibid., 256.
89. Ibid., 257.
90. Ibid., 222.
91. Ibid., 156.
92. Ibid., 157.
93. Ibid., 159.
94. Ibid., 162.
95. Ibid., 232.
96. Ibid., 295, 296, 296.
97. Ibid., 300.
98. Ibid., 226.
99. Ibid., 306.
100. *Still Glides the Stream*, 5.
101. Ibid., 18.
102. Thompson used the same metaphor in *Candleford Green* when describing the changing "tastes and ideals" in the village and in the culture at large. The passage begins with a line from the hymn "A Mighty Fortress Is Our God": "Time like an ever-rolling stream, bears all its sons away," and then continues, "and its daughters, too, and the tastes and ideas of each generation, together with its ideals and conventions, go rolling down-stream with it like so much debris. But, because the generations overlap, the change is gradual" (*Lark Rise to Candleford*, 462).
103. *Still Glides the Stream*, 232–33.
104. Ibid., 6.
105. Ibid., 8, 12.
106. Ibid., 13.
107. Ibid., 37.
108. Ibid., 226–27.
109. Ibid., 22.
110. Ibid.
111. Ibid., 23.
112. Ibid., 144.
113. Ibid., 148.
114. Ibid., 47.
115. Ibid., 194.
116. Ibid., 196.
117. Ibid., 29.
118. Ibid., 26.
119. Ibid., 29.
120. It is interesting to note that, although she was a wife and the mother of three children, Thompson's protagonist in *Still Glides the Stream*, like her narrative persona in *The Peverel Papers*, is a solitary woman who has no husband or children.
121. *Still Glides the Stream*, 17, 38.

122. Snell, "The Regional Novel," 27–28.

123. Cavaliero, *The Rural Tradition in the English Novel*, 11.

124. Snell, "The Regional Novel," 12. Around 1925, Thompson herself joined the Antiquarian and Field Society associated with the Haslemere Museum (Bloxham, *The World of Flora Thompson*, 214).

125. Cavaliero, *The Rural Tradition in the English Novel,* 6.

126. Leavis, "Regional Novels," 440.

127. Ibid., 442.

128. Snell, "The Regional Novel," 1.

129. Ibid., 43. In his analysis, Snell appears to conflate the role of the novelist and the role of narrators and characters in works of regional fiction.

130. Lane, Shuckburgh, and English's positions are discussed in Chapter 1.

131. These terms were originally devised by Franz Stanzel as neutral alternatives to the more familiar concepts of omniscient and limited narration (Keen, *Narrative Form*, 39).

132. Keen, *Narrative Form*, 39.

133. Ibid., 40.

134. Rabinowitz, *Before Reading*, 44.

135. Rabinowitz and Smith, *Authorizing Readers,* 43.

136. Rabinowitz, *Before Reading*, 158.

137. Ibid.

138. Ibid., 159.

139. Ibid., 209.

140. Ibid., 176.

141. Ibid., 44.

142. Ibid., 44, 53.

143. Ibid., 70.

144. Ibid., 58.

145. Ibid., 71.

146. Ibid., 58.

147. Ibid., 59.

148. Ibid., 44, 45.

149. Ibid., 126.

150. Ibid., 147.

151. Ibid., 227.

152. Ibid., 159.

153. Here, I paraphrase Sara Mills (in "Problems in the Analysis of British Working-Class Women's Writing in the Thirties: Flora Thompson's *Lark Rise to Candleford*"), who notes the tendency to downgrade working-class women's writing to a "less creative status" based on the assumption that such women "just transfer their experiences to the page" (56). See chapter 1.

154. Lindsay, *Flora Thompson*, 161.

155. Lane, introduction, *A Country Calendar*, 8.

156. Permission to quote from this letter, dated February 20, 1944, was given by Henry Westbury.

Chapter 4. The Minor Works

1. Copies of many of the short stories and literary essays can be found in the Flora Thompson archive.

2. A copy of the Peverel Society letterhead can be found in the Flora Thompson archive.

3. Lindsay, *Flora Thompson*, 115.

4. Ibid., 80. The *Lady's Companion*, subtitled "A Home Journal for Women and Girls," was also known as *Cartwright's Lady's Companion.*

5. Rose, *The Intellectual Life of the British Working Classes*, 419.

6. Lindsay, *Flora Thompson*, 80.

7. " Dorothea," *Our Book Club, Lady's Companion*, Feb. 25, 1911, 349.

8. Lindsay, *Flora Thompson*, 82.

9. " Dorothea," *Our Book Club, Lady's Companion*, July 22, 1911, 222.

10. Ibid., Apr. 1, 1911, 468.

11. Ibid., Apr. 29, 1911, 565.

12. Ibid., Sept. 16, 1911, 414.

13. Ibid., 532.

14. Lindsay, *Flora Thompson*, 86.

15. Ibid., 86–87.

16. *Victorian Women's Magazines*, 122.

17. The phrase "small sugared love tales" is found on page 306 of *A Country Calendar.* Writers such as Lane, Lindsay, and Shuckburgh have presented this phrase as Thompson's direct description of her short fiction. Since this phrase is actually found on the penultimate page of *Heatherley*, it is actually more indirect.

18. Lindsay, *Flora Thompson*, 92.

19. Ibid., 89.

20. Ibid. The religious writer Michael Fairless was born Margaret Fairless Barber (1869–1901). *The Gathering of Brother Hilarius* (1901) is a religious romance set in the time of the Black Death. Her most popular work, *The Roadmender* (1902), is a religious meditation on the road to heaven (Room, "Barber").

21. White, *Women's Magazines*, 87.

22. Thompson, "The Toft Cup," *Lady's Companion*, Jan. 6, 1912, 178.

23. Thompson, "His Lady of the Lilac," *Lady's Companion*, May 9, 1914, 618.

24. Ibid., May 9, 1914, 619.

25. Ibid., 620.

26. Eden Phillpots (1862–1960) was a popular and prolific writer of novels, short stories, poems, and one-act plays (Moult and Dayananda, "Phillpots," 161).

27. Thompson, "The Mistress of Boldre Farm," *Lady's Companion*, Aug. 2, 1913, 267.

28. Journalism plays a significant role in "His Lady of the Lilac," "The Uphill Way," "Our Contemporary," "Sign and Countersign," "Bluebell's Luck," and "Ambrose."

29. Thompson, "The Toft Cup," *Lady's Companion*, Jan. 6, 1912, 178.

30. Thompson, "His Lady of the Lilac," *Lady's Companion*, May 9, 1912, 618.

31. Thompson, "The Toft Cup," *Lady's Companion*, Jan. 6, 1912, 178.

32. In the *Out of Doors* essay, this passages reads: "During the night the frost had cast its spell over the woods and glades of the New Forest. This morning every branch and twig bore a pearly burden of hoar frost. Over the narrow lane which leads to my retreat, the morning star still glittered coldly; the silence of the winter dawn was only broken by the rumbling of wheels upon the frosty ruts, and the *crop, crop* of the forest ponies as they munched their scanty breakfast beside my garden hedge" (*Out of Doors, Lady's Companion*, Jan. 6, 1921, 2.)

33. Thompson, "The Toft Cup," *Lady's Companion*, Jan. 6, 1912, 180.

34. *Heatherley*, 255.

35. Thompson, *Lark Rise to Candleford*, 25.

36. Lindsay, *Flora Thompson*, 92.

37. Ibid., 97.

38. Bloxham, *The World of Flora Thompson*, 213.

39. Thompson made this statement in her interview with the *Civilian* in May 1921.

40. Interestingly, "The Mervyn Mystery" and "The Hidden Power" differ significantly from the other stories that Thompson published in the *Catholic Fireside* from 1920 to 1922. "The Mervyn Mystery" opens with the mysterious death of General Mervyn, known by his contemporaries as "The Strong Silent Man of India." A cruel colonial official, Meryvyn dies after being bitten by a poisonous snake purposely planted in his locked bedroom. In "The Hidden Power," the hero is summoned to a remote country estate to be the guest of the eccentric "Sir Owen." The story features a young woman being held captive in a tower, an attempted murder, and a conventionally romantic happy ending.

41. "The Hermit's Yew," *Catholic Fireside*, Sept. 11, 1920, 306.

42. Seaman, *Life in Britain Between the Wars*, 23.

43. "The Uphill Way," *Catholic Fireside*, Apr. 27, 1920, 80.

44. Ibid., 81.

45. Ibid., 80.

46. "Bluebell's Luck," *Catholic Fireside*, Feb. 26, 1921, 226.

47. Seaman, *Life in Britain Between the Wars*, 122.

48. "Our Contemporary," *Catholic Fireside*, Dec. 31, 1921, 349.

49. Ibid., 350.

50. Ibid., 359.

51. Ibid.

52. Ibid., 350.

53. White, *Women's Magazines*, 93.

54. "The Profiteers," *Catholic Fireside*, Apr. 16, 1921, 59.

55. Women who joined the VAD (Voluntary Aid Detachment) were trained to provide basic nursing care to wounded men in the war zone and in hospitals located throughout England during World War I.

56. "The Profiteers," *Catholic Fireside*, Apr. 16, 1921, 60.

57. Ibid., 59.

58. Ibid., 61.

59. Thompson published four of her poems in the *Catholic Fireside.*She published "To a Poet" in February 1921. "April" and "A Villanelle of Spring" were both published in April 1921. The fourth poem, "Emancipation," was published in "March" 1922.

60. Lindsay, *Flora Thompson*, 101.

61. The reviews of *Bog Myrtle and Peat* quoted in this chapter are from a collection of press clippings found in the Flora Thompson archive.

62. "Woman of Letters: Village Postmistress Poetess," *Daily Chronicle*, Mar 2, 1921. According to Thompson's daughter, Winifred, Thompson was embarrassed by this description of herself (Lindsay, *Flora Thompson,* 102).

63. Review of *Bog Myrtle and Peat*, *Times* [London] *Literary Supplement*, Mar. 17, 1921.

64. "Mother and Poetess," *Ideas*, Mar. 16, 1921.

65. Review of *Bog Myrtle and Peat*, *Evening Standard*, Mar. 28, 1921.

66. Review of *Bog Myrtle and Peat*, *Bookman*, Apr. 1921.

67. Review of *Bog Myrtle and Peat*, *Tit-Bits*, Apr. 16, 1921.

68. Review of *Bog Myrtle and Peat*, *Lady*, May 12, 1921.

69. "C," "Flora Thompson: Poet and Nature Lover," *Civilian*, May 14, 1921, 171.

70. Ferns, "Flora Thompson," *Dictionary of Literary Biography*, 262.

71. Ibid., 263.

72. Ibid., 265.

73. *Bog Myrtle and Peat*, 10.

74. "The Choice of Words," *The Peverel Literary Society Verse Writing Course*, 2. This writing course, an unpublished typescript, is found in the Flora Thompson archive.

75. Ibid., 3.

76. The texts of these poems are found in appendix B.

77. *Bog Myrtle and Peat*, 14.

78. Ibid., 15.

79. Ibid., 26.

80. Ibid., 10.

81. Ibid., 21–22.

82. Ibid., 10.

83. Ibid., 23.

84. Ibid., 28.

85. Thompson was familiar with Skerryvore because she often visited it during the fourteen years (1903–16) that she lived in Winton, a suburb of Bournemouth. Skerryvore was destroyed by a bomb during World War II.

86. A number of Thompson's *Fireside Reading Circle* essays can be found in the Flora Thompson archive.

87. For a complete list of *The Fireside Reading Circle* essays and their month and year of publication, see appendix C.

88. The edited copy of this essay can be found in the Flora Thompson archive.

89. Untitled, *Fireside Reading Circle, Catholic Fireside,* Jan. 6, 1923, 7.

90. Ibid., 8.

91. Ibid.

92. "Stabat Mater Dolorosa" is a Latin hymn that describes the Virgin Mary weeping at the foot of the cross.

93. "The Three Brontës," *Fireside Reading Circle, Catholic Fireside,* June 2, 1923, 231.

94. Ibid., 232.

95. Ibid., 233.

96. Ibid., 234.

97. Untitled, *Fireside Reading Circle, Catholic Fireside*, Apr. 7, 1923, 8.

98. Untitled. *Fireside Reading Circle, Catholic Fireside*, May 5, 1923, 119.

99. "The Three Brontës," *Fireside Reading Circle, Catholic Fireside*, June 2, 1923, 232.

100. Barker, *The Brontës*, 419.

101. Lindsay, *Flora Thompson*, 157.

102. "The Women Poets," *Fireside Reading Circle, Catholic Fireside*, Oct. 6, 1923, 385.

103. Ibid.

104. Ibid., 386.

105. Ibid.

106. Ibid., 387.

107. Alice Meynell had died on November 27, 1922.

108. "John Ruskin," *Fireside Reading Circle, Catholic Fireside*, Aug. 2, 1924, 134.

109. Ibid., 132.

110. Ibid., 133.

111. The poets discussed in "Modern Nature Poetry" are Alfred Lord Tennyson, Robert Browning, George Meredith, Jean Ingelow, Christina Rossetti, Matthew Arnold, John Davidson, R. L. Stevenson, Rudyard Kipling, Hilaire Belloc, A. E. Housman, Arthur Cripps, Sir Arthur Quiller Couch, Mary Coleridge, Mrs. Meynell, Gerald Gould, William Davis, and Francis Thompson.

112. "Evolution of the Novel," *Fireside Reading Circle, Catholic Fireside*, Jan. 3, 1925, 20.

113. In the course of her essay, Thompson also discusses the sonnets of Wyatt, Sidney, Elizabeth Barrett Browning, Dante Gabriel Rossetti, Mrs. Meynell, and Rupert Brooke. She also provides excerpts from the sonnets of Spenser, Shakespeare, Milton, Wordsworth, Sir William Watson, and Sir William Rowan Hamilton.

114. White, *Women's Magazines*, 96.

115. The full name of the society appears on the society's letterhead and on its membership booklet. Copies of both can be found in the Flora Thompson archive.

116. Lindsay, *Flora Thompson*, 109.

117. Bloxham, *The World of Flora Thompson*, 214.

118. Lindsay, *Flora Thompson*, 114.

119. Ibid., 115.

Chapter 5. The Working Classes

1. Altick, *The English Common Reader*, 316, 356.
2. Rose, *The Intellectual Life of the British Working Classes*, 84.
3. Altick, *The English Common Reader*, 5.
4. Ibid., 87.
5. Ibid., 90.
6. Rose, *The Intellectual Life of the British Working Classes*, 121.
7. Altick, *The English Common Reader*, 95.
8. Thompson, *Lark Rise to Candleford*, 100.
9. Ibid., 30.
10. Ibid., 100.
11. Ibid. Altick, *The English Common* Reader, 258.
12. *Drelincourt on Death*, a theological work written by the French Protestant divine Charles Drelincourt (1595–1669), was first published in France in 1651 as *The Defense Against the Fears of Death*. Giovanni Battista Belzoni, a late eighteenth-century explorer of Egypt and its antiquities, published his *Narrative of the Operations and Recent Discoveries within the Pyramids, Temples and Tombs and Excavations in Egypt and Nubia* in 1820.
13. Rose, *The Intellectual Life of the British Working Classes*, 121.
14. Altick, *The English Common Reader*, 307, 308.
15. Ibid., 300.
16. *Lark Rise to Candleford*, 358.
17. Ibid., 426.
18. Ibid., 426–27.
19. Ibid., 426.
20. Thompson, *Heatherley*, 206.
21. *Lark Rise to Candleford*, 174.
22. Rose, *The Intellectual Life of the British Working Classes*, 354.
23. *Lark Rise to Candleford*, 175
24. Ibid., 337.
25. Ibid., 186.
26. Ibid., 222.
27. Ibid., 237.
28. Ibid., 337–38.
29. Ibid., 337.
30. Rose, *The Intellectual Life of the British Working Classes*, 62.
31. *Lark Rise to Candleford*, 251.

32. Rose, The *Intellectual Life of the British Working Classes*, 386–87.
33. Rose, *The Intellectual Life of the British Working Classes*, 387.
34. Kelly, *History of Public Libraries in Great Britain*, 3.
35. Ibid., 16.
36. Ibid., 129.
37. *Lark Rise to Candleford*, 428.
38. *Heatherley*, 156.
39. Ibid., 175.
40. Ibid., 176.
41. Altick, *The English Common Reader*, 355.
42. *Lark Rise to Candleford*, 258.
43. Altick, *The English Common Reader*, 349.
44. Ibid., 355–56.
45. *Lark Rise to Candleford*, 47.
46. Altick, *The English Common Reader*, 360.
47. Ibid., 361.
48. *Lark Rise to Candleford*, 99.
49. Ibid., 373.
50. Altick, *The English Common Reader*, 363.
51. *Lark Rise to Candleford*, 516.
52. Altick, *The English Common Reader*, 363.
53. *Lark Rise to Candleford*, 516.
54. Law, *Serializing Fiction in the Victorian Press*, 137.
55. *Lark Rise to Candleford*, 101.
56. Ibid., 547.
57. Altick, *The English Common Reader*, 304.
58. Ibid., 226, n. 34.
59. *Lark Rise to Candleford*, 515.
60. Ibid.
61. Ibid., 447.
62. Ibid., 448.
63. Ibid., 449.
64. Ibid., 448–50.
65. Ibid., 449.
66. *Heatherley*, 187.
67. Ibid., 188.
68. Ibid., 187.
69. Ibid., 188.
70. Rose, *The Intellectual Life of the British Working Classes*, 83.
71. *Heatherley*, 242.
72. Ibid., 241.
73. Ibid.
74. Ibid., 240.
75. Ibid., 164.
76. *Lark Rise to Candleford*, 87.
77. Ibid., 31–32.
78. Ibid., 69.
79. Ibid., 66.
80. Ibid., 71, 70.
81. Ibid., 70.
82. Ibid., 68.

83. Ibid., 71.
84. Ibid., 74, 75.
85. Ibid., 77.
86. Ibid., 72.
87. Ibid., 73.
88. Ibid., 72.
89. Ibid., 84.
90. *Heatherley*, 199.
91. Ibid., 204.
92. Ibid.
93. Ibid., 205.
94. Ibid., 206.
95. Ibid., 155.
96. Ibid., 199.
97. Ibid., 283.
98. Ibid., 285.
99. Ibid., 286.
100. Ibid., 287.
101. Ibid., 288.
102. Ibid., 367.
103. Ibid., 368.
104. *Heatherley*, 228.
105. Ibid., 232.
106. *Lark Rise to Candleford*, 273.
107. Ibid., 274.
108. Ibid., 273.
109. Ibid., 274.
110. Ibid., 277.
111. Ibid., 277–78.
112. Ibid., 95.
113. Ibid., 96.
114. Ibid., 96, 97.
115. Ibid., 250.
116. Ibid., 281.
117. Ibid., 291.
118. Ibid., 349.
119. Ibid., 350.
120. Ibid., 351.
121. Ibid., 502.
122. Ibid., 503.
123. Ibid., 272.
124. Ibid., 273.
125. Ibid., 276.
126. Ibid., 384.
127. Ibid., 58.
128. Ibid., 55.
129. Ibid., 56.
130. Ibid., 57.
131. Ibid., 56.
132. Ibid., 265.
133. Ibid., 295.

134. Ibid., 506.
135. Ibid., 507.
136. Ibid., 216.
137. Ibid., 44.
138. Ibid., 213.
139. Ibid., 134.
140. Ibid., 134–35
141. Ibid., 141, 142.
142. Ibid., 201.
143. Ibid., 230.
144. Ibid., 234.
145. Ibid., 456.
146. Ibid., 329.
147. Ibid., 267.
148. Ibid., 211.
149. Ibid., 202.
150. Ibid., 501.
151. Ibid., 493.
152. Ibid., 215.
153. Ibid., 250.
154. *Heatherley*, 186.
155. Burnett, Vincent, and Mayall, *The Autobiography of the Working Class*, xvi.

Chapter 6. Thompson Revalued

1. Batsleer et al., *Rewriting English*, 43.
2. Ibid., 42.
3. Ibid., 44.
4. Ibid., 45.
5. Ibid., 44.
6. Klaus, *The Literature of Labour*, 160.
7. Swindells, 126.
8. Ibid., 128.
9. Ibid., 174.
10. Klaus, *The Literature of Labour*, 128.
11. Ibid., 130. Klaus quotes from page 143 of *Grierson on Documentary.*
12. Ibid.
13. Ibid., 131.
14. Ibid., 161.
15. Peterson, *Traditons of Victorian Women's Autobiography*, 177.
16. Snell, "The Regional Novel," 53.
17. White, *Women's Magazines*, 96.

Bibliography

Primary Sources

Poetry and Novels

Thompson, Flora. *Bog Myrtle and Peat.* London: Philip Allan, 1921.

———. *Heatherley. A Country Calendar.* Edited by Margaret Lane. Oxford: Oxford UP, 1979.

———. *Lark Rise to Candleford.* Oxford: Oxford UP, 1947.

The Peverel Book of Verse. Edited by Flora Thompson. Liphook, Hants, UK: The Peverel Society, 1926.

———. *Still Glides the Stream.* London: Oxford UP, 1948.

Collected Works

———. *A Country Calendar.* Edited by Margaret Lane. Oxford: Oxford UP, 1984.

———. *The Peverel Papers: A Yearbook of the Countryside.* Edited by Julian Shuckburgh. London: Century Hutchinson, 1986.

———. *The Peverel Papers.* Headley Down, UK: John Owen Smith, 2008.

Short Fiction and Essays

———. "Ambrose." *Catholic Fireside,* Oct. 30, 1920, 118–20.

———. "Bluebell's Luck." *Catholic Fireside,* Feb. 26, 1921, 226.

———. "The Call." *Catholic Fireside,* Mar. 6, 1920, 272–73.

———."A Country Child Taking Notes." *The Readers News,* Mar. 1947, 5–7, 10.

———."The Education of a Genius." *Lady's Companion,* Nov. 23, 1912, 25–26.

———. *Guide to Liphook Bramshott and Neighbourhood.* 1925. Reprint, Liphook, Hants, UK: Bramshott and Liphook Preservation Society, 2003.

———. "The Hermit's Yew." *Catholic Fireside,* Sept. 11, 1920, 306.

———. "The Hidden Power." *Catholic Fireside,* July 22, 1922, 83–86.

———. "His Lady of the Lilac." *Lady's Companion,* May 9, 1914, 617–20.

———. [Frances Stuart Thompson] "Homes Afloat." *The Farmer's Home,* June 22, 1936, 11.

———. "The Leper." *Catholic Fireside,* Jan. 24, 1920, 92–93.

———. "May Day in the 'Eighties." *The National Review,* May 1938, 649–54.

———. "The Mervyn Mystery." *Catholic Fireside,* Jan. 29, 1921, 135–36

———. "The Mistress of Boldre Farm." *Lady's Companion,* Aug. 2, 1913, 265–68.

———. "The Nut Brown Maid." *Lady's Companion*, Sept. 28, 1912, 457–61.
———. "Old Queenie." *Lady,* April 29, 1937.
———. "Our Contemporary." *Catholic Fireside*, Dec. 31, 1921, 349–51, 359.
———. "An Oxfordshire Hamlet in the 'Eighties." *National Review*, Aug. 1937, 222–28.
———. "The Profiteers." *Catholic Fireside*, Apr. 16, 1921, 59–62.
———. "Sign and Countersign." *Catholic Fireside*, July 17, 1920, 66–67.
———. "Skerryvore." *Catholic Fireside*, June 5, 1920, 264.
———. "The Tail-less Fox." *Lady*, Dec. 3, 1936, 1,046–47.
———. "The Toft Cup." *Lady's Companion*, Jan. 6, 1912, 177–80.
———. "The Uphill Way." *Catholic Fireside,* Apr. 27, 1920, 80–81.
———. "Where the Apple Reddens." *Catholic Fireside*, Sept. 23, 1922, 319–22.

Out of Doors and The Peverel Papers

———.*Out of Doors. Catholic Fireside*, Jan 1, 1921, 2.
———.*Out of Doors. Catholic Fireside*, Feb. 5, 1921, 142.
———.*Out of Doors. Catholic Fireside*, Mar. 5, 1921, 254.
———.*Out of Doors. Catholic Fireside*, Apr. 2, 1921, 2.
———.*Out of Doors. Catholic Fireside*, May 7, 1921, 134 and 150.
———.*Out of Doors. Catholic Fireside*, June 4, 1921, 238.
———.*Out of Doors. Catholic Fireside*, July 2, 1921, 2.
———.*Out of Doors. Catholic Fireside*, Aug. 6, 1921, 130 and 139.
———.*Out of Doors. Catholic Fireside*, Sept. 3, 1921, 234.
———.*Out of Doors. Catholic Fireside*, Oct. 1, 1921, 2.
———.*Out of Doors. Catholic Fireside*, Nov. 5, 1921, 134.
———.*Out of Doors. Catholic Fireside*, Dec. 3, 1921, 238.
———. *Peverel Papers. Catholic Fireside*, Jan. 7, 1922, 7–8.
———. *Peverel Papers. Catholic Fireside*, Feb. 4, 1922, 119–20.
———. *Peverel Papers. Catholic Fireside*, Mar. 4, 1922, 223–24.
———. *Peverel Papers. Catholic Fireside*, Apr. 1, 1922, 15–16.
———. *Peverel Papers. Catholic Fireside*, May 13, 1922,171–73.
———. *Peverel Papers. Catholic Fireside*, June 3, 1922, 249–51.
———. *Peverel Papers. Catholic Fireside*, July 1, 1922, 7–9.
———. *Peverel Papers. Catholic Fireside*, Aug. 5, 1922, 134–36.
———. *Peverel Papers. Catholic Fireside*, Sept. 2, 1922, 241–42.
———. *Peverel Papers. Catholic Fireside*, Oct. 7, 1922, 25–26.
———. *Peverel Papers. Catholic Fireside*, Nov. 4, 1922, 119–21.
———. *Peverel Papers. Catholic Fireside*, Dec. 2, 1922, 239–41.
———. *Peverel Papers. Catholic Fireside*, Jan. 20, 1923, 65–66.
———. *Peverel Papers. Catholic Fireside*, Feb. 17, 1923, 175–76.
———. *Peverel Papers. Catholic Fireside*, Mar. 17, 1923, 288–89.
———. *Peverel Papers. Catholic Fireside*, Apr. 21, 1923, 64–65.
———. *Peverel Papers. Catholic Fireside*, May 19, 1923, 183–85.

———. *Peverel Papers. Catholic Fireside,* June 16, 1923, 288–89.
———. *Peverel Papers. Catholic Fireside,* July 21, 1923, 77–78.
———. *Peverel Papers. Catholic Fireside,* Aug. 18, 1923, 188–89.
———. *Peverel Papers. Catholic Fireside,* Sept. 15, 1923, 299–300 and 304.
———. *Peverel Papers. Catholic Fireside,* Oct. 20, 1923, 428–30.
———. *Peverel Papers. Catholic Fireside,* Nov. 17, 1923, 540–41.
———. *Peverel Papers. Catholic Fireside,* Dec. 15, 1923, 651–53.
———. *Peverel Papers. Catholic Fireside,* Jan. 19, 1924, 63–65.
———. *Peverel Papers. Catholic Fireside,* Feb. 16, 1924, 186–88.
———. *Peverel Papers. Catholic Fireside,* Mar. 15, 1924, 315–17.
———. *Peverel Papers. Catholic Fireside,* Apr. 19, 1924, 435–37.
———. *Peverel Papers. Catholic Fireside,* May 17, 1924, 547–49.
———. *Peverel Papers. Catholic Fireside,* June 21, 1924, 679–81.
———. *Peverel Papers. Catholic Fireside,* July 19, 1924, 63–65.
———. *Peverel Papers. Catholic Fireside,* Aug. 16, 1924, 183–85.
———. *Peverel Papers. Catholic Fireside,* Sept. 20, 1924, 315–17.
———. *Peverel Papers. Catholic Fireside,* Oct. 18, 1924, 438–40.
———. *Peverel Papers. Catholic Fireside,* Nov. 15, 1924, 547–49.
———. *Peverel Papers. Catholic Fireside,* Dec. 20, 1924, 682–84.
———. *Peverel Papers. Catholic Fireside,* Jan.17, 1925, 65–67.
———. *Peverel Papers. Catholic Fireside,* Feb. 21, 1925, 211–14.
———. *Peverel Papers. Catholic Fireside,* Mar. 21, 1925, 327–29.
———. *Peverel Papers. Catholic Fireside,* Apr. 18, 1925, 427–29.
———. *Peverel Papers. Catholic Fireside,* May 16, 1925, 547–49.
———. *Peverel Papers. Catholic Fireside,* June 20, 1925, 679–81.
———. *Peverel Papers. Catholic Fireside,* July 18, 1925, 35–37.
———. *Peverel Papers. Catholic Fireside,* Aug. 15, 1925, 162–64.
———. *Peverel Papers. Catholic Fireside,* Sept. 19, 1925, 287–88.
———. *Peverel Papers. Catholic Fireside,* Oct. 17, 1925, 399–401.
———. *Peverel Papers. Catholic Fireside,* Nov. 21, 1925, 539–541.
———. *Peverel Papers. Catholic Fireside,* Dec. 19, 1925, 651–53.
———. *Peverel Papers. Catholic Fireside,* Jan. 15, 1926, 73–75.
———. *Peverel Papers. Catholic Fireside,* Feb. 19, 1926, 244–46.
———. *Peverel Papers. Catholic Fireside,* Mar. 26, 1926, 390–92.
———. *Peverel Papers. Catholic Fireside,* Apr. 16, 1926, 486–88.
———. *Peverel Papers. Catholic Fireside,* June 4, 1926, 657–59.
———. *Peverel Papers. Catholic Fireside,* June 25, 1926, 746–48.
———. *Peverel Papers. Catholic Fireside,* July 16, 1926, 94–96.
———. *Peverel Papers. Catholic Fireside,* Aug. 13, 1926, 205–7.
———. *Peverel Papers. Catholic Fireside,* Sept. 17, 1926, 365–67.
———. *Peverel Papers. Catholic Fireside,* Oct. 15, 1926, 491–93.
———. *Peverel Papers. Catholic Fireside,* Nov. 19, 1926, 651–53.
———. *Peverel Papers. Catholic Fireside,* Dec. 17, 1926, 779–81.

———. *Peverel Papers. Catholic Fireside*, Jan. 21, 1927, 77–79.
———. *Peverel Papers. Catholic Fireside*, Feb. 25, 1927, 231–32.
———. *Peverel Papers. Catholic Fireside*, Mar. 25, 1927, 365–67.
———. *Peverel Papers. Catholic Fireside*, Apr. 15, 1927, 468–470.
———. *Peverel Papers. Catholic Fireside*, May 20, 1927, 619–21.
———. *Peverel Papers. Catholic Fireside*, June 17, 1927, 748–50.
———. *Peverel Papers. Catholic Fireside*, July 15, 1927, 73–75.
———. *Peverel Papers. Catholic Fireside*, Aug. 19, 1927, 233–35.
———. *Peverel Papers. Catholic Fireside*, Sept. 16, 1927, 363–65.
———. *Peverel Papers. Catholic Fireside*, Oct. 21, 1927, 533–35.
———. *Peverel Papers. Catholic Fireside*, Nov. 18, 1927, 661–63.
———. *Peverel Papers. Catholic Fireside*, Dec. 16, 1927, 778–89.

The Fireside Reading Circle

———. *Fireside Reading Circle. Catholic Fireside*, Jan. 6, 1923, 7–9.
———. *Fireside Reading Circle. Catholic Fireside*, Feb. 3, 1923, 120–21.
———. *Fireside Reading Circle. Catholic Fireside*, Mar. 3, 1923, 231–33.
———. *Fireside Reading Circle. Catholic Fireside*, Apr. 7, 1923, 8–10.
———. *Fireside Reading Circle. Catholic Fireside*, May 5, 1923, 118–20.
———. *Fireside Reading Circle. Catholic Fireside*, June 2, 1923, 231–34.
———. *Fireside Reading Circle. Catholic Fireside*, July 7, 1923, 7–9.
———. *Fireside Reading Circle. Catholic Fireside*, Aug. 4, 1923, 133–35.
———. *Fireside Reading Circle. Catholic Fireside*, Sept. 1, 1923, 242–45.
———. *Fireside Reading Circle. Catholic Fireside*, Oct. 6, 1923, 385–87.
———. *Fireside Reading Circle. Catholic Fireside*, Nov. 3, 1923, 484–86.
———. *Fireside Reading Circle. Catholic Fireside*, Dec.1, 1923, 607–9.
———. *Fireside Reading Circle. Catholic Fireside*, Jan. 5, 1924, 19–22.
———. *Fireside Reading Circle. Catholic Fireside*, Feb. 2, 1924, 131–33.
———. *Fireside Reading Circle. Catholic Fireside*, Mar. 1, 1924, 244–46.
———. *Fireside Reading Circle. Catholic Fireside*, Apr. 5, 1924, 383–85.
———. *Fireside Reading Circle. Catholic Fireside*, May 3, 1924, 497–99.
———. *Fireside Reading Circle. Catholic Fireside*, June 7, 1924, 635–37.
———. *Fireside Reading Circle. Catholic Fireside*, July 5, 1924, 10–12.
———. *Fireside Reading Circle. Catholic Fireside*, Aug. 2, 1924, 132–34.
———. *Fireside Reading Circle. Catholic Fireside*, Sept. 6, 1924, 270–72.
———. *Fireside Reading Circle. Catholic Fireside*, Oct. 4, 1924, 383–86.
———. *Fireside Reading Circle. Catholic Fireside*, Nov. 1, 1924, 483–85.
———. *Fireside Reading Circle. Catholic Fireside*, Dec. 6, 1924, 626–28.
———. *Fireside Reading Circle. Catholic Fireside*, Jan. 3, 1925, 18–20.
———. *Fireside Reading Circle. Catholic Fireside*, Feb. 7, 1925, 150–52.
———. *Fireside Reading Circle. Catholic Fireside*, Mar. 7, 1925, 272–74.

———. *Fireside Reading Circle. Catholic Fireside*, Apr. 4, 1925, 371–73.

———. *Fireside Reading Circle. Catholic Fireside*, May 2, 1925, 484–86.

———. *Fireside Reading Circle. Catholic Fireside*, June 6, 1925, 623–25.

———. *Fireside Reading Circle. Catholic Fireside*, July 4, 1925, 738–40.

———. *Fireside Reading Circle. Catholic Fireside*, Aug. 1, 1925, 92–95.

———. *Fireside Reading Circle. Catholic Fireside*, Sept. 5, 1925, 234–37.

———. *Fireside Reading Circle. Catholic Fireside*, Oct. 3, 1925, 345–48.

———. *Fireside Reading Circle. Catholic Fireside*, Nov. 7, 1925, 486–88.

Archival Material

The Flora Thompson archive is held at the Harry Ransom Center at the University of Texas in Austin. This collection includes a variety of published and unpublished works by the author, as well as a collection of press clippings. The following archival materials are discussed in this book.

UNPUBLISHED MANUSCRIPTS

Dashpers (typescript—57 numbered pages, plus 7 unnumbered pages)

Gates of Eden (typescript—352 pages)

The Stythy (typescript—41 pages)

The Peverel Literary Society Verse Writing Course (typescript)

Lesson 1: Subject and Form (7 pages)

Lesson 2 : Rhythm and Metre (5 pages)

Lesson 3: The Choice of Words (5 pages)

Lesson 4: Rhyme (5 pages)

Lesson 5: Poetic Form (6 pages)

Lesson 6: The Sonnet-Marketing Verse (7 pages)

REVIEWS OF BOG MYRTLE AND PEAT

Most of these clippings do not include page numbers.

"Mother and Poetess." Review of *Bog Myrtle and Peat*, by Flora Thompson. *Ideas*, Mar. 16, 1921.

Unsigned review of *Bog Myrtle and Peat,* by Flora Thompson. *Bookman*, Apr. 1921.

Unsigned review of *Bog Myrtle and Peat,* by Flora Thompson. *Evening Standard,* Mar. 28, 1921.

Unsigned reveiw of *Bog Myrtle and Peat,* by Flora Thompson. *Lady*, May 12, 1921.

Unsigned review of *Bog Myrtle and Peat,* by Flora Thompson. *Times* [London] *Literary Supplement*, Mar. 17, 1921.

Unsigned review of *Bog Myrtle and Peat,* by Flora Thompson. *Tit-Bits*, Apr. 16, 1921.

"Woman of Letters: Village Postmistress Poetess." Review of *Bog Myrtle and Peat,* by Flora Thompson. *Daily Chronicle*, Mar. 2, 1921.

SHORT STORIES

The following short stories do not include complete publication information.

———. "The Leper." *Literary Monthly* (1913) 132–34.

———. "The Silent Piano."

Secondary Sources

Altick, Richard D. *The English Common Reader: A Social History of the Mass Reading Public, 1800–1900.* Columbus: Ohio State UP, 1998.

Ashraf, Phyllis. *Englische Arbeiterliteratur vom 18. Jahrhundert bis zum ersten Weltkrieg: Entwicklungstendenzen im Uberblick.* Berlin: Aufbau-Verlag, 1980.

Ballaster, Ros, Margaret Beetham, Elizabeth Frazer, and Sandra Hebron. *Women's Worlds: Ideology, Femininity and the Woman's Magazine.* Houndsmills, Basingstoke, UK: Macmillan Press, 1991.

Barker, Juliet. *The Brontës.* London: Phoenix Giant, 1997.

Batsleer, Janet, Tony Davies, Rebecca O'Rourke, and Chris Weedon. *Rewriting English: The Politics of Gender and Class.* London: Methuen, 1985.

Beetham, Margaret. *A Magazine of Her Own? Domesticity and Desire in the Women's Magazine, 1800–1914.* London: Routledge, 1996.

Bloxham, Christine. *The World of Flora Thompson.* Oxford: Robert Dugdale, 1998.

Blythe, Ronald. *Akenfield: Portrait of an English Village.* New York: Pantheon, 1969.

———. "Natural Involvements." Review of *A Country Calendar,* by Flora Thompson. *Times* [London] *Literary Supplement*, Nov. 1979, 9.

Bourne, George. *Change in the Village.* London: George Duckworth, 1959.

Burnett, John. *Destiny Obscure: Autobiographies of Childhood, Education and Family from the 1820s to the 1920s.* Harmondsworth, UK: Penguin, 1964.

———. *Useful Toil: Autobiographies of Working People from the 1820s to the 1920s.* Harmondsworth, UK: Penguin, 1984.

Burnett, John, David Vincent, and David Mayall. Introduction to *The Autobiography of the Working Class: An Annotated Critical Bibliography.* Vol 1. New York: New York UP, 1987,. xiii-xxxv.

———. "Thompson, Flora." *The Autobiography of the Working Class: An Annotated Critical Bibliography.* Vol 1. New York: New York UP, 1987.

Burt, Struthers. "Panorama of English Rural Life." Review of *Lark Rise to Candleford* by Flora Thompson. *New York Times Book Review*, Sept. 23, 1945, 4.

"Candleford Again." Review of *Candleford Green,* by Flora Thompson. *Times* [London] *Literary Supplement*, Mar. 13, 1943, 128

Casson, Sir Hugh. Introduction to *Lark Rise.* London: Folio Society, 1979, 9–16.

Cavaliero, Glen. *The Rural Tradition in the English Novel, 1900–1939.* London: Macmillan Press, 1977.

Change and Tradition in Rural England: An Anthology of Writing on Country Life. Edited by Denys Thompson. Cambridge: Cambridge UP, 1980.

Chase, Malcom. "Massingham, (Harold) John (1888–1952)." *Oxford Dictionary of National Biography.* Edited by H. C. G. Matthew and Brian Harrison. Vol. 37. Oxford: Oxford UP.

———. "This is no claptrap: this is our heritage." In *The Imagined Past: History and Nostalgia.* Edited by Christopher Shaw and Malcolm Chase. Manchester: Manchester UP, 1989.

Clinton-Baddeley, V. C. Review of *Lark Rise to Candleford,* by Flora Thompson. *Spectator,* June 22, 1945, 582.

Dangerfield, George. "English Village Life." Review of *Lark Rise* by Flora Thompson. *Saturday Review,* July 8, 1939, 12.

Davidson, Alan. "Europeans Wary Encounters with Tomatoes, Potatoes, and Other New World Foods." In *From Chiles to Chocolate: Food the Americas Gave the World.* Edited by Nelson Foster and Linda S. Cordell. Tuscon: University of Arizona Press, 1992.

Davin, Anna. *Growing Up Poor: Home, School and Street in London, 1870–1914.* London: River Oram Press, 1996.

Dewhurst, Keith. *Lark Rise to Candleford: Two Plays.* London: Hutchinson, 1980.

"Dorothea." *Our Book Club. Lady's Companion,* Feb. 25, 1911, 349.

———. *Our Book Club. Lady's Companion,* Apr. 1, 1911, 468.

———. *Our Book Club. Lady's Companion,* Apr. 29, 1911, 565.

———. *Our Book Club. Lady's Companion,* July 22, 1911, 222.

———. *Our Book Club. Lady's Companion,* Sept. 16, 1911, 414.

———. *Our Book Club. Lady's Companion,* Oct. 21 1911, 532.

Dudgeon, Piers. *The Country Child: An Illustrated Reminiscence.* London: Headline, 1992.

Dusinberre, Juliet. "The Child's Eye and the Adult's Voice: Flora Thompson's *Lark Rise to Candleford.*" *Review of English* 35.137 (1984): 61–70.

Edwards, P. D. *Idyllic Realism from Mary Russell Mitford to Hardy.* New York: St. Martin's Press, 1988.

English, Barbara. "*Lark Rise* and Juniper Hill: A Victorian Community in Literature and History." *Victorian Studies* 29.1 (1985): 7–34.

"The English Village: Passing of an Era." Review of *Lark Rise,* by Flora Thompson. *Times* [London] *Literary Supplement,* May 13, 1939, 278.

Evans, Ernestine."Fresh from an Ancient Spring." Review of *Still Glides the Stream,* by Flora Thompson. *New York Herald Tribune Weekly Book Review,* Aug. 1948, 2.

Federico, Annette R. "Flora Thompson." In *The Cambridge Guide to Women's Writing in English.* Edited by Lorna Sage, Germaine Greer, Elaine Showalter. Cambridge: Cambridge UP, 1999, 623–24.

Fernihough, Anne. "Thompson, Flora." In *British Women Writers: A Critical Reference Guide.* Edited by Janet Todd. New York: Continuum, 1989.

Ferns, John. "Flora Thompson." In *Dictionary of Literary Biography.* Vol. 240. Detroit: Gale Research, 2001, 261–67.

"Flora Thompson." In *The Feminist Companion to Literature in English.* Edited by Virginia Blain, Patricia Clements, and Isobel Grundy. New Haven, CT:Yale UP, 1990.

Forbes-Boyd, Eric. "The Texture of a Victorian Village." Review of *Still Glides the Stream,* by Flora Thompson. *Christian Science Monitor,* July 15, 1948, 11.

Frederick, John T. "A Candid Account of 'The Good Old Days.'" Review of *Lark Rise to Candleford,* by Flora Thompson. *Chicago Sun Book Week,* Aug. 19, 1945, 2.

Gomme, Alice Bertha. *The Traditional Games of England, Scotland, and Ireland.*2 vols. New York: Dover, 1964.

Hampson, John. Review of *Candleford Green,* by Flora Thompson. *Spectator,* Feb. 12, 1943,156.

Hastings, Selina. "Lane, Margaret Winifred." In *Oxford Dictionary of National Biography.* Edited by H. C. G. Matthew and Brian Harrison. Vol. 32. Oxford: Oxford UP, 2004, 432–33.

Hey, D. Review of *A Country Calendar,* by Flora Thompson. *Lore and Language* (1988): 129–30.

Hobson, Harold. "True Serenity Lingers in the Close of Salisbury Cathedral." Review of *Four Victorian Ladies of Wiltshire,* by Edith Olivier, and *Lark Rise to Candleford,* by Flora Thompson. *Christian Science Monitor,* June 16, 1945, 12.

Hoffman, Ruth C. "An Appreciation." In *The Peverel Papers* by Flora Thompson. Headley Down, UK: John Owen Smith, 2008.

Horn, Pamela. *Victorian Countrywomen.* Oxford: Basil Blackwell, 1991.

———.*The Victorian Country Child.* Phoenix Mill, UK: Alan Sutton, 1997.

Howkins, Alun. "The Discovery of Rural England." In *Englishness: Politics and Culture, 1880–1920.* Edited by Robert Colls and Philip Dodd. London: Croom Helm, 1986, 62–88.

Hughes, Ted. *Selected Poems, 1957–1994.* New York: Farrar, Straus, and Giroux, 2002.

"In a Victorian Village." Review of *Candleford Green,* by Flora Thompson. *New York Herald Tribune Weekly Book Review,* June 20, 1943, 22.

Jordan, Thomas E. *Victorian Childhood: Themes and Variations.* Albany: State University of New York Press, 1987.

Judge, Roy. "Fact and Fancy in Tennyson's 'May Queen' and in Flora Thompson's "May-Day.'" In *Aspects of British Calendar Customs.* Edited by Theresa Buckland and Juliette Wood. Sheffield, UK: Sheffield Academic Press, 1993, 167–87.

Keen, Suzanne. *Narrative Form.* New York: Palgrave Macmillan, 2003.

Keith, W. J. *The Rural Tradition: A Study of the Non-Fiction Prose Writers of the English Countryside.* Toronto: University of Toronto Press, 1979.

Kelly, Thomas. *A History of Public Libraries in Great Britain, 1845–1975.* London: Library Association, 1977.

Kitchen, Fred. *Brother to the Ox.* London: J. M. Dent and Sons, 1948.

Klaus, Gustav. *The Literature of Labour: Two Hundred Years of Working Class Writing.* Brighton, Sussex, UK: Harvester Press, 1985.

Kodish, Deborah G. "Moving Towards the Everyday: Some Thoughts on Gossip and Visiting as Secular Procession." *Folklore Papers of the University Folklore Association* 9 (1980): 93–104.

Lane, Margaret. *Flora Thompson.* Ilkley, Yorkshire: Scolar Press, 1976.

———. Foreword to *A Country Calendar.* Edited by Margaret Lane. Oxford: Oxford UP, 1979.

———. Introduction to *A Country Calendar.* Edited by Margaret Lane. Oxford: Oxford UP, 1979, 3–31.

Law, Graham. *Serializing Fiction in the Victorian Press.* New York: Palgrave, 2000.

Leavis, Q. D. "Regional Novels." *Scrutiny* 4.4 (1936): 440–447.

Lindsay, Gillian. *Flora Thompson: The Story of the Lark Rise Writer.* London: Robert Hale, 1990.

———. "Thompson, Flora Jane." In *Oxford Dictionary of National Biography.* Edited by H. C. G. Matthew and Brian Harrison. Vol. 54. Oxford: Oxford UP.

Malcomson, Robert W., and Stephanos Mastoris. *The English Pig: A History.* London: Hambledon and London, 2001.

Massingham, H. J. Introduction to *Lark Rise to Candleford.* Oxford: Oxford UP, 1945, vii-xv.

McAleer, Joseph. *Popular Reading and Publishing in Britain, 1914–1950.* Oxford: Clarendon Press, 1992.

Mills, Sara. "Problems in the Analysis of British Working Class Women's Writing in the Thirties: Flora Thompson's *Lark Rise to Candleford.*" In *Working-Class and Feminist Literature in Britain and Ireland in the 20th Century: Proceedings of the 3rd conference in Berlin, 20 to 22 March 1989.* Edited by Hanna Behrend and Isolde Neubert. Berlin: Der Rector, Humboldt-Universität zu Berlin,1990, 49–60.

Mingay, G. E. *The Victorian Countryside.* London: Routledge and Kegan Paul, 1981.

Moult, Thomas. "Phillpotts, Eden (1862–1960)." In *Oxford Dictionary of National Biography.* Edited by H. C. G. Matthew and Brian Harrison. Vol. 44. Oxford: Oxford UP.

Murphy, Paul. *Toward a Working Class Canon: Literary Criticism in British Working Class Periodicals, 1816–1858.* Columbus: Ohio State UP, 1994.

Neilson, Keith. "Kitchener, Horatio Herbert, Earl Kitchener of Khartoum (1850–1916)." In *Oxford Dictionary of National Biography.* Edited by H.C. G. Matthew and Brian Harrison. Vol. 31. Oxford: Oxford UP.

Notes on Flora Thompson's Lark Rise. Study-Aid Series. London: Methuen Educational, 1971.

Oakeshott, Edna. *Childhood in Autobiography.* Cambridge: Cambridge UP, 1960.

Opie, Iona and Peter. *The Singing Game.* Oxford: Oxford UP, 1985.

O'Rourke, Rebecca. "Were There No Women? British Working Class Women Writers in the Inter-War Period." *Literature and History* 14.1 (1988): 48–63.

Pascal, Roy. *Design and Truth in Autobiography.* Cambridge, MA: Harvard UP, 1960.

Peterson, Linda H. *Traditions of Victorian Women's Autobiography: The Poetics and Politics of Life Writing.* Charlottesville: University of Virginia Press, 1999.

Pickering, Michael. "Popular Song at Juniper Hill." *Folk Music Journal* 4.5 (1984): 481–503.

Rodway, Avril. *A Literary Herbal.* New York: Putnam, 1980.

Room, Adrian. "Barber, Margaret Fairless (1869–1901)." In *Oxford Dictionary of National Biography.* Edited by H. C. G. Matthew and Brian Harrison. Vol. 3. Oxford: Oxford UP.

Rose, Jonathan. *The Intellectual Life of the British Working Classes.* New Haven, CT: Yale UP, 2001.

Ruthe, Monika. "20th Century Working-Class Autobiography—Changing Features and Functions." In *Working-Class and Feminist Literature in Britain and Ireland in the 20th Century: proceedings of the 3rd conference in Berlin, 20 to 22 March 1989.* Edited by Hanna Behrend and Isolde Neubert. Berlin: Der Rector, Humboldt-Universität zu Berlin, 1990, 43–48.

Sampson, Anthony. *The Scholar Gypsy: The Quest for a Family Secret.* London: John Murray, 1997.

Scott-James, Anne. *The Language of the Garden: A Personal Anthology.* London: Viking, 1984.

Seaman, L. C. B. *Life in Britain Between the Wars*. London: B. T. Batsford, 1970.

Shiach, Morag. *Discourse on Popular Culture: Class, Gender and History in Cultural Analysis, 1730 to the Present*. Stanford, CA: Stanford UP, 1989.

Shuckburgh, Julian. Introduction to *The Peverel Papers: A Yearbook of the Countryside*. Edited by Julian Shuckburgh. London: Century, 1986, 7–15.

Shumaker, Wayne. *English Autobiography. Its Emergence, Materials and Form*. Berkeley: University of California Press, 1954.

Smith, John Owen. *Flora's Heatherley*. Headley Down, UK: John Owen Smith, 1996.

———. *Flora's Peverel*. Headley Down, UK: John Owen Smith, 1996.

———. *On the Trail of Flora Thompson: Beyond Candleford Green*. Headley Down, UK: John Owen Smith, 1998.

Snell, K. D. M. "The Regional Novel: Themes for Interdisciplinary Research." In *The Regional Novel in Britain and Ireland, 1800–1990*. Edited by K. D. M. Snell. Cambridge: Cambridge UP, 1998, 1–53.

Southron, Jane Spence. "A Village Chronicle." Review of *Candleford Green*, by Flora Thompson. *New York Times Book Review*, May 2, 1943, 24.

Spengemann, William C. *Forms of Autobiography: Episodes in the History of a Literary Genre*. New Haven, CT: Yale UP, 1980.

Swindells, Julia. *Victorian Writing and Working Women: The Other Side of Silence*. Minneapolis: University of Minnesota Press, 1985.

Taylor, Pamela. "Golden Time." Review of *Still Glides the Stream*, by Flora Thompson. *Saturday Review*, July 24, 1948, 9.

Thompson, E. P. *The Making of the English Working Class*. New York: Vintage, 1966.

"Thompson, Flora." In *The Oxford Guide to British Women Writers*. Edited by Joanne Shattock. Oxford: Oxford UP, 1993.

"Thompson, Flora Jane." In *The New Cambridge Bibliography of English Literature*. Edited by I. R. Wilson. Vol. 4. Cambridge: Cambridge UP, 1972.

"Thompson, Flora Jane." In *The Oxford Companion to English Literature*. Edited by Margaret Drabble. Oxford: Oxford UP, 1985.

Trodd, Anthea. *Women's Writing in English: 1900–1945*. London: Longman, 1998.

Trotter, W. R. *The Hilltop Writers: A Victorian Colony Among the Surrey Hills*. Headly Down, UK: John Owen Smith, 2003.

Unsigned review of *Over to Candleford*, by Flora Thompson. *Spectator*, Aug. 22, 1941, 189–90.

Unsigned review of *Still Glides the Stream*, by Flora Thompson. *San Francisco Chronicle*, July 11, 1948, 14.

Vicinus, Martha. *The Industrial Muse: A Study of Nineteenth Century British Working Class Literature*. London: Croom Helm, 1974.

Victorian Women's Magazines: An Anthology. Edited by Margaret Beethan and Kay Boardman. Manchester: Manchester UP, 2001.

"Village Annals." Review of *Still Glides the Stream*, by Flora Thompson. *Times* [London] *Literary Supplement*, May 22, 1948, 284.

"Village Childhood: A Vanished Life." Review of *Over to Candleford*, by Flora Thompson. *Times* [London] *Literary Supplement*, July 12, 1941, 338.

Vincent, David. *Literacy and Popular Culture*. Cambridge: Cambridge UP, 1989.

Violets and Vinegar: An Anthology of Women's Writing and Sayings. Edited by Jilly Cooper and Tom Hartman. London: Allen and Unwin, 1980.

Wade, Stephen. *In My Own Shire: Region and Belonging in British Writing, 1840-1970.* Westport, CT: Praeger, 2002.

Warson, Gillian R. *Fact and Fiction: Flora Thompson and the Fewcott Part Book*. UK: G. R. Warson, 2003.

White, Cynthia L. *Women's Magazines, 1693–1968.* London: Michael Joseph, 1971.

Williams, Raymond. *The Country and the City.* New York: Oxford UP, 1973.

Wolfe, E.A., "Village and Grandmother." Review of *Lark Rise,* by Flora Thompson and *Grandma Called It Carnal,* by Bertha Damon. *Time and Tide*, Apr. 14, 1939, 479.

"Yesterday in England." Review of *Lark Rise,* by Flora Thompson. *New York Times*, Aug. 6, 1939, 9.

Zagarell, Sandra A. "Narrative of Community: The Identification of a Genre." *Signs: Journal of Women in Culture and Society* 13.3 (1988): 498–527.

Index